THE
GROWTH
DELUSION

THE
GROWTH
DELUSION

WEALTH, POVERTY,
AND THE
WELL-BEING OF NATIONS

David Pilling

TIM
DUGGAN
BOOKS

New York

TIM DUGGAN BOOKS and the Crown colophon are trademarks
of Penguin Random House LLC.

The writing of this book was made possible by the generous award of a
Journalist Fellowship from the Friends Provident Foundation.

Library of Congress Cataloging-in-Publication Data
Names: Pilling, David (Editor), author.
Title: The growth delusion: wealth, poverty, and the well-being of nations /
David Pilling.
Description: 1st American Edition. | New York: Tim Duggan Books, 2018.
Identifiers: LCCN 2017046122| ISBN 9780525572503 (hardcover) |
ISBN 9780525572527 (ebook)
Subjects: LCSH: Economic development. | Poverty. | Wealth. |
BISAC: BUSINESS & ECONOMICS / Economic History. |
BUSINESS & ECONOMICS / Econometrics.
Classification: LCC HD82 .P495 2018 | DDC 338.9—dc23
LC record available at https://lccn.loc.gov/2017046122.

ISBN 978-0-525-57250-3
Ebook ISBN 978-0-525-57252-7

Printed in the United States of America

Jacket design by Christopher Brand
Diagrams by Philip Beresford

10 9 8 7 6 5 4 3 2 1

First U.S. Edition

To Kimiko
whose love can neither be
weighed nor measured

CONTENTS

THE
GROWTH
DELUSION

THE CULT OF GROWTH

For over seventy years the advanced societies of the world have preened in the mirror and mostly admired what they saw: growth. The mirror is called gross domestic product and it has become our principal means of judging how beautiful we are, both as economies and as societies. The economy—the thing that GDP seeks to measure—is all around us. You can't smell it or touch it. But it is the background noise of the modern world. It is the staple fodder of headlines, business channels, and political debate. Yet, for such a fundamental concept, surprisingly few know precisely what the economy is or how we gauge its progress. All we know is that it must constantly be moving forward, like a shark.

We define the economy in terms of GDP.* In modern times, and against its inventor's warnings, GDP has become a proxy for a country's well-being. If the economy is growing, then things must be good. If it is shrinking, then not so much. But the mirror into which we have been staring is more of the fairground than the bathroom variety. The image reflected back is grossly distorted and increasingly at odds with reality. Our economic mirror is broken.

---

*For the purposes of this book, unless otherwise stated, "the economy" and "GDP" are interchangeable terms since we define the economy by the size of its GDP. The economy will also sometimes appear as "national income." GDP growth is synonymous with growth.

We are living in an "age of anger," defined by popular backlash and rejection of previously cherished institutions and ideals, up to and including Western liberalism itself.[1] In the US that has led to the rise of Donald Trump. Britain has voted for Brexit, and in Europe unconventional parties, both on the right and the left, have shaken the status quo. There are political convulsions, caused by popular revolt, from India to Brazil and from the Philippines to Turkey.

There are many competing explanations for what has caused popular rage in countries that have, judged by conventional measures, never been richer. There is, though, a common thread. People do not see the reality of their lives reflected in the official picture, the picture painted principally by economists. Some of the forces at play in this backlash stem from issues of identity, a sense of helplessness, lack of affordable housing, an absence of community, and anger against money politics and rising levels of inequality. Some stem from the fact that our definitions of "growth" and "the economy" no longer fit people's lived experience. This book aims to explain the gulf between what experts say about our lives and what our lives actually feel like.

Though almost everyone has heard of GDP, few know it was invented as recently as the 1930s as a tool to counter the Great Depression and then reworked as a means to prepare for the Second World War. The first thing to understand is that the economy is not a natural phenomenon, a truth to be discovered. Before 1930 it practically didn't exist. It is a man-made thing, like cotton candy or car insurance or double-entry bookkeeping.

If GDP were a person, it would be indifferent, blind even, to morality. It measures production of whatever kind, good or bad. GDP likes pollution, particularly if you have to spend money clearing it up. It likes crime because it is fond of large police forces and repairing broken windows. GDP likes Hurricane Katrina and is quite OK with wars. It likes to measure the buildup to conflict in guns, planes, and warheads, then it likes to count all the effort in reconstructing shattered cities from the smoldering ruins. GDP is good at counting, but a pretty poor judge of quality. It has terrible table manners. For GDP, a dinner setting of three forks does just as well as a knife, fork, and spoon.[2]

GDP is mercenary. It doesn't deign to count transactions where no money changes hands. It doesn't like housework (here, at least, I find common cause) and it shuns all volunteer activities. In poor countries it struggles to account for most human endeavor, the bulk of which takes place outside the moneyed economy. It can count a bottle of Evian in the supermarket but not the economic impact of a girl in Ethiopia who trudges for miles to fetch water from a well.

Growth is a child of the manufacturing age, and GDP was designed primarily to measure physical production. It struggles to make sense of modern service economies, quite a defect in rich countries where services, like insurance and landscape gardening, dominate. It is not bad at accounting for production of bricks, steel bars, and bicycles—"things that you can drop on your foot."[3] But try it out on haircuts, psychoanalysis sessions, or music downloads and it becomes distinctly fuzzy. It is bad at measuring progress, precisely the thing we imagine it is good at. To our principal measure of growth, an antibiotic is worth pennies, even though a syphilitic billionaire from a century ago might have handed over half his fortune for a seven-day course.

Our definition of the economy, in short, is pretty crude. As someone remarked casually to this author, "If you're stuck in traffic for an hour, that contributes to GDP. If you go around to a friend's house to help out, that doesn't." It was, he said, "all you need to know." In the hope that he was wrong about that, I hope you'll read on.

We all sense instinctively that something is wrong. But we struggle to put our finger on it. The global financial crisis of 2008 was the ultimate signal that economics had let us down. In the run-up to the collapse of Lehman Brothers and the onset of recession in virtually the whole Western world, the cult of growth had led us to celebrate our economies. People like Alan Greenspan, chairman of the Federal Reserve, said everything was going swimmingly and that the markets should be left alone to create ever more wealth.

In fact, our standard measures had told us little about how growth was being created: that it was built on a foundation of exploding household debt and ever cleverer (for which read "ever more stupid") financial engineering by bonus-crazed bankers. Advanced economies had supposedly reached a new nirvana known as the Great Moderation, in which booms and busts had been consigned to history by clever technocrats and in which the market, if left to its own devices, always reverted to a happy state of equilibrium.

Economic growth told us little about rising inequality nor about huge global imbalances. The US was running huge trade deficits financed by Middle Eastern oil exporters and China, both of which were busy recycling their trade surpluses into US Treasury bonds. The Chinese were in effect lending Americans money so that they could afford all the stuff being produced in the factory of the world. That's what kept the growth merry-go-round spinning. Until it stopped. Years later, many Western countries, especially in Europe, are still struggling to bring their economies back to pre-2008 levels. Much of the growth of the previous years had, it turned out, been an illusion.

One problem with growth is that it requires endless production and, its close cousin, endless consumption. Unless we want more and more things and more and more paid experiences, growth will eventually stall. For our economies to keep on moving forward, we must be insatiable. The basis of modern economics is that our desire for stuff is limitless. Yet in our heart of hearts we know that way lies madness.

Several years ago the satirical magazine the *Onion* ran a piece about Chen Hsien, a fictional Chinese worker producing fictional "plastic shit" for bored Americans. In true *Onion* style, the piece was borderline offensive, yet it cut to the bone of a real issue. Chen was constantly shaking his head in wonder at the incredibly useless things he was being asked to make, from salad shooters and plastic-bag dispensers to microwave omelet cookers, glow-in-the-dark page magnifiers, Christmas-themed file baskets, animal-shaped contact-lens cases, and adhesive-backed wall hooks. "And I also hear that, when they no longer want an item, they simply throw it away. So wasteful and contemptible," he scoffs. "Why the demand for so many kitchen gadgets? I can understand having a good wok, a rice cooker, a tea kettle, a hot plate, some utensils, good china, a teapot with a strainer, and maybe a thermos. But all these extra things—where do the Americans put them? How many times will you use a taco-shell holder? 'Oh, I really need this silverware-drawer sorter or I will have fits.' Shut up, stupid American."[4]

Chen's rant hits a nerve because most of us in the rich world know that we are constantly buying things we never knew we wanted and will never use again. Advertising and envy of our friends and neighbors prompts us to buy more and to upgrade constantly. By the time you read this, my iPhone 5 will be a joke. We know too that goods like washing machines and toasters are deliberately designed to break so that we will purchase still more in a never-ending cycle of consumption.

The sort of things Chen makes sound ridiculous. But they are far from fictional. The SkyMall shopping catalog, which enables airline passengers to order from the comfort of their seats, has offered a variety of must-have items, including a portrait of your pet dressed as seventeenth-century nobility ($49), a mounted squirrel head ($24.95), a life-size hanging jungle-monkey statue ($129), and, most important, rubber lips for your dog ($29.95). When economists say the world's current problems are caused by a chronic lack of demand, one wonders what else we might possibly want.[5]

From the perspective of economics, the world has never looked so good and our spending power has never been so prodigious. The US has been growing more or less relentlessly since the first set of national accounts was published in 1942. The same is true of Britain and most of Europe. After a blip following the 2008 financial crash, most economies have resumed their upward trajectory, albeit at a more sedate pace. So even if growth has slowed, our economies have never been bigger. If accumulated growth is a proxy for well-being, then we must never have been so content.

One obvious problem with putting too much faith in growth is that its fruits are never evenly shared. Our standard gauge of average income—or well-being—is calculated by taking the size of a country's economy and dividing it by the number of people living there. Averages are a trap. They are deeply misleading.

Bankers earn more than bakers, who earn more than the unemployed. To take an extreme, if the entire economic pie of a wealthy country went to one individual and nothing went to anyone else, then the average person would be doing very nicely, thank you. But the typical person would have starved to death.

The real world is not quite so extreme—outside North Korea at any rate—but even in countries like the US averages can be grossly skewed. Let's just imagine for a moment that a large proportion of the wealth created each year goes to just 1 percent, or even 0.1 percent, of the population. Sounds far-fetched? In fact, the top 0.01 percent of Americans, just 16,000 families, has seen its share of national wealth quintuple since 1980. They now enjoy a bigger slice of America's economic pie than their counterparts did in the so-called Gilded Age of the late nineteenth century.[6] If your country's economy is growing solely because the rich are getting richer and if you are working harder and harder just to maintain your living standard, then you are entitled to ask what, precisely, is all this growth for?

That is particularly true since study after study shows that people's happiness depends not on their absolute wealth, but rather on their wealth relative to those around them. In an experiment written up in a paper called "Monkeys Reject Unequal Pay" two capuchin monkeys were initially perfectly content with a reward of cucumbers when they successfully performed a task. But when one monkey was subsequently given tastier grapes as a reward, the monkey receiving plain old cucumbers became enraged, angrily flinging the previously satisfactory salad vegetable at its handler.[7] The monkeys' economy had grown, since grapes are better than cucumbers. But the resulting inequality brought only discontent. Humans are the same. When employees at the University of

California were given information about the salaries of their peers, those discovering they were paid below the median suddenly became less satisfied and more likely to seek a new job. The attitudes of those earning above the median were blithely unaffected.[8]

Economic growth, then, is partly the aggregate effect of an arms race between individuals who must always stay one step ahead of their neighbors. Imagine going to your local restaurant to discover that no one is any longer prepared to work for a waiter's or chef's wages. Your relative wealth depends on someone else's relative poverty. And it is that individual compulsion to get ahead or to stay ahead that keeps us running faster and faster on the economic hamster wheel, propelling the economy forward without making us any happier. If a waiter earns $100,000 a year, you must earn $200,000 to keep him bringing you food. If he earns $200,000, you must earn $400,000, and so on.

It was not always thus. For thousands of years no one had heard of growth. Agricultural economies were basically static. Only with the Industrial Revolution did humans become capable, slowly at first, of increasing output from year to year. That is why Britain, then Europe, then America and Australia and New Zealand gradually began to pull away from the pack, leaving the still predominantly agrarian economies of Asia, Africa, and Latin America behind.

If growth is a relatively new concept for human societies, then the economy is an even newer one. Before the invention of GDP, it was pretty difficult to define what an economy was, even if you wanted to. Before then, an economy was pretty much a cost saving, what Jane Austen meant when she wrote to her sister in 1808, "I shall eat ice and drink French wine and be above vulgar economy."[9]

Now we are all too familiar with the concepts of the economy and economic growth. One could go as far as to say that they rule our lives. But what do they mean precisely? If the experts have designed a system that does not help us understand our reality, then the government is also left without a reliable metric with which to understand society. And if what we are measuring is wrong, or insufficient, then what we get, in terms of direction and policy, will be wrong and insufficient too. Governments make policies to maximize measured outcomes. For decades that has meant maximizing growth.

In Britain former prime ministers Tony Blair and David Cameron both launched projects to measure well-being as well as economic growth. Although these endeavors petered out in public, they have begun to shift the debate as well as to affect how policymakers think about the economy. Britain, for example, led the way in attempts to measure public services such as health and education, which are undercounted by conventional economic yardsticks.

In France, Nicolas Sarkozy, a right-of-center former president not exactly known for chiseling at the foundations of capitalism, set up the Commission on the Measurement of Economic Performance and Social Progress. In a foreword to the final document he wrote, "We will not change our behavior unless we change the ways we measure economic performance." Experts had long known, he said, that we were not properly measuring our economies, let alone our well-being. "We knew that our indicators had limitations, but we went on using them as if they didn't . . . We have built a cult of the data, and we are now enclosed within."[10]

The danger, said Sarkozy in remarks that foreshadowed a populist backlash across the world, was that people knew instinctively when the wool was being pulled over their eyes. "That is how we begin to create a gulf of incomprehension between the expert certain in his knowledge and the citizen whose experience of life is completely out of sync with the story told by the data. This gulf is dangerous because the citizens end up believing that they are being deceived. Nothing is more destructive of democracy."

We live in a society in which a priesthood of technically trained economists, wielding impenetrable mathematical formulas, sets the framework for public debate. Ultimately, it is the economists who determine how much we can spend on our schools, public libraries, and armies, how much unemployment is acceptable or whether it is right to print money or bail out profligate banks.

Bill Clinton's "It's the economy, stupid" meant voters only cared about the state of the economy. At the time this carried more than a grain of truth. Though few people could give a precise definition of what the economy actually was, many did vote according to their perception of how it was performing. That might be based on personal experience: whether their job felt secure and their mortgage payments manageable. But two quarters of something as nebulous as negative growth—the technical definition of a recession—could be enough to bury a political career. Voters had been hijacked by an abstract concept.

Since then something has changed. The backlash we are witnessing suggests that people are calling time on the economists and their faulty representation of our lives. That can be very liberating. It can also be very dangerous. We don't want non-experts building our bridges, flying our planes, or performing open-heart surgery. Do we want non-economists running our economies? The problem with economists is that they often claim a scientific precision that their profession does not merit. They also speak a language that fails to resonate with people's lived experience. That is why it is so important for citizens to learn the rudiments of the economists' lingo, to gain the tools to analyze what they are being told and to demand change if necessary.

Defenders of GDP say it was never meant to reflect well-being. To criticize it for failing to capture everything important in life is like blaming a tape measure for not telling us about a person's weight or personality. That would be a valid rejoinder if the economy were just another concept, one of many we used to judge how we are doing as societies. But economic growth has become a fetish, a proxy for everything we are supposed to care about and an altar on which we are prepared to sacrifice all. In pursuit of growth, we are told, we may have to work longer hours, slash public services, accept greater inequality, give up our privacy, and let "wealth-creating" bankers have free rein. If environmentalists are right, the pursuit of growth without end could even threaten the very existence of humanity, ransacking our biodiversity and driving us to unsustainable levels of consumption and CO_2 emission that wreck the very planet on which our wealth depends. Only in economics is endless expansion seen as a virtue. In biology it is called cancer.[11]

Guiding you gently through the technicalities of GDP is one of the purposes of these chapters. So too is fleshing out the possible alternatives—none of them perfect—from measures of wealth, equality, and sustainability to indicators of "subjective well-being" (happiness to you and me).

The aim of this book is not to declare war on growth. Some will fault it for that. Rather it is to show what is wrong with our measurement of growth in the hope that we can knock it from its pedestal. The way we measure our economies has its logic, though it is becoming less logical as we shift from manufacturing to services and from analog to digital. But it is a very narrow measure, a slit of a window through which to view our world. We need to broaden our perspective so that the image we capture is more reflective of our lives.

This book came about because, after twenty years of reporting for the *Financial Times* from five continents, I have reached the conclusion that our habit of seeing everything through the prism of economic growth is distorting our view of what is important. I know because I learned how to do it. From my very first days reporting from Latin America in the 1990s I taught myself how to compare every number to GDP and to mention it in almost every article—to lend a bit of gravitas. I didn't spend too much time worrying about what exactly GDP was or what it was supposed to mean.

Only years later did I begin to give it more thought. One catalyst was my experience in Japan in the mid-2000s, reporting on a country whose economy, in conventional terms, had stalled. Japan was regularly written about as though it were some kind of basket case stuck in perpetual stagnation and without the wits to haul itself out of misery. None of this felt right. Certainly, Japan had problems and it was true that its economic miracle, which had so astonished the world in the 1980s, had run out of steam. But Japan's supposed misery—as measured by nominal GDP—really didn't feel like misery at all.[12] Unemployment was extremely low, prices stable or falling, and most people's living standards rising. Communities were intact, certainly in comparison to those in America, Britain, and France. Crime was low, drug use almost nonexistent, the quality of food and consumer goods world class, and health and life expectancy among the highest in the world.[13] And yet, viewed through the prism of economics, Japan was an abject failure.

Economics can present a distorted view of the world. So much of what is important to us, from clean air to safe streets and from steady jobs to sound minds, lies outside its range of vision. Of course, we could just throw up our hands and let others worry about the precise definition of economic growth. But that would mean recusing ourselves from the debate. It would mean leaving everything that matters in life to the self-designated experts. And look where that has got us.

PART ONE

THE PROBLEMS WITH GROWTH

1
KUZNETS'S MONSTER

F or most of human history the workings of what we casually
refer to as "the economy" were pretty much a black box. Indeed, for millennia the concept of an economy hardly existed
at all. There were at least two reasons for this. First, before the
eighteenth-century Industrial Revolution, there was really no
such thing as economic growth. That made the economy an awful
lot duller. The output of agricultural societies was pretty much a
function of the weather. If rains were good, the harvest was good.
If not, it wasn't. Nor, in this pre-industrial world, were there huge
productivity gaps between one region and another. Most people
were just scraping by. Thus the size of a region's economy was
largely determined by the size of its population. In AD 1000 China
and India accounted for just over half of global economic output,
a proportion that remained unchanged for 600 years (and may be
heading that way again).[1]

Second, in an era of monarchs—especially those lucky enough
to have been ordained by God—what was going on in the broader
economy was of no great concern. For an absolute monarch there
was no distinction between his own wealth and that of his realm.[2]
Given the lack of distinction between the wealth of the monarch
and the wealth of the nation, there was little room for anything
we might call an economy. Apart from keeping the court in its

17

accustomed luxury, the only thing required of a national economy was to finance war. A nation grew only if it conquered new dominions. If the king could muster armies to grab new territory, the national weal would be increased. But how could you tell whether your nation could bear the cost? Most early attempts to catalog the size of an economy were driven by the need to work out the monarch's capacity to wage war.[3]

So it was in France. In 1781 Jacques Necker, the Swiss finance minister of Louis XVI, presented his famous *compte rendu au roi*, his "report to the king," the first attempt to take serious stock of France's finances. Necker, formerly a wildly successful banker—are the alarm bells going off yet?—showed that France's finances were in rude health. Revenues were said to exceed expenditure by the enormous sum of 10 million livres. The main purpose of the report was to demonstrate that France could easily afford its involvement in the American Revolutionary War, in which, as was customary, it found itself on the opposite side to Britain. Necker, who had made his own fortune through speculation, wanted to prove that France's finances were so solid it could easily borrow money to finance its war effort. What the *compte rendu* cleverly omitted, however, was that France had already borrowed heavily under Necker's own direction. One of the earliest attempts to present a set of national accounts was also a piece of fiction.

Necker's stab at national accounting was not the first. That distinction is usually given to William Petty, whose publication of the Down Survey in 1652 is considered by many to be the first systematic effort to survey a country's economy—in this case, that of Ireland.[4] With the help of simple instruments and a thousand unemployed soldiers, Petty undertook the comprehensive mapping of land in thirty counties covering 5 million acres. The principal motivation was to carve up Catholic land conquered by

Oliver Cromwell and to use it to pay back those who had financed the war as well as the arrears of soldiers' wages. In addition to mapping the land, Petty conducted a fairly rigorous survey of assets, including ships, houses, and personal estates. From this he worked out flows of income that would be generated, a crucial distinction from earlier efforts to catalog stocks of wealth such as the Domesday Book of 1086.

Later, after the restoration of King Charles II, Petty did the same in England and Wales. This time the objective was to improve the monarch's capacity to tax his subjects. Petty recommended keeping records on domestic consumption, production, trade, and population growth and started to develop methods for assessing the value of labor as well as land.

If early attempts to survey the economy had common themes of war, taxation, and subservience to the monarch's needs, there were other schools of thought pulling in a different direction. In France in the eighteenth century the so-called physiocrats emphasized that the wealth of a nation was rooted in farm production and productive work. Subtly different from Petty, in the physiocrats' interpretation the "productive class" consisted of mainly agricultural laborers, while the so-called sterile class included "artisans, professionals, merchants and, lo and behold, the King himself."[5] Viewed from this perspective, the invention of the economy—as something distinct from the monarch—was a profoundly democratic act.

Adam Smith, in his *An Inquiry into the Nature and Causes of the Wealth of Nations*, first published in 1776, also divided labor into productive and unproductive categories. A man, he wrote, "grows rich by employing a multitude of manufacturers: He grows poor by maintaining a multitude of menial servants." It wasn't a very flattering view of the leisured classes. Along with hosts of servants performing useless tasks for do-nothing aristocrats, the monarch, as well as the army and the navy, were put into the category of unproductive labor.

What unites these early attempts to catalog national wealth is an effort to draw what economists today call the production boundary—between activities that should be counted and those that should not. In short, they were trying to answer a question that is still relevant today: precisely what is an economy? In the great economic ledger should the king appear on the plus side, the embodiment in flesh and blood of the national patrimony? Or, as the physiocrats and Adam Smith implied, should he be on the negative side of the ledger, an unproductive spender of the nation's resources?

The same question of what should be included and what should be excluded has rumbled on ever since. Should we include government spending? How about providers of services, whose contributions to society—healthy minds (psychoanalysts), humor (clowns), education (teachers)—may be harder to count than horseshoes or bushels of wheat? In the twentieth century communist countries largely ignored services altogether. Even today we struggle to measure their economic contribution.

Modern national accounts of the type used by virtually every country in the world today only really began to take shape in the 1930s. Simon Kuznets is usually credited with the invention of GDP, the quintessence of the national accounting system. But Kuznets, rather like Victor Frankenstein, soon saw his creation take on a life—and a direction—of its own.

The man who is said to have invented our way of measuring growth was born in 1901 into a merchant family in the town of

Pinsk in what was then part of the Russian empire. Pinsk had a large Jewish population and Kuznets's parents were Belarusian Jews. As a child he lived under the rule of the tsar, and as an adolescent sympathized with the Mensheviks, whose hopes of reforming tsarist Russia were swept aside by the Bolshevik revolution of October 1917.[6] Kuznets then studied at Kharkiv University in Ukraine, where he attended the Institute of Commerce and studied economics, history, statistics, and mathematics. He was a young man of great social conscience and ideals.

His tutors at Kharkiv stressed the importance of basing opinions on empirical data, a lesson that stayed with him for life. There was also an emphasis on placing economic theory in a wider historical and social context. Kuznets was a brilliant student and by his early twenties had published his first paper on the wages of factory workers in Kharkiv. His studies at the university were interrupted by the Russian civil war, and in 1922 the family fled, via Turkey, to the US. It was here that the Belarusian émigré was to make a profound and lasting impact on global economics.

Kuznets continued his education at Columbia University, graduating in 1923 and receiving his PhD in 1926. The following year he joined the National Bureau of Economic Research, a think tank founded in 1920. Kuznets would become a distinguished academic economist with something any self-respecting economist aspires to—a curve named after him.[7] (Oh, and he also won a Nobel Prize in economics in 1971.) His most lasting achievement, however, came in the intersection between economics and the real world.

Kuznets loved data. He worked closely with the first director of research at the National Bureau of Economic Research, Wesley Mitchell, who was also chairman of President Herbert Hoover's Committee on Social Trends. That work took Kuznets into the heart of government policy. Hoover's election campaign had promised Americans "a chicken in every pot and a car in every garage." What they got instead was the Wall Street Crash and the Great Depression. Hoover's response to the terrible depression that followed, which at its trough saw at least one in every four Americans without work, was slow and inadequate. Essentially, he thought the economy would heal itself. Prosperity, he assured Americans, was just around the corner.

Hoover may not have been entirely to blame. There was no systematic methodology for drawing up an accurate picture of a national economy. A publication in 2000 by the US Department of Commerce, which praised GDP as "one of the great inventions of the 20th century," quotes an economist as saying, "One reads with dismay of Presidents Hoover and then Roosevelt designing policies to combat the Great Depression of the 1930s on the basis of such sketchy data as stock price indices, freight-car loadings and incomplete indices of industrial production." As hard as it is to believe now in this age of obsession with economic statistics, Hoover had only the crudest notion of what was actually going on.

That was about to change. When Franklin D. Roosevelt became president in 1933, Kuznets was entrusted with the task of creating national accounts. Kuznets outlined his ideas in an article for the *Encyclopedia of Social Sciences*. His notion was disarmingly simple: to squeeze all human activity into a single number.

Kuznets was the ideal man for the job. He had a near-obsession with measuring things. One writer compares his way of analyzing an economy to a doctor on his patient rounds. He based his assessment on observable data and symptoms. But understanding the patient's underlying condition also required judgment, knowledge, and a rigorous inquisition of the facts. For Kuznets, being thorough was more important than being brilliant.[8]

Kuznets began by categorizing American industry into different sectors, such as energy, manufacturing, mining, and agriculture. He was given a staff of three assistants and five statistical clerks. "Together they hit the road, visiting factories, mines and farms, interviewing owners and managers and writing down figures in notebooks."[9] Although the scale of data collection is vastly bigger these days, survey-based methodology hasn't changed that much even in the era of big data. To this day sizing up an economy remains primarily an extrapolation of survey data, not a summation of gathered facts.

Kuznets's team traveled the length and breadth of the USA asking farmers and factory managers what and how much they had produced and what they had purchased in order to make their final product. The team shared data so they could compare results and iron out anomalies. Kuznets knew the data were more or less meaningless in isolation. They had to be interpreted. Though it would take many more years before the first publication, in 1942, of a full set of gross national product statistics, Kuznets's work bore much earlier fruit.[10] In January 1934 he presented his first report to Congress. It ran to 261 pages and, for such a historic document, bore a name that only an economist could dream up: *National Income, 1929–32.*

The report began with much throat clearing about what the numbers could and could not reveal. His effort was, Kuznets said, "an amalgam of . . . estimates," at best "only well-considered guesses."[11] The welfare of a nation, he made clear, could "scarcely be inferred" from such an estimate. Contained within its pages, however, was a bombshell. In the three years following the Wall Street Crash the American economy had almost halved in size.

Kuznets's findings became the basis for the second, much more ambitious, phase of Roosevelt's New Deal, in which the government spent massively on public works, farm aid, and social security in order to pull the US economy out of its seemingly interminable recession. Kuznets had provided a more rigorous empirical foundation on which to take such radical action than freight-car loadings. Still, he had warned that the estimates of national income were "of little value in themselves." The headline number was not what was important, he said in words that should ring louder than ever today. For example, closer analysis showed that inequality had increased greatly during the Great Depression. Blue-collar wages had fallen much faster than white-collar salaries, and property owners had fared better than most. These findings provided Roosevelt with the evidence he needed to push through his radical employment policies, which included unemployment relief, the banning of child labor, and the right of labor unions to organize. Without Kuznets's report, much of this would have been impossible.

His work was far from finished. In 1936 Kuznets helped organize the first Conference on Research in Income and Wealth with high-level participants from both academia and government. It was during this conference that the term gross national product, or GNP, was first used. The proceedings of the first three annual conferences were published, revealing sharp differences among participants about what should be measured and what should be left out.

Although Kuznets is considered the father of GDP, in several important respects the methodology that evolved by the early 1940s—and which has remained largely in use ever since—went against his most profoundly held beliefs. Kuznets was striving for a measure that would reflect welfare rather than what he considered a crude summation of all activity. He wanted to exclude illegal activities, socially harmful industries, and most government spending. On many of these issues he lost. One student of national accounting goes so far as to suggest, "Kuznets, far from being the progenitor of GDP, was its biggest opponent."[12]

One of the most important consequences of the Second World War was the invention of the atomic bomb. It was developed by scientists, some of whom had fled Nazi Germany, working on the top-secret Manhattan Project in the New Mexico desert. The bomb was not only an outcome of the war; it also helped win it. Less well known is the case of GDP, the invention of which was hastened and molded by the life-and-death struggle with fascism. As with the atomic bomb, its invention had a material impact on the war. Like some of those who led the Manhattan Project, Kuznets was also a reluctant participant in his own creation.

Kuznets thought that a sensible definition of the economy should exclude defense spending. During the war he bent to pressure to include expenditure on armaments to defeat fascism, but in peacetime, he argued, a country's ability to wage war did not contribute to people's welfare. National income statements, he wrote in 1937, should be constructed from the viewpoint of an "enlightened social philosophy" and should discount activities that were detrimental or, in his word, a "disservice." The first item he listed for exclusion was "all expenses on armament." For Kuznets, spending on preparations for war subtracted from a nation's well-being because it reduced individuals' capacity to consume and because it was defensive in nature. If such spending was a necessary evil, then it should appear as a minus in the accounts rather than a plus.

But national income was a child of war. Kuznets lost the battle before it had begun. From 1940 the annual conferences that Kuznets had been holding on developing national accounts were held behind closed doors. Discussions of the state of the US economy had become a top-secret part of war planning. Making the link more explicit still, in 1942 Kuznets was transferred to the Planning Committee of the War Production Board. His main task there was to work out whether the economy had enough spare capacity to switch into the manufacturing of munitions. More generally, he needed to assess the economy's ability to sustain an all-out war in Europe as well as in Asia, where the Americans had been fighting Japan since the attack on Pearl Harbor the previous year.

Kuznets threw himself into the task. He sought to discover how America's economic capacity could best be employed so that it struck a balance between building a fighting machine and maintaining the domestic consumption necessary to keep the economy ticking over. Within the government and military establishment there was sharp disagreement between those who wanted to commandeer, even nationalize, the means of production so that they could be diverted to the war effort and others, including those working with Kuznets, who concluded that the economy had plenty of spare capacity that could be marshaled without curtailing domestic consumption. These economists may even have influenced the timing of America's entry into the war in Europe, having concluded that the US would better be able to sustain its effort if it delayed involvement until late 1943 or early 1944.[13]

Just as Germany had lacked an atomic bomb that could have tilted the war in its favor, so it was missing the statisticians and economists who could also have helped it. Germany ended the war without having made anything like the advances in national accounts secured by the US.[14]

26

There was another powerful force at play, namely John Maynard Keynes. In 1940, two years before Kuznets was drafted into the War Production Board, the famous British economist had written an instantly influential pamphlet with the less-than-ambiguous title *How to Pay for the War*. As Britain struggled to stave off the threat from Nazi Germany, Keynes complained that economic statistics were too fuzzy to work out the amount of resources that could be mobilized for the war effort. He sought, in the words of his pamphlet's opening sentence, "how best to reconcile the demands of war and the claims of private consumption."

Keynes wanted to work out the fairest way of sharing diminished resources while preserving the government's ability to raise debt to pay for the war. "In order to calculate the size of the cake which will be left by civilian consumption," he wrote, the government would have to estimate various things, including the economy's "maximum current output," the sustainability of drawing on foreign reserves to pay for imports, and the amount it would need to spend on guns, aircraft, and soldiers. According to his rough-and-ready calculations, output could probably be increased by 15–20 percent by bringing boys and women into the workforce and by lengthening overtime. But, he complained, "the statistics from which to build up these estimates are very inadequate. Every government since the last war has been unscientific and obscurantist, and has regarded the collection of essential facts as a waste of money." Only the state, he concluded, was in a position to collect and process such statistics. In their absence, the government was stumbling about in the dark.

That was not all. Until Keynes, attempts to define the scope of a national economy had excluded the government. But Keynes thought the government played a vital role in the economy, particularly during business downturns, when he advocated government spending to stimulate demand. If government expenditure were excluded from GDP, then its perceived role in the economy would be diminished. Until that point national income had been considered the sum total of market activity, or the spending of private individuals, including businesses, on investment and consumption.[15] In this definition there was no room for government.

Kuznets considered most government spending—including on such things as roads—as a so-called intermediary cost "implicit in our economic civilization." To Keynes, this was a conceptual error. If government expenditure was excluded, then whatever the state spent on the war effort would count against economic growth in the national accounts. The more the government spent, the less there was available for private consumption and investment. Keynes's economic views demanded that this definition of the national economy be turned on its head. The government had to be considered part of the economy.

This was an almost revolutionary assertion. It was nothing less than a redefinition of what the economy was. By baking this idea into our national accounts, Keynes continues to show his influence. Without this definitional shift, what we know today as Keynesian fiscal stimulus would be difficult to justify since it would detract rather than add to national income. Only if the government is considered part of the economy can its spending contribute to final output. In this way, "a British war-time definition of the economy has become a global consensus."[16]

Keynes's ideas had a huge impact in Britain, where a new system was being put into practice by two young economists, Richard

Stone and James Meade, who were appointed by the Treasury to produce Britain's first modern set of national accounts. These were duly published in 1941, bearing the distinct imprimatur of Keynes's theoretical input. Keynes's ideas also quickly took hold on the other side of the Atlantic, where financing the war had become the *raison d'être* for producing an accurate set of accounts. Kuznets's objections were swept aside by realpolitik, underpinned by the intellectual contribution of the forceful and influential British economist. That Keynes was the true inventor of GDP, writes one commentator, is "one of economic history's best kept secrets."[17]

There was a third area in which Kuznets lost influence over his invention. Kuznets thought anything detrimental to social welfare should also be excluded. This included not only things like armaments, but also advertising, speculation and all illegal activities, such as gambling, extortion, and prostitution. What should be added and what should be left out is a bit like making a cake. The type of recipe you select will affect the flavor and texture: you can have the plain sponge of growth or the chocolate cake with extra filling. Kuznets's tastes were restrained, even prim. He thought national accounts should measure only economic activity that was good for you—definitely on the sponge-cake side of things, then. Kuznets lost that debate and we have been left with a recipe for double chocolate fudge cake with whipped cream and sugar sprinkles. Everything, good and bad, goes into it. Economic growth—like butter and cream—is not always good for your health.

In his slightly dry style, this is what Kuznets had to say on the matter:

It would be of great value to have national income estimates that would remove from the total the elements which, from

29

the standpoint of a more enlightened social philosophy than that of an acquisitive society, represent disservice rather than service. Such estimates would subtract from the present national income totals all expenses on armament, most of the outlays on advertising, a great many of the expenses involved in financial and speculative activities."[18]

The way we calculate economic growth today ignores Kuznets's warnings. The bigger our banks, the more persuasive our advertisers, the worse our crime and the more expensive our health care, the better our economies are seen to be performing. That is not what Kuznets wanted. But it is what we got.

2

THE WAGES OF SIN

One day in 2012 two accountants working at Britain's Office for National Statistics embarked on an unusual project: they started counting prostitutes. Joshua Abramsky and Steve Drew were not bored; they were responding to a diktat from Eurostat, the statistical arm of the European Union, which wanted EU nations to standardize how they calculated national income.

One of the anomalies in how countries compile their national accounts is their treatment of illegal activities, such as gambling, prostitution, and the handling of stolen goods. Simon Kuznets thought only activities that contribute to human welfare should be counted, but who was to decide what they were? He thought advertising was worthless. Perhaps someone else would judge video games a waste of time, or stop counting alcohol and cigarettes or junk food on the grounds that they are bad for one's health.

Years before, Eurostat had settled the dispute by ruling that any monetary transaction in which parties willingly consent to take part should be counted as economic activity.[1] After all, in some European countries, including Holland, where prostitutes famously sit in window displays along the canals of Amsterdam, prostitution is legal. So, in some countries, are certain types of drugs. And in those European countries such activities are counted as part of the economy. For consistency, Eurostat wanted other countries to adopt the same approach.[2] National income, it reasoned, is supposed to measure the goods and services produced in a country over a certain period. It can't distinguish between "good" and "bad" activity. If bombs and derivative products (the toxic and occasionally exploding creations of the banking world) are counted, then why not a shot of heroin or an hour of paid-for sex?

But how were Abramsky and Drew to work out the contribution of prostitution to the British economy? Where were they to go for information? They didn't, as one might assume, head straight to the nearest red-light district to see how many prostitutes they could spot. Being statisticians, they did what came naturally: they turned to research papers.[3] Information was sketchy. There was no easy way to calculate how many prostitutes there were working in Britain. In the standard household survey there was, hardly surprisingly, no question about the use of sexual services. Abramsky and Drew turned instead to a 2004 survey of off-street prostitutes in London, which they supplemented with an estimate from the Metropolitan Police of the number of on-street prostitutes in the capital.[4] They then scaled that up to arrive at an estimate of the number of prostitutes in Britain in 2004. Using census data of males over sixteen, they brought the figure up to date under the assumption that the number of prostitutes would rise in proportion with the male population.

From these back-of-a-condom-packet calculations they estimated—with an alarming if spurious accuracy—that there were 60,879 prostitutes working in Britain in 2009. As if to underline the arbitrariness of the exercise, only female prostitutes were counted.[5] How much were their services worth? For that the statisticians would need to know how many customers each prostitute saw and how much they charged for sex. Again they turned to research. This time they relied on Dutch academic work for an estimate of how many clients prostitutes saw each month, and for prices they went to PunterNet, a website where men rated the services of women they had visited. At about 25 clients per prostitute per week charging an average of £67.16 per "personal service," they worked out a number for the total expenditure on prostitution in Britain in 2009.

Abramsky and Drew performed a similar exercise with illegal drugs. They restricted their search to crack cocaine, powder cocaine, heroin, cannabis, ecstasy, and amphetamines. (So if your drug of choice is not on this list, you're really not doing your bit for the economy.) They also made similar assumptions about intermediate consumption—the raw materials needed to make the final product—for example by discounting the electricity used to grow marijuana from the final sale price in order to arrive at a value-added amount.[6]

The exercise, which provoked a minor commotion in the British press, feels faintly ludicrous, but what we choose to count and what we don't has real consequences. This was a letter to the *Financial Times* in response to the newspaper's report that sex work and illegal drugs had added £9.7 billion to the British economy and a quite unrelated editorial urging Britain to keep its defense expenditure at 2 percent of GDP.[7]

The 2 percent of GDP Nato benchmark to which you refer in your editorial "Fight or flight will be the UK's choice on defence" is surely a very strange way in which to calculate a country's defence budget. Applying this criterion to the UK has meant that the targeted expenditure figure has recently risen as a result of prostitutes' earnings and the consumption of illegal drugs being included in the composition of GDP, which seems mildly ridiculous. If only prostitutes worked a bit harder the army could have a few more guns!

Applying different methodologies to how we calculate the size of economies distorts international comparisons, one of the very things for which GDP is regularly used. The US, for example, does not count illegal activity. It does, of course, count guns, which are legal in America but illegal in much of Europe.

The treatment of drugs in America (a heavy user) and Colombia (an important supplier) is entirely different. Colombia has traditionally counted drugs as part of its economic activity, though their contribution has been declining. In 2010 it fell sharply following the demise of Pablo Escobar's Medellin cartel. At its peak, in the late 1980s, according to Ricardo Rocha, an economist at Bogotá's Rosario University, cocaine amounted to 6.3 percent of Colombia's GDP.[8] By 2010 the cartels were no longer pulling their weight and their contribution had slipped to a measly 1 percent.

These things make a difference. In 1987, in what became known triumphantly as *Il Sorpasso* (after a cult movie), Italians awoke to find that their economy had overtaken that of Britain to become the fifth biggest in the world. The reason? The Italian statistical agency had improved its measurement of the notoriously large, untaxed gray economy. The result was an 18 percent jump in the size of the economy courtesy, at least in part, of the Mafia. "All of a sudden we're waking up and discovering that we're richer and better than we thought," Massimo Esposito, an editor of *Il Sole-24 Ore*, Italy's business daily, said.[9]

What we measure can, and frequently does, affect how we see ourselves. It can also affect policy. Now that we recognize the sterling contribution of crack cocaine and prostitution to Britain's economy, the logical next step might be to legalize (and tax) these goods and services. That might be no bad thing. But we should acknowledge the effects our measurements have on policy. Who doubts, for example, that Western governments encourage arms manufacturers because they contribute to the economy, no matter the toll in death and injury?

Similarly, governments around the world go easy on tobacco companies, which contribute to economies and pay tax to treasuries. The (not-so) hidden cost to society of cigarettes—ill health, medical expenditure, and early death—is accepted as a necessary by-product of their economic contribution. Besides, the resulting hospital care and cancer treatment also contribute to economic output. It is a good example of how we prioritize growth without stopping to think why. Because we view policy almost exclusively through the lens of economics, we are tempted to see lung cancer as a necessary trade-off for growth. Subtracting tobacco from economic activity rather than adding it would not cure us of nicotine craving, but it would likely change government incentives and thus its policy toward the tobacco industry.

Woe betide any politician who is willing to advocate a drop in growth in the interests of some greater cause, be it social or environmental. In the US the idea of sacrificing growth by, say, taxing gasoline or carbon more heavily as a measure against global warming would be politically unthinkable. Indeed, Donald Trump's decision to quit the Paris accord on climate change in the name of growth won strong support among sections of the American public. When Kevin Rudd, Australia's former prime minister, tried to introduce a carbon emissions trading scheme, his bill was defeated on the grounds that it would raise business costs and damage the economy. He was unceremoniously drummed out of office.[10]

Adding drugs and prostitution to British national income helps draw out more clearly these questions about what we are measuring and the sort of society we are endorsing. If we take the exercise to its logical conclusion, should we not, for example, also count hit men and protection rackets as part of our national economy? If a hit man takes a fee and performs a service, doesn't that meet Eurostat's definition of something that should be counted: a monetized transaction between willing parties?

Shouldn't we also count trade in stolen goods? Well, we do. As Sanjiv Mahajan, an expert on national accounts, explains, there is a distinction between the initial act of theft and the sale of stolen goods. If I steal your Ferrari that is an involuntary transaction, which does not appear in national income. But if I then sell your Ferrari and go out and "buy caviar and a bottle of claret at Fortnum & Mason" with the proceeds, that will turn up as retail sales, thus boosting the economy. "I wouldn't want to see a headline in the *Sun* newspaper saying, MORE THEFT CONTRIBUTES TO THE ECONOMY," says Mahajan. "But it does in a way because you've got money without producing anything. You've used the same good twice."

Mahajan is aware of how arbitrary, even illogical, this way of thinking might seem. But national income, he says, has never pretended to be a moral measure, nor a proxy for well-being. "If you want to increase GDP, you should raise value-added tax, increase use of illegal drugs and prostitution and have a war," he offers. "Sounds like a right happy time, doesn't it?"

On the outskirts of the Welsh cathedral city of Newport, not far from the River Usk, is a windswept business park. There sits a drab squat building of brick and glass. It is the sort of structure that gives modern architecture a bad name, just the type of place where you might expect rows of statisticians to be laboring away over rows of statistics. Outside on the lawn an off-white sign, held aloft by two metal posts, completes the picture. The notice reads OFFICE FOR NATIONAL STATISTICS, followed by some words in Welsh, SWYDDFA YSTADEGAU GWLADOL, which presumably mean, "Beware: statisticians at work."

In 2007 the Office for National Statistics, ONS for short, moved almost lock, stock, and barrel from London to this part of south Wales. Virtually all of the London-based staff quit rather than make the move to Newport. It's not an episode the Welsh Tourist Board likes to brag about.

Compiling Britain's statistics can be a thankless task. In spite of the expertise and diligence of those who have built careers at the ONS, a survey in the *Financial Times* found that only 10 percent of Britons thought the figures it produced were accurate. Most believed data were manipulated for political purposes.[11] Still, woe betide the compilers of Britain's national accounts if these figures—apparently trusted by no one—are late. In June 2010 the statistics office delayed release of national income data after admitting it had discovered potential errors in the numbers. The two-week postponement caused ripples in the markets, which speculated about possible revisions to growth data already released. The update, when it came, did indeed show that the recession had been deeper than thought, with the economy having shrunk from peak to trough by 6.4 percent rather than 6.2 percent as previously stated.

The ONS has not only had to move location; it has also been subject to budget cuts of millions of pounds. That has obliged it to trim the sample size of its surveys and to contemplate abandoning some series of statistics altogether. The government even threatened to scrap the next census, the foundation of many other data sets, on the grounds that it cost too much. The 2011 census set Britain back a hefty £480 million.[12] Collecting good statistics is expensive. It has not always been a political priority, as Keynes pointed out more than sixty years ago.

For the 650 or so people working on national income in Newport the end of each quarter is like a starting gun. They have only twenty-five days to produce their first estimate, a tall order given that it can take up to three years for all the relevant information to come in. The first published release, therefore, is a rough-and-ready estimate which is gradually refined as more data become available. For each quarter, the ONS publishes estimates after 25 days, 55 days, and 85 days, by which time 90 percent of the relevant data are available.[13] Statistics agencies around the world work to slightly different schedules, but in broad terms their methodology is the same.

There are three recipes for GDP. Although each uses different ingredients, in theory they should end up tasting exactly the same. In practice, because of the dizzying array of data and assumptions that goes into each method, they often turn out quite different. That leaves national accountants having to reconcile the three sets of numbers by weeding out dodgy-looking outliers.

Before we get on to the three recipes, let's start with a definition. The Office for National Statistics—whose motto is the wonderfully pithy and entirely laudable "Better statistics, better decisions"—says GDP is "the value of goods and services produced during a given period." That makes it sound awfully simple and begs the question of why it took hundreds of years to come up with.

Of GDP's three little words, the first is "gross," which simply means a number with nothing subtracted.[14] Kuznets had also considered net national product, which would have removed various things, including wear and tear on the machinery used to produce finished goods. Next, "domestic" means in the home country. That makes it distinct from gross *national* product, which includes everything produced by a country's companies whether at home or abroad. In the age of the multinational, this distinction matters. Finally comes "product," which means everything produced, both goods and services.

The three recipes are known as the expenditure, income, and production methods.[15] They measure what is spent, what is earned, and what is made. An economy should only produce what is bought (once imports and exports are taken into account), and people can only spend what they earn. That's why, in theory, the three measures should come out the same.

The production method is the sum of everything produced by factories and farmers, hairdressers and patisseries. Working out the value of production is not straightforward, as it is easy to double-count. Take the example of a bakery.[16] You can't simply add up the value of the doughnuts, loaves, croissants, and doughnuts— did I mention doughnuts?—in order to arrive at the right number. That is because you'd be counting in these goods items that you have tallied up earlier. You'd have counted the flour when you were totting up the output of the miller. And you'd have counted the wheat that went to make the flour when you were adding up the output of wheat farmers.

So when it comes to working out the contribution of bread to an economy, you're actually trying to count what's known as the "value-added," the additional value that has been created in the process of turning flour—as well as butter, electricity, labor, and rent—into a loaf of crusty farmhouse or German pumpernickel. You have to subtract the value of all the intermediate goods that go into making the finished product. The production formula is deceptively simple: the value of all goods and services produced over a given period minus the value of intermediate goods.

Next comes the expenditure method, which calculates something economists sometimes refer to as "aggregate demand." That is everything "spent," whether by households, businesses, or government. Because we're calculating domestic product, we need to add in exports, since these were made at home, and subtract imports, since these were made abroad. The formula for this recipe is: consumer spending plus government spending and investment plus business investment plus exports less imports. It is, perhaps, the best-known recipe in the economic cookbook.[17] The final recipe is the income approach, which measures all the income earned in an economy, mostly in wages, profits, dividends, rent, and taxes. When it comes to measuring our economy, we are what we earn.

As in the US, Europe, and many other countries, most of the numbers on which the ONS relies come from sample surveys. They are not a full reckoning of every transaction made in the economy. "There's no computer in the sky counting up all the receipts," says Umair Haque, an author who has criticized our economic measures. "It's a very crude survey and so we shouldn't treat it as sacrosanct."[18]

To take a mundane example, the ONS cannot know every time I pop down to the shop to buy a packet of Fig Newtons or a toilet plunger. Information on the former comes from a variety of sources: from the biscuit company, which should know roughly how many packets it produced; from supermarkets and shopkeepers, who should know roughly how many they have sold; and from households, who should know exactly how delicious Fig Newtons are. But the ONS cannot ask every household in the land how many Fig Newtons and toilet plungers they bought last week. "Oh, and while we're at it, did you perchance purchase anything else?" Instead it relies on sample surveys. An important one is the Living Costs and Food Survey. An interviewer sent by the ONS conducts an initial face-to-face interview and then leaves a diary in which each person in the family, including children, records their expenditure over a week or more. Each year about 5,000 people in Britain fill out such forms, from a population of about 65 million.

Businesses are more intensively sampled. Each month the ONS sends out 45,000 surveys to UK companies of all description. Just as Kuznets did, statisticians categorize businesses by sector and subsector, so that information from one can be scaled up to form a representative picture of the whole. Guidance is provided by something called the International Standard Industrial Classification (Revision 4), which is compiled by the United Nations. If you're a nerd, it can make fascinating reading. In its more than 290 pages every conceivable business is classified, from, to take two random examples, "fishing cruise" companies to "manufacture of luggage, handbags and the like, saddlery and harness." Each category is further subdivided into dozens of items. Then the results are scaled up to represent the sector as a whole. Think of it as an exit poll. Not all people leaving the polling station are asked how they voted, but a large enough sample is collected to present a fairly reliable picture.

The ONS is also trying to harvest more information from what statisticians call "administrative data." This is information collected by the government for non-statistical purposes in the day-to-day course of running the country. Examples might include driving licenses, registration of births or deaths, customs clearances, tax records, and so on. These provide rich pickings for statisticians because they often cover the entire population and contain real data as opposed to estimates derived from surveys. For a cash-strapped agency, administrative data have another advantage: they have already been collected and come free of charge. In 2015 the ONS announced plans to take data directly from Her Majesty's Revenue and Customs VAT returns. It estimated that using this data could halve the amount of surveys it would need to send out in future.

Once data start to come in, the statistical work begins. Different numbers go into each of the three formulas outlined above. Then, all three estimates must be reconciled using something called a "supply and use table," which is really a set of matrixes in which different results can be compared.

Finally, numbers have to be adjusted for seasonality and for inflation. It's not much use reporting that car sales went up dramatically in one month if people always buy lots of cars at one particular time of year. Far better to smooth out the numbers by adjusting for seasonal factors. Otherwise, just imagine the headlines in January: SLUMP IN CHRISTMAS TREE SALES, ECONOMY ON ROCKS.

Inflation is harder, and even more important, to account for. Growth is normally adjusted for inflation. It would be misleading to say that the economy had expanded by 15 percent if 14 percentage points of that increase were accounted for by price rises. People are more interested in the "real" rate of growth. Statisticians either compare volumes of production (rather than value) or apply a deflator, which discounts the effect of inflation.[19] Now all we need is to wait for Abramsky and Drew to finish counting all those drugs and prostitutes, and, hey presto, there's your GDP.

3

THE GOOD, THE BAD, AND THE INVISIBLE

In the summer of 2012 Janice S, a sixty-four-year-old former sales assistant living near Stamford in Connecticut, felt pains in her chest.[1] She was driven four miles by ambulance to a hospital, where she underwent three hours of tests and had some fleeting encounters with a doctor. Eventually she was told she had nothing more than indigestion and was sent home. That was the good part. The bad part was the bill: $995 for the ambulance, $3,000 for doctors, and $17,000 for the hospital—altogether $21,000 for a routine screening.[2] Heartburn has never been so expensive.

What could have possibly cost so much? Among the hospital's charges were three "troponin I" tests for $199.50 each. A troponin test measures the levels of certain proteins in the blood associated with heart attacks. The hospital charged patients using a "chargemaster," a price list that seemed to bear no relation to cost—or reality. When hospital administrators were asked about the chargemaster they grew nervous and changed the subject.

If Medicare, the US government insurance scheme, had covered the cost of the troponin test, it would have paid the hospital $13.94 for each one rather than the $199.50 Janice was charged. Because Janice was out of work she was not insured. Nor was she covered by Medicare, which starts at age sixty-five. Janice was also charged $157.61 for a complete blood count test. Medicare would have reimbursed the hospital $11.02 for the same procedure. Other huge markups included the charge for a simple acetaminophen tablet—a generic version of Tylenol—the price of which had been inflated by 10,000 percent. According to Stamford Hospital's filings, its total expenses on lab work like Janice's over a twelve-month period were $27.5 million, while its total charges were $293.2 million, not a bad little earner for what is officially a nonprofit organization.

Each year the US spends around 17 percent of GDP on health care.[3] That is almost twice the amount spent in most advanced countries. The UK puts 9 percent of GDP into health care, Japan 10.2 percent, and France, which has a world-class health system, 11.5 percent. Singapore, which also has an exceptionally good health service, spends just 4.9 percent, less than a third of the US. Each and every week Americans lay out more than $55 billion on medical expenditure, close to what it cost to clean up after Hurricane Sandy in 2012.

You'd have thought that all this money would produce spectacular results, but you'd be wrong. Health outcomes in the US are no better than in most developed countries, and in some cases considerably worse. The US comes in at number 31 in the life-expectancy league tables, just below Costa Rica.[4] Its average life expectancy of 79.3 years for both sexes compares with 83.7 for Japan, the best-placed country. In other words, the Japanese spend half as much and live four years longer.

The US is likely to fall farther behind. By 2030 women in South Korea are likely to have a life expectancy of nearly ninety-one, according to a recent study published in *The Lancet*, which put the achievement down to universal health care, good childhood nutrition, and the rapid take-up of new medical technology. By contrast, the study found, the US was expected to have the lowest life expectancy of any rich country by 2030.[5] In infant mortality, which measures the number of infants who die before the age of one, the US doesn't fare any better. In 2015 it came 57th in the world, just behind Bosnia and Herzegovina, with 5.72 deaths per thousand live births. Monaco was best at 1.82.

Defenders of the US health care system dispute these numbers. Such raw data, they say, fail to account for differences between countries in diet, ethnicity, levels of inequality, and social problems such as drug abuse. They also don't take into account the very high levels of violent deaths in the US, especially from shootings. Infant mortality numbers may not be comparable, these people argue, because they are measured differently in different countries. Some of those objections may be valid, although the lobbying of the US health industry means one should take such objections with a huge dose of sodium (presumably marked up 10,000 percent).[6]

You'd need to be drawing a pretty sizable check from Big Pharma to argue that Americans are getting good value for their health care dollar. So what exactly accounts for the inflated costs? The health industry's formidable lobbying machine ensures that laws in Washington are made with the interests of health care providers in mind.[7] As a result the patient sometimes comes out second best. The pharmaceutical and health-care-product industries, combined with groups representing doctors, hospitals, nursing homes, and insurers, spent $5.36 billion between 1998 and 2012 on lobbying, according to Steven Brill, who has researched the US health care industry extensively. That compared with $1.53 billion spent by the defense and aerospace industries and $1.3 billion spent by oil and gas interests over the same period. In other words, the "health-care-industrial complex spends more than three times what the military-industrial complex spends in Washington."[8]

The profit motive is a big factor, both in inflating costs and in encouraging practitioners to overtest, overprescribe, and overoperate. In cities up and down America hospitals are among the most profitable enterprises, employing administrators whose salaries frequently run into millions of dollars. Fear of litigation also drives costs higher. Behind every well-paid doctor stands an even better paid lawyer. In Janice's case, certain of the tests administered were more about protecting the hospital from potential lawsuits than providing the best patient care.

What does all this extra health care spending bring, if not improved health? The answer, of course, is economic activity. Lots of it. All those profits, insurance assessments, malpractice suits, and unnecessary CT scans are contributing to the growth of America's economy. But it is an odd sort of contribution. The more inflated the prices, the bigger health care's seemingly positive impact on the national economy.

If you accounted for it differently—say as Kuznets proposed—you might consider the huge bill a minus rather than a plus. You could even subtract it from the size of your economy as a negative "defensive expenditure." But that's not how it's done. As things stand, all that is required to boost American growth would be to double health care costs. You could call this growth-enhancing policy proposal the $42,000 heartburn.

If it is easy to count up the revenues and profits of private health care providers, we have a much harder time figuring out how much the government contributes to our economy. Much as Keynes wanted to ensure that government expenditure appeared as national income, all too often government spending doesn't count for very much. That is no small matter. Even in the most market-oriented economies, governments provide all sorts of services, often for free. Because there is no charge, it is not easy to price them or to work out how much they contribute to the economy. A private school, for example, makes profits, which count as national income. A hospital in America can positively rake in the cash, measurably adding to the size of the economy. But government services—from an accounting point of view—are less visible. Depending on the country, the state may run trains, collect rubbish, build roads, provide fire and ambulance services, and invest in science. Governments in most countries of the world provide free schooling up to a mandatory age. Some even provide free, or heavily subsidized, university education. Many offer free health care.

National accountants have never cracked the problem of how to value government services. It is almost impossible to measure properly something that is provided for free. Why is that? Take state schools. All you can do is count inputs: wages for teachers, rents for buildings, the cost of electricity, and so on. Since no one pays for the output—education—you cannot measure the value-added. Similarly, with state health systems you can't measure all those inflated profits. Again, you simply count the inputs: doctors' and nurses' pay, the wholesale price of medicines, and so on. A successful hernia operation or a woman sent home with a touch of heartburn is invisible.

To raise the economic contribution of the UK's National Health Service—which provides health care free to patients—you'd need to increase the cost of all those inputs. You would pay doctors and nurses higher wages, pay drug companies more for their medicines, and perhaps throw in some more litigation and lobbying activities for good measure. In other words, the only way to raise a public health system's economic contribution—as conventionally measured—is to make it *less* efficient.

Not all growth is good and the apparent absence of growth is not always bad. You can conjure a bigger economy out of thin air simply by wasting money: just look at US health care. Conversely, you could drastically improve a free state-provided health service without it adding to growth one iota. Another implication, therefore, is that the bigger a country's public sector, the more we underestimate the true size of its economy. The way we account for national income is biased in favor of private over public provision.

In Britain the government of Tony Blair tried to solve the problem by directly measuring public service efficiency. In 2001 Blair appointed Michael Barber, a former teacher, to head the so-called Delivery Unit. Barber appeared before skeptical journalists flourishing a dizzying array of targets and flip charts. He would, he said, benchmark the provision of public services and hold public servants accountable. Journalists mocked his new-fangled approach as "deliverology." Barber adopted the term and never looked back.

The Delivery Unit was attempting to come up with actionable alternatives to the conventional way we measure growth. It started with the recognition that the government couldn't measure public provision well, so simply pouring more money into hospitals and schools and hoping for the best could end up being a colossal waste of money. Instead, it wanted measurable outcomes, whether in successful hip replacements, shorter waiting times at government offices, fewer train delays, or better exam grades by eighteen-year-olds. You'd set a target, say that 90 percent of trains would arrive with less than a ten-minute delay. And then you'd track results and take action—fire the management or invest in updated technology—if targets were being missed. Barber has since helped export the concept as far afield as Malaysia, Indonesia, and Ethiopia.

The verdict on how the Delivery Unit did is mixed. It was often too easy to game the system. Even Barber admits that hospitals improved their waiting times by the simple ruse of not letting patients through the door. (Only once they were admitted were they deemed to be waiting.) Although the intention was good, it created perverse incentives. Hospitals would seek to meet targets for heart patients by treating the easy cases and shunning the harder ones. Schools stopped admitting less gifted children. You could make the statistics look good without necessarily improving the quality of service.

Still, an urgent task of national accounting is to improve measurements of public services so that their true value is better reflected. Public services tend to be better value for money than our economic indicators suggest. And, of course, they are not really free. We pay for them with our taxes. Which is why it is so important to measure them properly.

In 2012 Shinzō Abe was elected prime minister of Japan with a radical plan to get the economy growing again.[9] There were several elements to his strategy, including a commitment to a daring monetary policy designed to rekindle inflation. One idea was more simple. He was going to put Japanese women to work. The plan even had a catchy title: Womenomics.[10]

Japan's post-war economy was built around the male worker, the so-called salaryman. The stereotypical arrangement was for a man to enter a company from school or university. He would then stay at the same firm his whole career, his salary increasing each year, until retirement. The successful life path for a woman was to marry one of those men. At home she would take care of the house, including the household finances, bring up the children, and help look after her own and her husband's parents as they grew older. When her own children went to school or university, she might go back to work, but probably only part-time. That pattern was encouraged by a tax system that effectively penalized married women for working too many hours.

Of course, there were exceptions. Many women broke the mold. Besides, by the time Abe came to power, Japan's job-for-life system had long been crumbling. Still, it was obvious to almost everyone that Japanese women could be contributing more economically. When Abe launched his plan, about 49 percent of working-age women had jobs. That compared with 56 percent in the US and the UK and 60 percent in Sweden.

Trying to shift people into paid employment—or attracting new labor in the form of immigrants—is an obvious way to increase the size of an economy. In fact, there are really only two ways to produce economic growth as we now measure it. One is to add people. The other, usually achieved by investing capital, is to raise productivity by getting those people to work more efficiently. Instead of producing, say, 1,000 cars a day, a factory will produce 2,000 cars using the same workforce or, better yet, with half the workforce and a cast of supporting robots.

Adding people is in many ways easier than raising productivity. You simply take people who were not earning money and put them into paid employment. Whatever they produce contributes to the national economy. The unspoken assumption here is that whatever these people were doing before was, from an economic standpoint, worthless. They may have been pillars of their community or unpaid performance artists or hardworking mothers. But only paid work counts.

If a Japanese housewife cooks her aging father-in-law meals, helps him in and out of bed, helps him use the toilet, and washes his clothes and sheets, none of her efforts count toward the economy. If, however, she works in a care home looking after someone else's father-in-law—and earning a wage while she's at it—then the exact same activities contribute to national income. In the same way, if I charge to paint someone's house, I am adding to the economy. But if I volunteer to paint my neighbor's living room for free, my work is statistically invisible.

In Japan women did enter the workforce in record numbers after Prime Minister Abe came to power, although this may well have had more to do with pinched family finances than a direct response to his plan. Many of the women who joined the labor force took on low-paid part-time work. More than half of all paid work done by women in Japan falls into this category. Still, after being well behind, the proportion of female workers in Japan is now higher than in America, where more and more people from both sexes have dropped out of the labor force altogether.[11]

Few doubt that Japan's gender relations and its labor market need shaking up. It is good for the country to have more women in work, particularly if—as is presently not happening much—they climb the management ladder and begin to affect how companies are run. Corporate Japan could do with a dose of female creativity and a fresh injection of ideas. But much of the "economic gain" to Japan came about simply by encouraging women to ditch their often valuable unpaid work at home and to do paid—and taxable—jobs in the workplace. As a result, the economy grew marginally faster. But it is debatable how much extra work was actually being done.

Like the government's contribution to the economy, housework and volunteer work is hard to count. Because there is no price attached to "home production," such as making a bed, cooking a dinner, or sweeping the *tatami* matting, it is not easy to put a value on such activity. Nor is it clear where we should draw the line. Should we count it when we scratch our own nose, since this also brings an unrecorded benefit?[12]

Advocates of counting household chores and volunteer work say these activities are routinely ignored because they are performed mainly by women. That's why they are undervalued. Or, more precisely, not valued at all. One author lists some of the activities that are not part of the economy as "giving birth to babies, raising children, cultivating a garden, cooking food for her siblings, milking the family cow, making clothes for her relatives or taking care of Adam Smith so he can write *The Wealth of Nations*."[13] Even the woman whose housework freed up time for the economist Adam Smith to write his most famous work contributed nothing to the economy, as we define it. Smith is known for his concept of the "invisible hand," which describes the market forces and pricing signals that are supposed to make economies work smoothly without a central plan. He wrote less about the invisible sex.[14]

In Jonathan Franzen's novel *The Corrections* Enid's husband, Al, is irritated that she has not cleared up magazines and jars from the top of the stairs.

> But it seemed to her that he'd asked her to do more than "one thing" while he was gone. He'd also asked her to make the boys three meals a day, and clothe them and read to them and nurse them in sickness, and scrub the kitchen floor, and wash the sheets and iron his shirts, and do it all

without a husband's kisses or kind words. If she tried to get credit for these labors of hers, however, Al simply asked her whose labors had *paid* for the house and food and linens?[15]

Presumably Enid did something else for her children that Al never bothered to consider worth putting on the same footing as paid work: she literally fed them on her own milk. Nutritionists are almost unanimous in recommending that mothers breastfeed babies for the first six months.[16] Because of the antibodies in colostrum, the first milk a mother produces, more than one-fifth of deaths in newborn babies could be prevented if all infants were breastfed within the first hour of life. All the women of the world could suddenly decide that they were going to breastfeed their children for the first six months to the enormous benefit of the next generation. Yet this would not affect growth in any way. In fact, economic activity would decrease because of the loss of sales of paid-for infant formula. This is a classic example of perverse accounting: we value precisely the opposite of what is actually beneficial. Those who advocate government policies to encourage breastfeeding are outgunned by lobbyists working for baby-formula companies, who can point to the economic benefits of their industry.

Julie P. Smith, an Australian academic, attempted to estimate the hidden contribution of breast milk to the economies of Australia, Norway, and the US.[17] She used the European market price for breast milk of $100 a liter, based on the cost of milk at human milk banks. She then worked out a value of average milk produced per day and the average length of time that mothers breastfeed their babies in those three countries. She found that Australian mothers produced 42 million liters of milk with a market price of $4.2 billion. Norwegian mothers produced $1.1 billion worth of milk, and

American mothers $53 billion worth. She also calculated what she called "lost milk," the milk that would have been produced if mothers had breastfed to the recommended six months. Doing so would have raised milk production to $8.9 billion, $1.8 billion, and $127 billion respectively.

Not counting "women's work" diminishes its perceived importance. In this case we value a precious health elixir that only women can produce at precisely zero. The danger is that, if we do not measure something, it is undervalued. In often invisible—even subconscious—ways, policymakers and regulators are biased toward what they can see and what they can count. They support industries, say the baby formula industry, because it employs people, pays taxes, and contributes to the economy. The invisible and the uncountable, almost by definition, get sidelined.

If we can put a price on breast milk, surely all kinds of housework could be incorporated into a new definition of what constitutes an economy? After all, national income already includes one important item where no money changes hands: something known as "imputed rent." If I live in a rented apartment, then the monthly rent I pay is part of the economy, recorded as my expenditure and my landlord's income. But what if I live in my own house or apartment? I pay no rent even though I still have a roof over my head. From the point of view of the economy—unless we make some kind of adjustment—my house is invisible.

That is a problem. Imagine comparing a country where most people rent to one where most people own their own home. The home-owning country would look poorer relative to the home-renting country since the value of people's homes would be effectively invisible. To get around this anomaly, statisticians use something called imputation. They work out how much rent an owner-occupier would have to pay if she were living in rented accommodation. This is done by comparing her own home to a similar rented property, say the house next door. The imputed rent figure appears in the national income accounts as if it had actually been paid—even though no transaction has taken place and no money has changed hands. Through this accounting trick, the rent we would have to pay if we didn't already own our home becomes part of the economy. (Remember, what we confidently call the economy is basically a figment of our imagination.)

Couldn't exactly the same be done for housework? The answer is that it could. In fact, the exercise of counting the imputed economic contribution of housework is now routinely performed by national statistics agencies in many countries. The results, though, are not incorporated into the official statistics. That would be just a bit too right-on. Instead, they are left in occasional "satellite accounts," orbiting around the central body in the economic solar system: Planet GDP.

The man who figured out the size of the US economy for nearly twenty years, Steve Landefeld, former director of the Bureau of Economic Analysis, is on the whole enthusiastic about counting housework. He has done extensive research on the subject, starting in 2000 with a paper entitled, in the enticing language beloved of economists, "Accounting for Nonmarket Household Production Within a National Accounts Framework."[18] But Congress has been less than supportive, particularly when it comes to stumping up cash to pay for all the surveys that would be necessary to make this a regular exercise. For Congress, "statistics just can't compete with stuff like cops on the street," says Landefeld. "Statistics is about as far down the list as you can get in terms of priorities."

In 2012 researchers in America published a paper building

on Landefeld's work.[19] The headline finding was that if cooking, cleaning, washing, driving and so on were counted, these activities would add roughly $3.8 trillion to the total size of the American economy. That would make the economy 26 percent bigger. The paper uses what is known as time use data, basically a diary filled in to record activities performed throughout a twenty-four-hour period. After excluding a few activities—such as sleeping (which personally I'd very much like to see counted as a productive economic activity)—the researchers boiled these down to seven main tasks from gardening to childcare. The hours are aggregated and a wage applied, using the hourly rate for a general housekeeper.

By tracking similar surveys back to 1965, researchers found that the amount of housework had actually dropped over the years. In 1965, it estimated, household production accounted for 39 percent of the economy, significantly more than today. It attributed the fall largely to changing lifestyles, as more women took paid jobs and as families ate out more, knitted fewer sweaters, and became less picky about cleaning up potato chips lurking under the sofa.

The UK's Office for National Statistics has been conducting a similar exercise since 2002, when it published its first satellite account for household activity.[20] It chose a different approach from the one adopted by American researchers. Instead of counting up hours of activity and applying a standard wage, it attempted to put a monetary value on household "output," such as the number of meals prepared and children cared for. Studies have found that households can easily identify how often they use the washing machine, the type and quantity of meals prepared and so on. That still leaves the question of quality. A househusband might heat up a can of spaghetti hoops or prepare a cordon bleu dinner following a recipe. Unless you adjust for quality, these would both be counted exactly the same.

The paper divides household work into seven categories: shelter, including do-it-yourself maintenance; providing transport (all those car rides to ballet class); nutrition (those lukewarm spaghetti hoops); laundry services; childcare; care for elderly or disabled members of the household; and volunteer activities. As with traditional national income accounts, in each case intermediate consumption is removed. If a mother gives her child an apple that she has already paid for at the supermarket, it should not be counted again. If a father knits a sweater for his daughter then the cost of the wool must be deducted so that only the value-added of his labor counts and so on. Then a proxy price must be found. For example, the cost of taking the bus to school as opposed to getting a ride from your mother. At each stage one assumption is piled on another, from the amount and quality of the work done to the equivalent market price.

After making all these complex calculations for the year 2000, British statisticians found that total unpaid household work was worth £877 billion or about 45 percent of all economic activity for that year.[21] Of that, £221 billion was attributed to the value of childcare, £164 billion to nutrition (perhaps more cordon bleu than spaghetti hoops after all), and £156 billion to transport. Laundry accounted for £46 billion. Voluntary activity came in at just £13 billion, which struck me as either an underestimate or an indication that the British are more interested in cleaning and pressing their shirts than helping out their neighbors. Similar exercises have been carried out in many countries, including Australia, Finland, Hungary, Germany, Mexico, and Nepal. Finland is typical in showing unpaid housework as contributing some 40 percent to total economic activity.[22]

One interesting finding of the 2012 American study was that counting home production lowers measured inequality. The reason is that poor people make their own beds just like rich people (unless the rich people have paid staff to do it for them). The imputed dollar value of a millionaire making his bed or ironing his shirt doesn't vary much from a pauper performing the same task. Adding a small chunk of home production "income" to a poor family thus has a bigger effect, proportionately, than adding it to a rich one.[23]

The more we formally count housework as part of the economy, therefore, the more relatively equal our societies look. That is a counterintuitive result. Trying to count housework as part of economic activity would normally be considered a progressive idea, one designed to highlight the invisible work done disproportionately by women. Yet doing so would tend to de-emphasize the inequalities that are causing so much anger in many of our societies. Messing with economic statistics is never easy.

4

TOO MUCH OF
A GOOD THING

The road from Reykjavik's sleek airport to the Icelandic capital passes through a landscape of black lava, rocky scabs from previous molten eruptions that go on for mile after wide-open mile. A cold wind blows in from the Atlantic Ocean and the strewn rock is bathed in a brooding, beautiful light. The capital is sophistication itself. Home to roughly half of Iceland's population of 334,000 people, its buildings resemble little ski chalets or competition-winners from architectural magazines. Icelanders are fashionably dressed. Prosperous, liberal and chic, Reykjavik is the kind of place where the cafés serve toasted date and kale sandwiches (open-face on dark brown bread, of course) and play warbling Ethiopian jazz.[1]

Still, eight years after the financial crisis, the scars of one of the most dramatic banking collapses in modern times are as visible as the rocks scattered by the volcanic eruptions. Six months before I arrived in October 2016, Sigmundur David Gunnlaugsson, the prime minister, had resigned after revelations that he and his wife had owned an offshore investment trust with multimillion-dollar claims on Iceland's failed banks. The scandal, the latest in a cavalcade of post-crash revelations, had helped give life to the Pirate Party, an anarchist-leaning group with roots in online activism which was now threatening to upend the island's cozy politics. The party was Iceland's version of the radical movements—from both left and right—that had sprung up across Europe in the aftermath of the 2008 financial meltdown. Its logo was a black pirate flag.

Elections triggered by Gunnlaugsson's resignation were just a few days away. Twelve parties were jostling for control of Iceland's ancient parliament, founded in AD 930. There was a palpable sense of anger over what people saw as betrayal by the country's elites.

At sixty-two, Sigmunder Knutsson, a man who wore his scowl on his sleeve, described himself as a poet and an economist. Many Icelanders think of themselves as having twin vocations, and not a few, including Birgitta Jonsdottir, the leader of the Pirate Party, consider themselves poets. These days fewer admit to being economists.

"When I think about politics in Iceland, it makes me want to vomit," Knutsson told a reporter from the *New York Times*, tucking into a plate of fermented shark, a local treat, in a small café with worn tables and bare walls. "It's all about corruption among a very small elite," he said. "There is something that is not right. Something smells bad."[2]

Arnan, a thirty-two-year-old former banker with shoulder-length blond hair, stopped in the street in front of the Hallgrimskirkja, a modern cathedral that looks like an about-to-blast-off space rocket, to voice much the same opinion. Iceland had traditionally been a farming country with an economy dominated by the big landowning families, he said. Those same families had used their wealth and influence to secure a monopoly over the island's rich fishing quotas. In the latest iteration, he said, the self-same elite had taken over a banking sector that had expanded exponentially in the first years of this century.

The story of Iceland's banking industry illustrates one of the messages of this book. Not all economic growth is good. Rapid growth comes in many flavors, and some of them are less appetizing than others. In the 1990s David Oddsson, Iceland's longest-serving prime minister, oversaw a Thatcherite orgy of deregulation that transformed Iceland from sleepy fishing nation to pioneer of turbocharged "Viking capitalism."[3] After the banks were privatized in 2002, three institutions, Glitnir, Kaupthing and Landsbanki, went on an incredible expansion binge fueled by cheap borrowing from other cash-flush banks. They lent money to friends and to each other and set off on a madcap spending spree, picking up assets all across Europe, from English football teams to Danish airlines. Stefan Olafsson, an Icelandic professor, called it "probably the most rapid expansion of a banking system in the history of mankind."

Iceland changed from a country into what one writer called a giant hedge fund.[4] Its gung-ho young business titans swallowed whole the economic philosophy they had learned at American business schools. Together with normally sober Icelandic citizens they participated in a bout of collective madness. It wasn't long before most Icelanders discovered the trick of borrowing cheaply in foreign currencies abroad and pumping the money into the local stock market, which increased in value nine times between 2003 and 2007. They invested in local property, whose value also went up and up and up, confirming their secret suspicion that they were investment geniuses. Consumption went wild. It became fashionable to hire helicopters to pop over to the other side of the island for picnics. One particularly exuberant Icelander paid $1 million to hear Elton John sing two songs for his birthday. By my reckoning, that's $500,000 a song.[5]

What ordinarily sober citizens did, the banks did on steroids. The business of banking is credit creation, and Iceland's institutions took their job seriously. At the peak of the insanity, the three main banks' assets were worth 14.4 trillion krona, or an astonishing ten times Iceland's national income. Not everything that was being done was, shall we say, legal. Michael Lewis, a financial author, quotes one hedge fund manager as describing some of the transactions between Iceland's banks. "You have a dog, and I have a cat. We agree that each is worth a billion dollars. You sell me the dog for a billion, and I sell you the cat for a billion. Now we are no longer pet owners, but Icelandic banks with a billion dollars in new assets."[6]

As banks' activity expanded, so did their apparent contribution to the economy. While the fishing industry's share of output dropped from 16 percent of GDP in 1980 to 6 percent in 2006, the share of finance, insurance, and real estate went rapidly in the other direction. In the eight years to 2006, it rose from 17 percent of economic output to 26 percent.[7] From the perspective of national accounting, bank expansion was a wonderful thing. It brought growth and yet more growth. Indeed, per-capita income exploded, reaching around $45,000 a head in 2006, making Iceland the sixth-richest country on earth. Kaupthing, the largest privatized bank, went on a binge of buying, merging and deal-making. It opened up an Internet bank, Kaupthing Edge, with branches in ten European countries, in a valiant effort to hoover up retail savings. Iceland had almost no track record in global finance, yet within a few years, according to one banker, Kaupthing began to think of itself as "the Goldman Sachs of the Arctic."[8]

Then—and you probably guessed this was coming—it all went horribly wrong. And I mean horribly. When Lehman Brothers went bust in September 2008, trust in the entire global financial system vanished overnight. Banks stopped lending to each other, unsure whether their counterparties were good for the money or whether their balance sheets too were riddled with toxic assets. For Icelandic banks, leveraged up to the hilt, it was the end of the road.

Within ten days, Glitnir, the third largest, asked for a government bailout. As the krona plummeted and news spread that the financial system was insolvent, Icelanders started removing cash from banks by the bag-load. Many were left with huge debts in foreign currency which they had to repay with a sinking krona. Within a few weeks all the banks had been nationalized. In Britain, where 300,000 people and some local councils had put money in Icelandic banks, Gordon Brown, the prime minister, invoked anti-terrorism laws to try to recoup lost savings. Geir Haarde, Iceland's prime minister at the time, was not exactly sugarcoating his words when he said, "The danger is real that the Icelandic economy would be sucked, along with banks, under the waves and the nation would become bankrupt."[9]

By the end of October, Iceland, just months previously an apparently roaring success, had gone cap in hand to the International Monetary Fund for a bailout. The stock market fell 85 percent and every Icelandic man, woman, and child was on the hook for their $330,000 share of the $100 billion in losses racked up by reckless banks.

I strolled over to the annex of Iceland's parliament, a modestly proportioned building that resembles a modern art gallery, to see Birgir Armannsson. A neatly dressed man in a soft gray suit, Armannsson is a senior member of the center-right Independence Party, which was part of the ruling coalition when Iceland was leaping, lemming-like, off the financial cliff. As a young lawyer in the 1990s, he had noticed attitudes to finance change. "Icelandic business people became richer than ever before and started to lose all connection with the Icelandic people, with the Icelandic community," he said. In the following decade it got worse. "They became international billionaires instead of being rather well-off local business people. They started to buy private jets and yachts, something we had never before seen in Iceland. Before, it was good, maybe, to have two cars."

Armannsson watched the process unfold at close hand. "Icelandic banks got cheap loans all over the world and they were pumping money into local companies. The stock market rose dramatically and nobody thought it would ever go into reverse." Were there no warning signs? I asked. Didn't the sudden rise in living standards and the massive paper gains look too good to be true? "Well into 2008, the outlook looked good. That was what parliamentarians thought, including myself. In retrospect we should have been quicker to respond to the rising problems," he said. "It has also come to light since the crisis that Icelandic bankers were manipulating the market and were deeply involved in insider trading. A lot of it was just a bubble."

I asked whether he thought conventional accounting had overstated the contribution of banks to the economy. "It would take someone with more expertise than me," he said. "This is a complicated issue." Then he added, as if it might be of some comfort, "I think we have limited possibility of the same crisis. Probably the next financial crisis will be a little bit different."

Just to be absolutely clear: the 2008 banking crisis, whose effects were still rippling through the world nearly a decade later, cannot be blamed on the way we account for financial services in our national accounts. The crisis had its roots in race-to-the-bottom deregulation, naive faith in the capacity of markets to self-correct, and a perverse "shareholder-value" ideology that allowed a few thousand masters-of-the-universe bankers to ransack their own institutions while simultaneously feeling good about themselves. There were many other factors, from the hugely increased (and unnecessary) mathematical complexity of financial instruments to the inherently corrupt relationship between the ratings agencies and the clients who paid them. The rampant fad of securitization was another ticking time bomb. This was the practice of dicing and slicing different revenue streams and smushing them together into a tradable asset, a practice that severed the traditional link between lender and borrower. After a while people were happily trading bits of paper—all triple-A rated, naturally—blissfully unaware of what the underlying assets actually contained. As we now know, much of it was mortgage debt taken out on homes by people who could not afford to make their payments.

Yet the banking crisis *was* linked to national accounting in two important ways. The first is as much psychological as anything else. This is what you might call the danger of the circular argument, one that goes like this: "We all know growth is good. Growth is measured by GDP. So when GDP is going up that must be good. Giving free rein to banks to do their thing is a recipe for higher GDP. Ergo giving free rein to banks must be good."

That led ambitious governments around the world, including Iceland's, to ape the Anglo-Saxon model, one that involved liberalization, deregulation, and privatization. Really anything with a "tion" on the end of it would do. Banks were allowed to get on with the business of "wealth creation"—which mostly meant shuffling bits of paper among themselves, lending recklessly, and paying themselves fat bonuses. The global cheerleaders for these policies were the US and the UK, where Ronald Reagan and Margaret Thatcher had set the deregulation agenda in motion and where Wall Street and the City of London were rampant. Not only was it obvious how much money bankers were making—you only had to look at the cars they were driving to see that—but they also spent formidable amounts of money lobbying governments to make life yet easier for them.

Banking became a bigger and bigger part of the US and UK economies. The "contribution" of the financial sector to national income grew enormously. In the 1950s, when banks were banks rather than "great vampire squids," they contributed about 2 percent to the US economy.[10] By 2008, that had quadrupled.[11] Similar things happened in Britain. Until 1978 financial intermediation accounted for around 1.5 percent of whole economy profits. By 2008, that ratio had risen to about 15 percent.

The perceived success of financial deregulation in generating economic dynamism encouraged other countries to do the same. New Zealand, Australia, Ireland, Spain, Russia, and even little Iceland were seduced by the Anglo-Saxon model. The financial industry exploded all over the world. For the year to April 2008, the largest 1,000 banks reported aggregate pre-tax profits of almost $800 billion.[12] Countries that adopted these policies, including ones that gave freer and freer rein to their "wealth-creating" banks, did well, while others appeared to lag. The way we think of economic growth tends to tell you one thing: the bigger the banks grow the better.

As the idea that an unbridled banking industry led to a strong economy took hold, governments did all they could to foster the growth of the financial sector. For the most part, that meant getting out of the way. From the mid-1980s, states rolled back banking industry regulations, many of them put in place after the 1929 Wall Street crash. In America the separation of investment from commercial banking was steadily eroded until it was abandoned altogether with the repeal of the Glass-Steagall Act in 1999. In the mid-1980s London had its Big Bang, which swept away regulations and paved the way for huge financial conglomerates. As in Iceland, banks that had once relied on steady retail depositors for their capital took to the wholesale markets, sucking up and recycling first petro-dollars from the Middle East and then the surplus savings of workers and peasants in booming China.[13]

A process now known by the hideously ugly term "financialization" took hold. Anonymous capital markets replaced the once-simple relationship between borrower and lender. New products sprang up to fill this new market, including complex derivatives, or bets on the future movement of prices. Soon banks were talking a new language of forward exchange rates, credit default swaps, and collateralized debt obligations. The less ordinary people understood about what was really going on the better. I remember in the mid-2000s being lectured by senior bankers who explained to me condescendingly how derivatives were making the world a safer place by spreading risk to the four corners of the earth. But like Easter eggs hidden in sundry parts of the garden, it wasn't long before everyone forgot where they were hidden—or precisely what color or shape the eggs were. Just for good measure, in keeping with those buccaneering times, the market in derivatives was not regulated at all.

Banks' biggest customers were each other in an insane shuffling of paper that added virtually nothing to real economic activity (properly measured). The vast bulk of bank assets were actually claims on other banks. In Britain actual lending to businesses and individuals engaged in productive activity amounted to about 3 percent of total assets.[14] That left the other 97 percent. What's more, banks were horribly incentivized to keep up the game of pass the parcel. From the bankers' perspective, there was no downside. If a bet came off, they would be rich beyond imagination—and praised as wealth-creating geniuses to boot. And if it didn't come off, well, what was the worst that could happen?

It turned out that the worst was the near-collapse of the entire financial system, a meltdown arrested only by taxpayer bailouts worth hundreds of billions of dollars. Banking, as has been said by more than one person, is socialism for the wealthy and capitalism for everyone else.

Throughout the whole hideous expansion, conventional economics was sending but one signal: Bigger is better. Banking's apparent contribution to the economy had seduced politicians for decades. When the industry blew up, the debt was transferred from private banks to the public purse. A whole generation was saddled with the bill, both in higher taxes and in lost economic opportunity. One report put the cost of the financial crisis at between one and five times annual world output.[15]

That brings us to the second, slightly more technical, matter of the way we account for banking activity in our national accounts. The system that has evolved is perverse. It stems from the fact that banks do not charge fees for many of their activities. If a bank lends you money, it may charge a one-off fee. But the bulk of its revenue comes from what is called the spread—the difference between the interest rate it charges you and the interest rate at which the bank itself can obtain money.

To measure the supposed economic value generated by this

interest-rate spread, a new accounting concept was introduced in the 1993 update to the UN System of National Accounts, the holy book of GDP. The concept is called financial intermediation services indirectly measured, or FISIM for short. Without going into technical details, the upshot is that the wider the spread the more value is judged to have been created. That is back to front. In banking, spreads increase when risk rises. If a banker judges you quite unlikely to repay a loan, she will raise the interest rate charged to reflect the higher risk of default. So, from an accounting point of view, the riskier the portfolio of loans the greater the contribution to growth. Put another way, the more catastrophically irresponsible bankers are, the more we judge them to be helping the economy to grow. It is as if a driving instructor rated your proficiency solely on the basis of your maximum speed.

As one report into the UK financial crisis put it, with the sort of understatement only the British can muster, "This can lead to some surprising outcomes."[16] In the fourth quarter of 2008, after Lehman Brothers went bust and the international financial system seized up, from the perspective of UK national income things had never looked better. Just as the economy was about to go into free fall, the report said, "the nominal gross value-added of the financial sector in the UK grew at the fastest pace on record."

As several huge banks in Britain were about to go under, the financial system made up a record 9 percent of total economic activity. Worse, after much of the financial system was nationalized, its "contribution" rose yet again, this time to an all-time high of 10.4 percent, within a whisker of all British manufacturing.[17] "At a time when people believed banks were contributing the least to the economy since the 1930s, the national accounts indicated the financial sector was contributing the most since the mid-1980s," the report notes. "How do we begin to square this circle?"[18] How indeed?

In the US the story was every bit as catastrophic. Taxpayers injected hundreds of billions of dollars to bail out some of the biggest names in banking, including Citigroup and American International Group, the world's biggest insurer. Merrill Lynch was folded into Bank of America, Washington Mutual was sold to JP Morgan, and Lehman Brothers—well, you remember Lehman Brothers. Even Goldman Sachs and Morgan Stanley, the last two independent investment banks left standing, had to agree to become bank holding companies, which subjected them to greater regulation. In October 2008 $700 billion of taxpayer money was pumped into the Troubled Asset Relief Program, but not before Congress had rejected it once, prompting the biggest points fall in the history of the Dow Jones Industrial Average. As the financial crisis spread to the real economy, General Motors and Chrysler came knocking on the government's door for relief.

Nearly a decade after these events, the US economy still had not recovered its pre-crisis growth rate. That was probably, in large part, due to the fact that much of that growth had been little more than fiction.

The conversation about how we should account for banking activity quickly leads to a discussion about what banks are for. It is worth a tiny digression. Banks fulfill two broad functions. One is to store and transfer money. The other is to allocate risk. Somewhere along the way, these functions got badly scrambled.

I went to discuss this with Gavyn Davies, a former partner at Goldman Sachs. Davies said I should think of banks as being in two categories: cloakrooms and casinos. Cloakroom banks are boring. They are essentially utilities, places to house your money. "People give you the money; you put it in a cupboard, and when they come and get it, you give it back." Another metaphor sometimes used for this kind of bank is the economy's plumbing or pipework. That's because banks, even boring ones, transfer money along a network of pipes, for example if I want to send cash from my account to pay a utility bill or to my grandma back home in Wichita.

The other, more interesting—yet potentially more dangerous—function of a bank is to allocate capital. That means allocating risk. It requires a bank to make decisions about the creditworthiness and potential profitability of those to whom it lends money. At its most simple, the bank chooses between two widget companies that both need working capital. The bank lends to the better widget company and starves the inferior widget company of funds. Society benefits through better widgets. "Now, you're going to measure that not necessarily through the banking system," Davies said. "You're going to measure it through the productivity and production of the widget manufacturer." If the bank is doing its job right, everyone benefits.

But if the bank's capital allocation is measured in the real economy, why do we have to measure it separately as if it were useful in itself? We pick up the contribution of banks to the economy in the production of excellent widgets and in the production of all the other businesses helped by having access to excellent widgets. Measuring capital allocation as a stand-alone activity smacks of double counting, like measuring the flour in bread or the electricity in the production of marijuana. Accountants used to think so too. In the 1950s finance was treated as an unproductive activity, and banking made a only small positive—or even a negative—contribution to

71

national income. Interest-rate flows were "treated as an intermediate input" and netted out of the final value-added contribution to GDP.[19] Only with FISIM did we become obsessed about measuring what the banks were up to themselves.

Davies thought about the issue slightly differently. "When I used to have existential crises about what am I doing wasting my life in the banking system," he said, a colleague would assure him that banks played a vital economic role. "What we're doing is actually the most important function of all. We're allocating capital in the right way."

Davies said this always made him feel better. "Then 2008 happens and it's obvious that we've allocated capital in totally the wrong way for the previous decade," he said. "Those two activities—allocating capital in the right way and allocating it in the wrong way—are measured the same." They both count toward economic growth, which is to say they're really not being measured at all.

5

THE INTERNET
STOLE MY GDP

t is a cold rainy night in New York. You are in your apartment
listening to contemporary jazz on Spotify when you are seized
by the desire to escape the chill of winter for a weekend in Baja
California, a place you've wanted to visit ever since an enthusiastic
review on TripAdvisor caught your eye. You ease open your laptop and start searching. At skyscanner.com you type in JFK and
San Jose Cabo airports, put in dates for next weekend, and select
"Direct flights only." Within minutes you've entered your credit
card details and booked the cheapest option available.

Next stop is Airbnb to find accommodation. After some searching you hit upon a reasonably priced beachfront condo with what
looks like a spectacular view of the ocean. You also go into your
own Airbnb account so that anyone looking will know that your
Brooklyn apartment is free to rent next weekend. Finally, you ar-
range some online insurance just in case anything goes wrong. On
the day of the trip itself you go to the airline's website, enter your
passport details, select an aisle seat, check yourself in, and print
out your boarding pass. Then you book an Uber and slide into
the back seat for the trip to the airport. Time to rest. You've been
working hard.

The digital economy has blurred the distinction between
work, leisure, and household chores, shifting what is called the

production boundary, between activities that we count and activities that we don't. It has made the job of measuring the economy harder than ever. Advanced economies have for decades been more about services than manufacturing, but this tendency toward the ethereal and uncountable has been exacerbated in the Internet age. Will Page, director of economics at Spotify, the Swedish music-streaming service, says, "GDP faces a square peg, round hole dilemma" because it was "originally designed to measure tangible manufactured goods, which are losing relevance in the modern economy."[1]

When I went to see Page in Spotify's London offices—open plan, help-yourself drinks fridge, mandatory games room—I had to print out my own security badge and attach it to my lapel, a job that would once have been done by a receptionist. "The goal of disruptive technology companies, in the statistical sense, is to reduce GDP," Page said when I found him lurking in one of the corridors. "To wipe out transaction costs, which are being measured, and to replace them with convenience, which is not being measured. So the economy is shrinking, but everyone is getting a better deal. Lots of what tech is doing is destroying what wasn't needed. The end result is you're going to have less of an economy, but higher welfare."

From the economy's perspective, he was suggesting that Spotify and similar companies are like dark matter. Instead of pumping GDP out, they suck it in and make it disappear. And yet they are providing a valuable service that people are willing to pay for. What this does to our economy, as conventionally measured, is a complicated subject about which there is considerable controversy. So it is worth unpicking into several strands.

The first is the question of home production. We have seen that washing your children's clothes or cooking Adam Smith's dinner is not counted as economic activity. But what about printing your own boarding pass? Or, as I had to do the other day, tagging your own bag at the airport and sending it on its merry way along the luggage belt? (Next thing you know you'll be flying the plane.) Until recently these activities would have been performed by a paid member of the airport staff and been counted in economic statistics. Now these jobs have been outsourced—to you. In terms of the measured economy, they have vanished.

Similarly, the work you've just done to book your fabulous weekend in Mexico would once have been performed by a paid employee. In national accounting terms it has moved outside the production boundary. From the perspective of measurable economic activity, printing your own boarding pass is the equivalent of scratching your own nose. It serves a purpose but is no longer part of what we call the economy.

Now the airline doesn't need a reservation clerk and the taxi company doesn't need anyone to take calls and dispatch vehicles. On the other hand, as with all technological advances, it is hoped that the reservation clerk and taxi dispatcher will find more productive work elsewhere. There's another possible way in which economic activity—even that captured by conventional measures—has been enhanced. Because the airline is saving money, it can either lower its fares or pay its shareholders bigger dividends from increased profits. Either way, someone has more money in their pocket to spend on extra consumption, which should add to growth.

The second strand is the tendency of prices to fall toward zero. In the 1980s, when I was living in America, I remember my father calling me long distance from London. The conversation would always go the same way. "I can't stay on long," he would bellow down the crackly line. "It's costing a fortune." Virtually the whole call was taken up with the subject of how much this was costing and how he'd soon have to hang up. Long-distance calls were stressful and unsatisfactory.

These days, if there is an Internet connection people can communicate for free for an unlimited amount of time. Services like FaceTime and Google Hangouts mean they can see each other in real time too. People can browse Facebook and chat to their friends, they can send out messages on Twitter (particularly useful if they've been elected to high office), or look up information on Wikipedia (ditto). Wikipedia, which theoretically can bring all human knowledge to anyone with an Internet connection, is valued at precisely zero. How is it possible that such amazing things cost nothing? And does this mean that much of what we truly value lies outside what we call the economy?

There are three main ways we pay for non-tangible digital services such as streamed music, YouTube, and Facebook. One is the old-fashioned way: we pay money. The second way is with our time, specifically by looking at advertisements displayed on sites. In that case, the content or service is paid for by advertising revenue.[2] The third method is similar to advertising, only instead of paying with time, you pay with data. Yours. Many companies make a business of selling on information about their customers. This means you may be contributing to growth in ways that only the National Security Agency truly understands.

Something else was going on that night in New York. You were participating in what has become known rather glibly as the sharing economy. Before Airbnb, if you were out of town, you would normally have left your apartment vacant. Post Airbnb, you can effectively exchange your apartment for one in Baja California by finding a third person to rent it on the online marketplace. Congratulations, you are helping to sweat the world's physical assets. You have turned what would have been an empty apartment into a hotel. That's good for the environment (if you discount the small matter of the flight to Mexico) because it means hotel companies won't need to build as much new accommodation. But, all else being equal, it is bad for the economy: less construction, cheaper rooms.

The same is true when you trade in your secondhand goods on eBay. Or donate old clothes to Africa. You are damaging the economy, though you might have fondly imagined you were helping the environment or clothing a poor child in Rwanda.[3] Remember Chen, the fictional Chinese worker. Given your sudden predilection for secondhand goods, he will no longer be required to produce so much stuff. As things become cheaper and more convenient, economic activity will fall. Or at least it will appear to fall. It feels as though our definition of the economy is failing to capture what is really going on.

Let's turn to your laptop, the one you used to do all that work. It probably cost the same as the laptop you bought three years ago. But in terms of memory, speed, and screen image, it is at least twice as good. So you're getting a better product for the same money. Put another way, the price has dropped. This is important in the calculation of GDP. That is because the growth figures you generally see are adjusted for inflation. With computers and other technology services, the improvement—and therefore the fall in prices—is faster than statisticians can keep up with. That means we are overestimating inflation and thus underestimating the real size of our economies.

In 1995 the US Senate ordered an inquiry into the problem. The following year the Boskin Commission reported that, partly because of rapid advances in equipment like computers and phones, the US had been overstating inflation by 1.3 percentage points a year before 1996.[4] That meant it had been understating growth by the same amount.[5] Other countries, including Japan and some European states, have made similar adjustments. But so fast is the pace of technological change that it is safe to assume everyone is behind the curve. That would imply that we are overestimating inflation—and that we are richer than we think.

A concept that sums up a lot of what is happening is the consumer surplus. This is the gap between what the consumer pays for something and what it is actually worth to them. The idea was popularized by Alfred Marshall, a nineteenth-century economist. It can apply to something as simple as water, for which you might be prepared to pay considerably more than the market price, particularly if you are very thirsty. Or the latest John Grisham thriller, for which an ardent fan would pay a lot more than the cover price to get a look at an early copy.

As technology races ahead and as the price of some products tends to zero, some economists argue that the consumer surplus is widening. One way of testing the theory is to see how much early adopters are willing to pay for, say, the latest iPhone. The gap between the opening-weekend price and the price at which the phone eventually settles is the consumer surplus, at least for them. Or you could threaten to take away someone's iPhone and see how much they would pay you to get it back. An iPhone is not just a piece of equipment, but also a means of connecting to networks of friends and business associates and of accessing information. "I think the real value is many thousands of dollars per person," says Gavyn Davies. "That's a humongous mismeasurement of the value that the iPhone has brought to most human beings."

Most experts agree that, because of these technological upheavals, national accounts underestimate economic growth. But estimates differ widely—not to say wildly—as to how much. Erik Brynjolfsson of the Massachusetts Institute of Technology noted in 2012 that the information sector accounted for the same official share of GDP in the US—about 4 percent—as it had done a quarter of a century earlier. This is implausible, to put it politely. Many people have taken a stab at calculating what we are missing in the official figures. Methods vary.[6] They include attaching an hourly wage to the time we spend on the Internet, estimated at $22 in one Google study, since that was the average US wage at the time.[7]

Brynjolfsson and a colleague, JooHee Oh, conducted their own exercise. They started with a finding that, between 2002 and 2011, the amount of leisure time Americans spent surfing the net, using services such as Facebook, Google, Wikipedia, and YouTube, rose from 3 to 5.8 hours a week. Since consumers could have used the time for something else, the authors assumed that the extra hours spent on the Internet reflected a growing consumer surplus that they calculated at $2,600 per user for a grand US-wide total of $564 billion in 2011. If included in national statistics, that would have raised growth by 0.4 percentage points a year. Other estimates have come up with nearly twice that.[8]

Not everyone agrees that staring at Facebook should be counted as economic activity, particularly if people do it at work when they could be doing something useful—like chatting to colleagues. Why should watching YouTube be counted when watching TV or playing with your children or walking in the park is not? Should we really put more of a value on watching a cat video than, say—to pick an entirely random activity out of thin air—watching a real cat? The benefits of the Internet can be overstated as well as understated.

...

There is, it says in Ecclesiastes 1:9, no new thing under the sun. Doubtless the dude who wrote that copied it from somewhere else. We have always had a hard time accounting for innovation. That applies equally to improvements in cars and photocopy machines as it does to faster Internet speeds. When new inventions first appear they can be incredibly expensive. One example is medicines, which are protected by patents. These allow pharmaceutical companies to charge hundreds, if not thousands, of dollars for their products. But when the patent runs out, the price of the same medicine falls to pennies and the product essentially vanishes from the economy.

If you think technology is accelerating faster than ever before, as many do, then the mismeasurement problem is getting worse. But there are serious academics who contend that the really important advances in technology are all behind us. Robert Gordon, an expert on productivity at Northwestern University, argues that all the truly transformative inventions came about after 1870 and more or less ran out of steam around 1970. He cites the invention of electricity and the internal combustion engine, and the provision of clean water and sewage disposal. These led to the invention of machines such as the telephone, the radio, the refrigerator, the car, and aircraft. Many of these technologies in turn produced huge ripple effects.

Ha-Joon Chang, a Cambridge economist, says the washing machine was a far more revolutionary invention (pun intended) than the Internet. Why? "The washing machine, piped gas, running water and all these mundane household technologies enabled women to enter the labor market, which then meant that they had fewer children, had them later, invested more in each of them, especially female children. That changed their bargaining positions within the household and in wider society, giving women votes and prompting endless other changes. It has transformed the way we live."[9] Gordon argues that technology has had a profound impact on society, but that this impact is diminishing. The speed of travel went from the horse and carriage to the jet plane, but plane speeds got stuck some fifty years ago. Urbanization and the transformation of women's lives by domestic appliances are one-off events. Once they have occurred, these technological leaps quickly fade in the statistics.

Still, it seems a fair bet that the computer revolution will transform our lives in ways we hardly yet comprehend. Robots and artificial intelligence will render many of the jobs we do today redundant, changes that are only hinted at with the automated answering services and supermarket auto-checkout machines that have already become part of everyday life. Cars will drive themselves, packages will come by drone, and robots will prescribe medicines and take care of the elderly. In Japan robots have been building other robots for many years.

If new inventions are all about the exchange of information and "standing on the shoulders of giants," then technological advances can only accelerate as more and more people get access to information. Increasingly, even in developing countries, people have instant access to virtually the entire body of human knowledge, something that would have been inconceivable even in 1990. In Rwanda there are plans to give 12 million people access to an AI doctor, which would give medical advice based on a description of symptoms over the phone.[10]

This debate about whether we are underestimating growth lies at the heart of what is perhaps the greatest conundrum faced by the economic profession. Amid all this innovation and technological change, why has productivity stagnated? The answer could be that improvements are simply not being picked up. Of course, it could also be that technology is somehow not bringing the expected jump in productivity that people expected, but this seems less likely.

The conundrum is central to how people feel about their circumstances. Many in Europe and America, particularly in the so-called shrinking middle class, are upset at the perceived stagnation of their living standards. But if growth is being underestimated, it could be that many are better off than they think. If we could only capture technological change better, maybe we would realize that our lives are not so bad after all. Alternatively, perhaps people are unhappy about other things, including the loss of meaningful work, rising inequality, and the fracturing of communities. The fundamental point is that, on these and other matters, the concept of growth—as currently measured—sheds little light.

If you've never ridden on a Japanese bullet train it is hard to imagine the awesomeness of the experience. The sleek white trains with their comically elongated noses slide into the station with such precision that passengers standing at designated spots on the platform find themselves right in front of the door to their allotted carriage. The trains glide off in a matter of seconds to resume racing across the countryside at near-airplane speeds, and you are left to gape as the landscape streaks by or to purchase some freshly made delicacy from the bowing women pushing trolleys noiselessly through the carriages. Between Tokyo and Osaka there are about 300 daily services, which make the 552-kilometer journey in 2½ hours with an average delay measured in fractions of a second.

It is hard to put a price on quality. An economist would say that the price is whatever the customer agrees to pay since the market finds a natural equilibrium between supply and demand. That might just about work within a country, but when it comes to comparisons between countries, especially in the context of non-tradable services like a train between Tokyo and Osaka, the price test breaks down. In the UK, no matter how much I may dread the prospect of long delays, shabby trains, and soggy bacon sandwiches on the London to Sunderland route, I cannot pay more to take a Japanese bullet train to the same destination.

The same is true of American Amtrak trains, which crawl along at speeds that belong in another century and have the odd fatal accident. (Not a single person has been killed by a bullet-train accident since Japan launched the service in 1964.) Imagine my surprise then when I came across a report from consultants McKinsey bemoaning the inefficiency of the Japanese service sector, up to and including its trains. Even the best Japanese companies, it said, reached only 85 percent the efficiency of the American system.[11] That was pure economist-speak. For anyone who has actually taken a train in both countries, to say American or British trains are more efficient than Japanese ones is laughable. Economists have little to say on questions of quality. Criticisms of Japanese inefficiency stem from the fact that economists are not comparing like with like, since very few countries can match—and none exactly replicate—the service available in Japan.

Kyoji Fukao, a professor at Hitotsubashi University's Economic Research Institute, helped provide much of the Japanese data that went into the international comparisons used by McKinsey and others. He agreed that the usual measures of service-sector efficiency—value added per man hour and total factor productivity, which incorporates capital and labor inputs—were crude and difficult to apply across borders. Fukao gave the example of Japan's retail sector, lambasted for its inefficiency in the McKinsey report. The basic measure of retail-sector productivity is how much of a product an employee can shift in an hour. On this measure, Germany does well. That turns out to be because of restricted opening hours, which oblige customers to make hefty purchases in concentrated bursts. Japan does badly. That is partly because there are tiny shops on every street corner that sell the most dazzling array of products. Many are open twenty-four hours a day. They are cheap but of excellent quality and incredibly convenient, yet looked at in purely numerical terms less efficient than cavernous US superstores on the outskirts of big cities. These experiences are incomparable. Nor, incidentally, is any allowance made for the fact that Japanese shops tend to be within walking or, at most, cycling distance. Data fail to capture the inconvenience of having to drive out of town, or the "externalities"—the unmeasured side-effects—associated with long shopping expeditions: traffic accidents, pollution, road maintenance, stress, and lost time.

Services are inherently subjective. An engineer is asked how to make the service on the London–Paris Eurostar more pleasant. He recommends spending £6 billion on new track to shorten the three-and-a-half-hour journey by forty minutes. An advertising executive is asked the same question. He comes up with a different solution. He recommends hiring male and female supermodels to walk up and down the aisles dispensing free Chateau Petrus throughout the journey. The train company will save billions on new track. And passengers will actually ask for the trains to slow down.[12]

Even without cross-border complications, working out the output of services is much harder than for manufactured products. How do you compare something as simple as one haircut with another? There's the boot-camp short-back-and-sides performed with an electric razor, or the three-hour session at a high-end salon in which every strand of hair is lovingly sculpted and the experience rounded off with a delicious head massage. But what about the decor of the salon and the skill of the hairdresser, not just in cutting hair but in artful conversation? And it's not good enough to say that the price of the haircut tells you all you need to know about the quality, because the price will vary from year to year. How does the poor statistician work out price changes from one year to the next—essential if national income accounts are to make sense—if the service in question is hard to quantify and in constant flux?

If you think haircuts are hard, try the services that landscape gardeners or computer engineers provide, each individually tailored to the customer's needs and virtually impossible to compare. National statistics agencies struggle with these questions daily. The US, for example, has more than 350 classification categories for manufactured goods, which account for less than a fifth of the economy, but fewer for the entire range of services, which make up some 80 percent of economic activity. The way we measure production was invented in the 1930s, but since then the nature of what we produce has changed beyond all recognition. Our standard measures of the economy struggle to tell us much at all about the vast bulk of things we actually consume. That is quite a flaw. It suggests we should take growth statistics less seriously than we do.[13]

In August 2016 the European Commission handed down its biggest ever tax judgment when it ordered Ireland to collect $14.5 billion (plus interest) in back taxes from Apple. The commission argued that Apple had engaged in a dubious profit-allocation scheme that allowed most of its profits to be moved to a "head office" on the outskirts of Cork, the southernmost county in Ireland. Effectively, the commission argued, Apple was tax-resident in no country in Europe, allowing it to shrink its European tax rate to well below 1 percent. For the record, Apple's chief financial officer called the EU's finding "legal mumbo jumbo" and said its calculation of Apple's tax bill used the "wrong denominator and the wrong numerator"—though apart from that it was presumably spot on.

The dispute stems from claims of tax avoidance, but the arguments apply to how we measure the economy, particularly in an age when multinational companies are ever more sprawling and the stuff they are selling ever more intangible. In Apple's case, much hinges on intellectual property. On paper Apple's subsidiary in Ireland—a country that accounts for only a fraction of its sales—is super-profitable because that's where Apple's intellectual property rights are held. In the digital age the value of a product is not primarily found in a physical asset, but rather in the brand or intellectual or artistic content. Even for something as seemingly tangible as a jet engine, customers pay not only for the piece of equipment but also for sophisticated service contracts in which the provider monitors the engine in real time and keeps it running smoothly throughout its life.

Many multinational companies are able to move the source of value of their products—whether intellectual property, service contracts, or legal services—around their international networks almost willy-nilly. You may buy your engine in Seattle, but the people ensuring the engine keeps running for twenty years are in Mumbai. Through a practice known as transfer pricing one sub-

sidiary charges another for the use of these intangible services and the profit is logged in one location—almost certainly the one with the lower tax rate. In 2014 Facebook caused an outcry in Britain by paying tax of just £4,327, a fact that helped provoke a tax revolt in one small Welsh town where tiny businesses were paying substantially more than that.[14]

GDP was conceived of in terms of the nation state, but businesses increasingly operate across borders. Gross national product, as it was originally called, measured everything produced by a country's nationals, wherever they happened to work. Under the administration of George H. W. Bush that changed to the more familiar GDP, which measures anything produced within a nation's borders, including by non-nationals. The reason for the switch may have been that Bush needed to boost his economic credentials. Switching to GDP, as opposed to GNP, increased the perceived US growth rate because it included the production of Japanese companies who had invested heavily in the American car and electronics industries.[15]

In these days of the multinational, when many Western companies have decamped to China, Mexico, or Vietnam, it makes more sense to use gross national product. Incidentally, that would make Western economies look better and the countries where the manufacturing takes place look worse than our current method of calculating the economy.[16] What constitutes national production, however it is configured, becomes almost meaningless when companies are registered in one country, make products in a second, sell them in a third, and pay taxes (if they really, really have to) in a fourth.

Apple's European tax dispute is a good example. But so is the manufacture of Apple's iPhones, most of which are assembled in

factories in the southern Chinese city of Shenzhen owned incidentally by Hon Hai, a company from the breakaway island of Taiwan. The fact that Apple and many other American companies have chosen China as a manufacturing base is the reason the US runs such a big trade deficit with that country. Yet, the ostensible size of the trade deficit—despite being so politically explosive—is not that significant. That is because most of the components assembled in China are made elsewhere: microchips in South Korea, capacitors in Japan, and processors in the US itself. You don't even need to open an iPhone to see what's going on. Just flip it over and you'll see "Designed by Apple in California. Assembled in China." One report found that only 2 percent of the cost of an iPhone went to Chinese labor, with 30 percent going to Apple's shareholders in the form of profits.

Even something as seemingly simple as an opal is hard to pin down. A book about Chungking Mansions, the dosshouse-cum-trading-hub in Hong Kong where people gather from all around the world to trade, recounts a dizzying example of low-end globalization.[17] Australian opals are shipped, via Chungking Mansions, to southern China, where they are polished, sent back to Australia, and sold as souvenirs to Chinese tourists visiting Australia (who presumably take them back to China). In such a world the idea of domestic production—our very definition of the economy—becomes almost meaningless.

6
WHAT'S WRONG WITH THE AVERAGE JOE

In September 2015 the scientific journal *Proceedings of the National Academy of Sciences of the United States of America* published a paper by two academics, Anne Case and Angus Deaton. It carried the less-than-riveting title "Rising morbidity and mortality in midlife among white non-Hispanic Americans in the 21st century." Buried in its careful language was a shocking revelation. From 1999 there had been a marked increase in the deaths of middle-aged white Americans. Nothing quite like it had been seen in the industrialized world since the breakup of the Soviet Union in 1991 when an entire generation seemed to succumb to despair and vodka, and life expectancy fell alarmingly. How on earth could this be happening in America, a country whose economy had been growing at solid rates—at least until the 2008 financial crisis—for decades?

Shockingly, the rise was the result of what the authors called "deaths of despair"—specifically suicides, drug and alcohol poisonings and chronic liver disease and cirrhosis. Up until 1999 deaths among white midlife Americans aged between forty-five and fifty-four had been falling at about 2 percent a year, in line with declines in other wealthy countries, but in that year this trend abruptly stopped and went into reverse.

The paper contained a striking graph in which deaths per

100,000 middle-aged white Americans were plotted against those of Australia, Canada, France, Germany, the UK, and Sweden. In all cases death rates in other countries continued to decline at pre-1999 levels. Death rates of Hispanic Americans and African Americans (not shown on the chart) also fell in line with international norms.[1] But those of white Americans did not: in fact, they started edging upward. That reversed decades of progress and was not happening in any other wealthy country. It added up to silent carnage. If mortality among white middle-aged Americans had continued falling at the trend rate, no fewer than half a million deaths would have been avoided between 1999 and 2013. Put another way, the phenomenon of "deaths of despair" in a previously

Figure 1

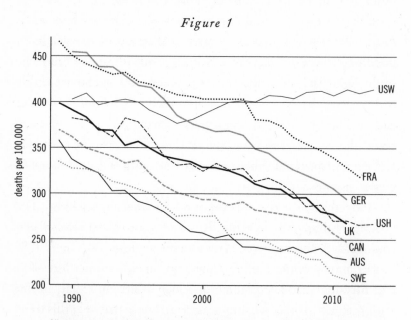

All-cause mortality, ages 45 to 54 for US white non-Hispanics (USW), US Hispanics (USH), and six comparison countries: France (FRA), Germany (GER), the United Kingdom (UK), Canada (CAN), Australia (AUS), and Sweden (SWE).

privileged part of the population was similar in scale to the AIDS epidemic that had ravaged America for much of the 1980s and 1990s. What on earth was going on?

Before we seek to answer that question, there are two broader points. One is that, whatever was happening, none of it was showing up in the usual economic statistics. In 2015, fifteen years after the reversal in mortality started happening, the economy was growing reasonably well. Notwithstanding the 2008 financial crisis, the size of America's economy had ballooned from $10.3 trillion in 2000 to $18 trillion in 2015, a gain of 80 percent.[2] Even adjusting for inflation, it had grown 30 percent.[3] If you went back forty-five years to 1970, the US economy was now three and a half times bigger, even adjusting for inflation.[4] The irony was that many Americans, particularly blue-collar workers, were harking back to the 1970s as a sort of golden age when jobs were good and prospects of a middle-class life decent. It might be stating the obvious to say that raw growth statistics cannot capture intangible feelings, such as the loss of community, job security, well-being, or even identity, but if that is the case, why have we made economic growth—measured by GDP—a proxy for what we are supposed to value in life? Somewhere hidden in the narrative of growth and increasing prosperity lurked something very troubling.

The second point concerns averages and aggregation. The trick of the Case–Deaton study was to disaggregate the numbers, here by age, race, and class. In doing so, subterranean trends obscured by headline numbers and averages were suddenly revealed. The average American was living a longer and healthier life, but a subsection had suffered a reversal in fortunes. Why? The explosion of opioid use, including of prescription drugs such as Oxycontin, was one strong factor. Not only did that explain direct deaths from overdoses, but the underlying pain, physical or mental, that made the growing use of opioids such a problem in the first place also helped explain higher suicides and alcoholism. Opioids were most likely a symptom, not the underlying cause.

Digging deeper, it seemed much of the rise in deaths and sickness was affecting people without a college education. Failure to reach university was somehow becoming a death sentence. In 1970 low-income middle-aged men had an average life expectancy five years below that of high-income men of the same generation. By 1990 that gap had widened to twelve years. Now it is more like fifteen. As one commentator put it, "Dying half a generation sooner than you might have is bad enough. Expecting to die younger than your parents is worse. It goes against what Westerners in general, and Americans in particular, have taken for granted."[5]

Growing inequality explained some of what was going on. Median wages had more or less stagnated since the 1970s, partly due to a loss of bargaining power by unions, a trend that has been replicated in most of the industrial world as the tenets of free-market capitalism encouraged a race to the bottom. In the US the share of economic output going to wages has been falling steadily for decades, with more going to corporate profits and capital. That exacerbates inequalities and penalizes people who have to work for a living, particularly those with skills that can be outsourced, mechanized, or computerized. Many of the best blue-collar jobs came with health benefits and on-the-job training, but some of those jobs have gone to China, southeast Asia, India, or Mexico. More still are being done by robots or strings of computer code. In wealthy countries the share of national income paid to workers fell from around 55 percent in 1970 to below 50 percent at the height of the 2007 financial bubble.[6] An expanding economy has not, in other words, primarily benefited the workers who produced all that growth, but rather the owners of capital. "There really is a decline of the American working class," Deaton said. "It reached its heyday with the 'blue-collar aristocrats' of the early 1970s with good union jobs, a job where you got . . . a promotion every year and you built a middle-class life for yourself and your family."[7] Without a decent job, a person's chance of finding a stable partner falls, and the risk of drug addiction, alcoholism, depression, and suicide rises.

The paper caused huge interest. The authors were accused by some of ignoring African Americans, whose rates of mortality were still far higher than white Americans, even though they were closing the gap as a result of the reversal in white fortunes. But it was the findings about the decline of the white middle class that chimed so well with the 2016 presidential election in which Donald Trump was swept to power. As the *Washington Post* pointed out, "President Trump won huge swaths of voters in 2016 by promising to address the grievances of the white working class, and white nationalists endorsed his campaign. Case and Deaton's research on white mortality seemed to speak directly to that political narrative."[8]

In 1964, according to a 2014 Pew Research Center report, the average hourly wage for non-management, private-sector workers in America was $2.50, an amount that had risen to $20.67 by 2014. That sounds great until you take inflation into account. In constant 2014 dollars the average hourly wage in 1964 was $19.18. Half a century of toil, all that growth and technological advance later—and all you've got to show for it is a lousy $1.50. "In real terms the average wage peaked more than forty years ago," the report said. One explanation is increasing benefit costs, particularly of employer-provided health insurance. If employers have to pay more and more for health costs, they tend to compensate by bearing down on wages.[9]

Certainly, many Americans are feeling the pinch. In the Pew survey 56 percent of respondents said their family's income was falling behind the cost of living, against 44 percent in September 2007. In other words, even when the economy was binging on credit in the run-up to the Lehman shock, more than four in ten Americans felt they were barely surviving. The recession that followed exacerbated the trend. In 2000, 33 percent of Americans described themselves as "working class," according to Gallup. By 2015 that number had risen to 48 percent. "Far from dying out, the working class now accounts for almost half of America by people's self-perception," wrote one author. "In some respects these measures are more revealing than statistics on median income, or income inequality. They express a feeling about being shut out from the benefits of growth. It is a very un-American state of mind."[10]

Inequality is not always bad. Progress depends on it since society never moves in lockstep. If you accept that, the only alternative to inequality is stagnation. In *The Great Escape*, a 1963 movie about the Second World War starring Steve McQueen, prisoners of war escape from a Nazi camp after secretly digging a tunnel. The escapees are indubitably better off than the prisoners left behind. Would it have been better if everyone had remained in the camp until the end of the war, or should we celebrate the fact that some people escaped first?[11]

That metaphor can be applied to almost any situation in which some people get an early advantage. Between 1550 and 1750 life expectancy in Britain showed no improvement. Nor, interestingly, did kings and dukes live any longer than peasants. Then something happened: the royal family gained access to an early small-pox vaccination brought from Turkey. Because of this and other medical advances, which spread from the court to the aristocracy, the wealthy in Britain opened up a twenty-year gap in life expectancy over the poor. It was unfair. The advantage was based on inherited wealth and privilege. But it was progress. In the end, vaccinations became widespread, bringing benefit not only to all the people of Britain, but also to people throughout the world.[12]

You could call this good inequality—a mechanism of progress, albeit an unfair one. But what about bad inequality? Imagine a dinner date in New York followed by a night at the opera.[13] To arrive on time, you have to get through the Lincoln Tunnel. The tunnel has two lanes, but you're not allowed to change from one to the other. Suddenly there's a traffic snarl-up. Both lanes stop moving. Time ticks away. There is a serious chance you'll miss dinner. More time passes. Now those opera tickets might turn into worthless bits of paper. When the lane next to you starts moving, you think to yourself, *Terrific. Soon we'll be moving too.* But your lane doesn't move and that hope slowly turns to anger as you watch cars in the next lane speeding along. Suddenly all you can think is how unfair life is, how the system is stacked against you. Before you know it, you're breaking the law, cutting into the other lane. This is bad inequality.

In America people have historically been quite tolerant of inequality. The attitude has been, *Good luck to them. It shows we can do it too.* But that is changing. If other people gain advantages by access to expensive education or inheritance or old boys' networks, your goodwill toward the success of others turns to resentment.

"If you're white and working class in America, you've had no income gain for thirty years," says Angus Deaton. "If everybody was getting no income gain and there was some good reason for it, a war or something, I think people would have no difficulty with it." But there is no war and some people are forging way ahead. "When they see these bankers with their enormous salaries or the head of New York–Presbyterian hospital, who gets paid $3 million a year, they see that these guys are getting really rich, and the white working classes are getting nothing."[14]

The middle class is flourishing. These are not words you see often these days. But it is true. So long as, that is, you're talking about the global middle class and not the middle class in the West—much of which has been treading water at best for decades. If you look at incomes globally, however, something not often done, you will see that those between the 45th and 65th percentiles (from the bottom) doubled their real incomes between 1988 and 2011. Many of these people were Chinese. Those between the 80th and 95th percentiles—the middle class of high-income countries—have seen real incomes stagnate.[15] The global top 1 percent—which includes the top 12 percent of US earners—receives nearly 30 percent of all income and owns about 46 percent of all wealth.[16]

The story of modern inequality is complex. Inequality is rising within most countries, especially high-income ones, but on a global level, inequality *between* some nations is actually shrinking.[17] At the very least, the gap between incomes in parts of Asia, on the one hand, and Western Europe, the US, and Australasia on the other, has narrowed, particularly since 2000. Much of that has occurred because of rapid industrialization in Asia, especially in China, and more recently, India. As growth in those two countries—which together account for nearly 40 percent of the world's population—gathers steam, the income inequalities opened up by the West after the Industrial Revolution are gradually being narrowed. Where once there was a great divergence of standards of living in the nineteenth and much of the twentieth century, now there is a great convergence.

So the income benefit gained thanks to the accident of birth is beginning to fall.[18] For humanists who support equality of opportunity regardless of nationality this is a wonderful thing. But if you're living in the former industrial heartlands of Europe or America, it may not seem like anything worth celebrating. Today what you do is more important than where you do it. A corporate lawyer or microbiologist in New York, Shanghai, or Bangalore is likely to be doing very well. If your job in the West is making shoes or furniture you may not be able to compete with someone doing the same work in Bangladesh, Ethiopia, or the Philippines. One explanation for the rise of nationalism and the reaction against immigration on both sides of the Atlantic is that those who are doing poorly because of globalization are fighting for their "citizenship rent," the advantage they once enjoyed by accident of birth.[19]

Since most politics is national and not global, it is the inequalities within countries, not between them, that have caused a political backlash around the world. Very high inequality is almost always unsustainable, especially in countries where this has not been the norm, and the story in almost all wealthy countries is one of increasing inequality, especially of wealth (as opposed to income). Or to put it in starker terms: the rich have been getting much richer while more or less everybody else has been falling behind. This is the uncomfortable reality lurking behind our narrative of endless growth. Whether Western liberalism can survive this jolt to the system is an open question.[20]

The rise in inequality preceded the global financial crisis by years if not decades. In 2008 the Organization for Economic Cooperation and Development, a club of the world's richest thirty-five countries, found that in the previous two decades the gap between rich and poor had increased in three-quarters of OECD countries.[21] In Canada, Finland, Germany, Italy, Norway, and America the gap had not only widened between the rich and the poor; it had also increased between the rich and the middle class.

Contrary to what most Americans are brought up to believe, social mobility is hard in the US. In fact, it is easier in socialist-leaning Nordic countries. (It is also relatively hard to move up in the world in the UK and Italy.)[22] Generally, the more unequal a society, the harder it is to move, as the wealthy entrench their advantages through education, political lobbying, inheritance, connections, and so on. The so-called Great Gatsby curve shows that, as inequality increases, social mobility decreases.[23] If you're in the wrong lane of the Lincoln Tunnel, the OECD report shows, you're likely to get stuck. "Greater income inequality stifles upward mobility between generations, making it harder for talented and hard-working people to get the rewards they deserve," it says.

Inequality has increased for three main reasons, according to the OECD. Wages have risen for those people who were already well paid, especially bankers, professionals, and corporate executives; there are fewer jobs for less well-educated people, who have been dropping out of the jobs market in large numbers; and there are more single-parent families. Poverty among the elderly has fallen, but among young adults, especially those with children, it has risen sharply.

Gradual recovery from financial crisis has done little or nothing to erode inequality. Normally, when economies recover, inequality falls as people find work, but this has been offset by a recovery in asset prices, which mainly benefits the better off. In the US in 2014 the bottom 10 percent of the population earned 1.6 percent of income, while the top 10 percent earned 29.2 percent. The same figures for Iceland, the most equal of OECD countries in that year, were 4.1 percent and 20.6 percent respectively. Put more starkly, in the US the top 10 percent earned more than eighteen times the bottom 10 percent. In Iceland the equivalent ratio was five times.[24] In Britain it was 10.5 and in France 6.9.

What does all this have to do with economic growth? The answer is nothing at all. That's the problem. The fact that an economy is growing tells you nothing about what is happening to the distribution of wealth. True, we cannot forget the lessons of the previous chapter, which are that quality improvements and technological advances could mean we are better off than we think.[25] Still, the fact that someone has a better mobile phone or a more powerful form of painkiller in their pocket may come as small consolation if they feel they are falling behind financially. Although our countries are getting richer and our companies more efficient, we're not creating more jobs, nor paying people more. Increased productivity has been decoupled from wages and employment.[26] And if most people are not feeling any benefit, what precisely—and who precisely—is all this growth for?

PART TWO

GROWTH AND THE DEVELOPING WORLD

7
ELEPHANTS AND RHUBARB

One day in 2015 some economists working in Kenya had a bright idea. Literally. Knowing how hard it was to obtain accurate economic statistics in a country with limited resources, a large informal sector, and an economy that went from Mercedes-Benz-driving urbanites to cow-herding Maasai tribesmen, they looked for another way of measuring activity. The idea they hit upon was to use satellite imagery from outer space to record the intensity of lights at night.

Their method was less outlandish than it appeared. In poor countries from India to Eritrea there is a close correlation between the size of an economy as conventionally measured and light-intensity data from satellites. When plotted on a graph, downward blips in economic activity, say caused by drought, war, or a recession, are closely matched by a corresponding dip in light intensity. The idea rests on the assumption that almost all nighttime consumption requires some sort of lighting, making a rise in light intensity a good proxy for growth.[1]

Lights at night are as good at capturing informal as formal economic activity. That is a huge advantage in a place like Kenya. The farmers, hawkers, traders, nomads, artisans, repairmen, con men, day laborers, truckers, and metal bashers who help make most African economies tick generally work outside the taxed economy and largely beyond the purview of national statisticians. One of the basic tenets of our economies is that, if you can't put a dollar sign against it, it doesn't exist, but much of what makes Africa go round economically is invisible.

The night-light method has been used to gain a better understanding of the massive informal economy in India, a country of 1.3 billion people where more than 90 percent of the working population toils outside the formal sector. One could theoretically ask electricity companies how much power they sell in each district. But satellite imagery provides a more accurate picture, since official figures don't count small off-grid schemes powered by solar or hydro. Nor do electricity companies properly account for the power that trickles away via inefficient grids or is stolen by poor communities adept at tapping power from overhead cables.

Light-intensity data has another advantage: it tells you more about economic activity at a local level than conventional data. Because of the high cost and practical constraints of conducting detailed surveys, poor countries rely on national extrapolations compiled from thin samples. The satellites that provide light-intensity data, by contrast, create a richer picture. Satellites circle the earth fourteen times a day, tracking data square kilometer by square kilometer. That is better than anything that could possibly be achieved by an employee of a national statistics bureau, clipboard in hand, going from village to village.

One surprising finding of the Kenya night-light study related to Nairobi, the capital, a city of at least 3 million people and a regional hub in east Africa. Light-intensity data indicated that Nairobi contributed about 13 percent to the national economy, a far smaller proportion than suggested by conventional national income statistics. If the night-light numbers are right, huge swaths of Kenya's rural economy are being routinely undercounted.

The quality of economic data in many poor countries is shockingly bad. We put great store in them nonetheless. We use economic data to compare countries' levels of poverty, to decide whether their policies are working, how much aid they receive, or what interest rates they must pay to borrow money. Yet a combination of methodological pitfalls and lack of institutional capacity renders many of the numbers on which we rely virtually meaningless. Different estimates of African GDP for the year 2000 compiled by the World Bank, the University of Pennsylvania, and the University of Groningen—three of the world's most prestigious sources of national income data—reveal wild inconsistencies. One, for example, ranked the west African nation of Liberia as the second-poorest country on the continent. Another had it a full twenty places higher.[2]

One problem is that in most African countries the so-called black or gray economy—much of which by definition takes place in the shadows—is very large. So little is known about it that statistical offices resort to all sorts of ruses, proxies, and accounting tricks to fill in the blanks. Many countries simply do not have the resources. In Zambia in 2010 the national accounts for the whole country were compiled by a lone statistician. "What happens if I disappear?" the man asked plaintively.[3]

Zambia is a relatively stable country. What on earth are we to make of the statistics gathered in a place like the Democratic Republic of Congo, formerly Zaire, a Western-European-sized nation of 80 million people racked by years of civil war and with little that resembles a functioning state? Even if it had a working statistics office in the capital, Kinshasa, most regions of the country are inaccessible by road, with many places reachable only by riverboat or canoe. In Zimbabwe, where only 6 percent of the workforce is formally employed, one cabinet member, the nephew of veteran leader Robert Mugabe, told me over dinner that measuring Zimbabwe's economy was "like trying to use a tape measure to figure out how much Coke is in this glass."[4]

Even in countries not quite so challenged, the method recommended by the UN System of National Accounts to calculate and cross-check GDP—using expenditure, income, and production—is practically impossible. Only a few African countries, one of which incidentally is Kenya, even attempt it. Many use only production. "GDP statistics from African countries are best guesses of aggregate production," says Morten Jerven, an expert on the subject. "Another way of phrasing this is that we do not know very much about income and growth in Africa."[5]

That is quite a thing to say about a continent containing 1 billion of the world's 7 billion people. We pretend our economic statistics and international comparisons have an accuracy that is simply not warranted by the facts. If even some of what happens in Africa is true of other developing countries in Asia and Latin America, then economies containing several billion of the world's people may be producing highly dubious figures. All sorts of decisions, from aid to investment, are based on these numbers and all sorts of conclusions drawn about which policies work and which don't, but we are mostly stumbling about in the dark. Kuznets thought his method was wholly unsuited to measuring poor economies where so much activity takes place in the informal sector. Yet that is precisely what we do. It is a pretty damning indictment of our capacity to paint a meaningful picture of the world.[6]

Terry Ryan is something of a celebrity. A local newspaper described the chairman of the Bureau of National Statistics as an "icon of Kenya's economic scene." Born and bred in the country, Ryan is baffled when outsiders look at his white skin and conclude he is not African. Brought up on a farm in Nakuru in the west of Kenya, where he worked briefly as a shamba boy—a field hand—he studied at two of the country's best schools before completing his studies in Australia and Ireland and then in the US, where he rounded off his education with a PhD at the Massachusetts Institute of Technology. He lectured in economics at the University of Nairobi until 1983, when he was asked to join the Kenyan government as director of planning. Though retired from the civil service, he continues to play an influential role in the compilation of Kenya's national statistics. The day I met him, in the spring of 2016, he was proofreading the latest set of GDP figures.

Ryan is a tall man with long, angular limbs, impeccable diction, and the slightly comic air of a character from a Dickens novel. When I went to see him on the top floor of the central bank, a dimly lit tower block in Nairobi's old business district, he was clutching a battered brown leather suitcase, an accoutrement that, by all accounts, rarely leaves his side and is said to contain sheets of statistics dating back to the 1960s. At eighty-two, he was as sharp as a razor.

Ryan is proud of Kenyan statistics, which he says are among the best in Africa. Kenya has a competent civil service and a reasonably sophisticated economy, with cash crops, a cut-flower industry, light manufacturing, and a well-developed tourism sector. It is also relatively prosperous by African standards, with income per capita of about $3,200 adjusted for local prices.[7]

Kenya follows the UN national accounts guidelines to the letter, though Ryan calls the income numbers it collects "very iffy." Adherence to standard methodology notwithstanding, Ryan is at pains to point out that Kenya's economic statistics are in no way comparable with those of, say, the US. "You are measuring elephants and rhubarb," he says, conjuring up a metaphor that makes the comparison of apples and oranges seem mundane. So he has adapted the "rhubarb" methodology designed by Simon Kuznets to measure the US economy to the realities of an "elephant" economy like Kenya's. "It's perfectly correct for the developed world," he says. "It makes admirable sense for the developed world. But it doesn't necessarily transfer neatly into a developing-country context."

Kenya is a country of roughly 45 million people. Some of its elite live like New Yorkers in expensive apartments or spacious houses in gated compounds, while others live in tin shacks or mud huts, or trek the vast open spaces as nomads. Nairobi is a modern city with skyscrapers, department stores, office blocks, motorways, prodigious slums, jazz clubs, restaurants, and one of Africa's most advanced technology hubs. Even here, amid the traffic and the commerce, so-called urban shepherds trudge along with their herds of cows, which graze by the four-lane motorways or on the lawns of millionaires' homes.[8] Outside Nairobi, in the wilderness of Kenya's beautiful landscape, is a whole other world. "We still have hunters and gatherers," says Ryan. "Not many, but they're there."

Among Kenya's patchwork of ethnicities are the Maasai, tall warrior cattle herders who once occupied the Great Rift Valley from modern-day central Kenya to northern Tanzania. The Maasai believe that all the world's cows belong to them, a conviction that has brought them into inevitable conflict with other pastoralists and settled farmers. For them cattle are more or less everything. A greeting in the Maa language, from which the Maasai take their name, is "I hope your cows are well." There are about 800,000

Maasai in Kenya, roughly the same number as the Turkana, a camel-herding people from the remote northwest.

The point is that much of Kenyan society lies outside the theoretical framework Kuznets was considering in America. That applies even to the many millions of sedentary subsistence farmers. In a good year they might produce a surplus, which they barter for other goods or sell at the local market. In a bad year almost everything they produce is eaten. Either way, most of their production never shows up officially.

Ryan takes the example of maize. He estimates that only half of all maize produced in the country is bought and sold. So the only way of counting the maize eaten by subsistence farmers is to impute its value. This is precisely the same concept used to impute the value of the rent that would be paid by owner-occupiers living in their own homes. "I know the number of households, and I know how much maize people actually eat," Ryan says, since household surveys have established an approximation of the dietary habits of rural Kenyans. So he has a good idea roughly how much maize is grown and eaten by subsistence farmers.

In theory you could do the same with all manner of less obvious subsistence products. Benjamin Muchiri, a senior official at Kenya's National Bureau of Statistics, says his office has tried theoretical exercises to work out the imputed value of non-marketed activities from the draft power of oxen working in the fields to the transport provided by camels. You could, say, compare the oxen to tractors and the camels to journeys by motorcycle taxi. One might even count the cow dung used to line the walls of huts as self-produced building material.

Including or excluding parts of the informal economy can make a big difference. In 2009 a study was made of milk, using data gathered in that year's population census. This concluded that national income statistics for 2009 underestimated the economic contribution of milk by about twenty times. It also found that the total contribution of "ruminant livestock"—including cows, goats, and camels—was nearly $2 billion more than was captured in official statistics, no small discrepancy in an economy nominally worth only $37 billion.[9] It estimated that 80 percent of beef consumed in Kenya was produced by pastoralists, including the Maasai, about a fifth of which was walked over the border from neighboring countries.

As well as providing meat and milk for their owners, livestock has other benefits not captured in normal economic exercises. Pastoralists, for example, use their cows as collateral that can be "cashed in" in emergencies. That saves the expense of taking out rural credit, which commands very high interest rates. Cows are walking bank accounts—literally cash cows. They have one further benefit. For protein, Maasai drink the blood of their cattle, which they siphon off sparingly from the jugular and mix with milk. The Maasai traditionally do not deign to plant crops, but live entirely off their livestock. Unless they kill a cow and sell it for money, they could spend an entire lifetime subsisting off their herd, practically invisible to GDP.

The difficulty of putting a dollar amount on such a rural economy might not matter so much if it wasn't so big. Officially, agriculture accounts for 20 to 26 percent of Kenya's economy, depending on the harvest. Even ignoring all the other problems of imputing the value of subsistence farming, this underestimates the sector's economic impact. That is because money earned in rural Kenya is quickly spent on basics, thus moving around the economy with what economists call a high-velocity or multiplier effect. "I spend 100,000 shillings in the countryside, I get a lot for it," Ryan says. "A high proportion of that will be generating more purchasing of toothpaste, more purchasing of dresses, hairdos. It really does circulate. It creates jobs, does all sorts of things." In poorer countries, where the success of a harvest can be decisive and irrigation is almost nonexistent, weather experts, who can predict rainfall, make better economic forecasters than economists.

Miles Morland, who has been successfully investing in Africa for years, is also scathing about the quality of statistics. "You would think the fact that over 80 percent of the adult population in a country like Kenya, where NGOs solemnly tell us that 'national income per head for half the population is less than a dollar a day,' have mobile phones might lead someone with a functioning brain to question the statistics and ask how people with effectively no money can afford to buy so many mobile phones," he snorts. He calls the hidden African economy Kioskenomics after the little kiosks where so many transactions are made beneath the radar of the taxman or statistician. "Anyone outside a Washington institution can see that income per capita in Africa must be vastly higher than the IMF figures indicate," he says. This matters because these figures, which we take so seriously, "are the prism through which economists, politicians, bankers and planners the world over pass judgments on developing countries."[10]

Ryan agrees that official statistics drastically underestimate the true size of Kenya's economy. They suggest that 72 percent of the population lacks enough money to eat properly, he says. "So 72 percent of my people are dead. Sorry. Beaten again," he says, throwing up his hands in mock resignation to the logic of standard economics. Yet clearly these Kenyans are managing to stay alive whatever the data tell us.

One explanation is that family and kinship structures mean wages earned by those in formal employment go farther. If averages are skewed in America and Europe because a few people have much more, in Africa it is generally the other way around. Of course there is gross inequality, but, typically, people with jobs support an extended family, from parents, uncles, sisters, brothers, and hangers-on to anyone who can claim even the most tenuous of connections. Ryan recalls an incident when someone walked into his office at the planning ministry complaining that Kenya's GINI coefficient—which measures inequality—was "disastrous." "I said, 'Yes, it's disastrous, but it doesn't mean what you think it means,'" Ryan recalls. "It so happened that the assistant minister in the planning ministry was an ex-student of mine. I knew him very well. So I said, 'Wait, wait, wait. Let's just go next door.' So we walked into the assistant minister's office, and I said, 'Sorry for interrupting. How many people are you keeping on your salary?' He thought for a while and he said, 'Probably about fifty.' I said, 'Thank you.' And we walked out."

Ryan's lesson is that you cannot take numbers at face value, even if they purport to be the definitive explanation of an economy. "You have to interrogate the data," he says in a phrase that could come straight from Kuznets. "GDP tells you things that are worth knowing, but don't think it tells you the answers to everything. See, what I'm trying to push," he says, "is that this number is not a meaningless number. But you have to understand what its meaning is."

•••

Yemi Kale was finding it hard to sleep. He was harboring a dark secret. Numbers were swimming around in his head. He was sure they were right, but they were controversial. They could cause trouble. He thought of postponing their release and leaving the whole nasty business for his successor to deal with. "I was extremely uncomfortable," he told me later.[11] "I was tempted not to publish at all."

Kale (pronounced Ka-leh) is a statistician. To be exact he is the statistician general of the National Bureau of Statistics of Nigeria, the most elevated number-cruncher in that huge west African country. You might consider a job in statistics, even one with such a grand title, to be one of the world's dullest, right up there with accountancy or chicken sexing. That is not true in Africa, where working out the size of an economy is fraught with risks, even dangers. There were times when Kale feared for his safety. More than once he has received threatening calls from state governors, boiling with rage over what he had revealed about levels of poverty or unemployment in their fiefdoms. "This job is extremely controversial," he says. "Our country is not very good at accepting the truth, whether it's good, bad, or ugly."

On the face of it, the secret Kale was keeping came under the category of "good." Based on his three-year study, Nigeria's economy was 89 percent bigger than previously imagined. When he eventually plucked up the courage to announce the results one Sunday afternoon in April 2014, the information proved electrifying. It carried huge symbolic significance, meaning Nigeria had leapfrogged South Africa to become the biggest economy on the continent.

For a country with an often puffed-up sense of its own importance, this was of no little import. Nigeria is by far the most populous country in Africa, with a population of around 180 million people. The country has oil—and it has attitude. If you listen to a Nigerian, you can easily imagine Nigeria is a rich country, such is the level of ambition, drive, and entrepreneurship on constant, flamboyant, display. Indeed, since Nigeria gained independence in 1960, its citizens have never tired of reminding their neighbors that Nigeria is a "big, big country." Here, at last, was proof that it was the biggest of them all, at least in Africa.

The discovery would also come as a pleasant surprise to many global investors, from beer companies looking for the next big market to portfolio managers allocating investment funds. Division chiefs at multinationals, who might have always nurtured the suspicion that Nigeria presented richer pickings than their bosses realized, would be able to go to their boards in New York or Shanghai with proof that they were right.

"The revision will have a psychological impact," said Ngozi Okonjo-Iweala, Nigeria's larger-than-life minister for economy and finance at the time. "It validates the investment thesis." The point of recalculating GDP, she was quick to point out, was "not to be the biggest." The main objective was "to measure the economy properly." But being the biggest evidently came as a nice bonus.

There were, however, downsides to being richer, as Kale knew only too well. On average, the figures were saying, Nigerians were much better off than they had previously thought. That came as news to the tens of millions of his countrymen who lived in squalor, without jobs, without water, or without electricity—all this in the continent's biggest oil producer. In 2010, according to Kale's own bureau, 61 percent of Nigerians were living in poverty, defined as subsisting on less than $1 a day. According to respondents in a survey, an astonishing 94 percent of Nigerians described themselves as poor, compared with "only" 76 percent six years earlier. "Despite the fact that the Nigerian economy is growing, the proportion of Nigerians living in poverty is increasing every year," Kale lamented.

Many Nigerians might legitimately ask why they were still poor in such a prosperous country, one that was now nearly twice as rich as previously thought. Presumably the answer was that the country's elite, notorious for guzzling the nation's wealth, was stealing even more than had hitherto been imagined. The truth, as Gloria Steinem, the women's rights activist, is said to have remarked, "will set you free. But first it will piss you off."

Kale is something of an evangelist. For all the difficulties associated with defining and measuring an economy, he saw the pursuit of more accurate statistics as an almost sacred mission, part of the process of democratic consolidation following the end of military rule in 1999. There was, he said in remarks he had prepared to coincide with the release of the new numbers, "an increased demand for accountability and good governance backed by evidence." People were sick of Nigeria's leaders stealing the country's patrimony. Much of the profit derived from pumping oil from Nigeria's coastal waters and swampy delta simply vanished into thin air. Forming a more accurate economic picture, Kale thought, would help ordinary Nigerians hold their government to account.

It was important to realize, he added, that growth could not be equated with well-being. "The fact that a country has a higher nominal GDP than the other does not, in itself, suggest that one country is 'more developed' than the other," he said. "Development encompasses a broader set of measures of human progress than GDP, which is strictly a measure of economic output." He highlighted both inequality and unemployment as societal ills missing in the national income statistics. Economic growth, he said, was of little use if the income generated was captured by a narrow elite and if it was not being used to create jobs and opportunity for most Nigerians.

Internationally too, being richer was a mixed blessing. On the positive side, if the economy was almost 90 percent bigger, then Nigeria was less indebted than previously thought. Such is the fixation on GDP that almost all numbers are measured against it. GDP is the denominator in many of public policy's most important ratios. For example, a country's indebtedness is usually expressed in terms of debt-to-GDP. If GDP rises, then debt falls. Hey presto. That meant Nigeria, in theory at least, would be able to borrow more money from abroad. It could also expect to pay less since interest is charged according to perceived risk. And if Nigeria was less indebted, then naturally it was less risky too.

Yet countries like Nigeria don't always want to be seen as better off. Even a country as big and important as China is not comfortable with economic statistics that suggest it is doing too well. For months Beijing fought fiercely behind the scenes to prevent the release in 2014 of data, compiled under the auspices of the World Bank, that showed China overtaking the US as the world's biggest economy measured in local prices.[12] The Communist Party had long adhered to Deng Xiaoping's dictum that China should mask its prodigious rise by "hiding its light" and biding its time. Here were meddling economists from the World Bank, of all places, blowing the gaff.

Kale had realized just how delicate a subject he was dealing with three years earlier. In 2011, when he had first been approached to oversee the recalculation of Nigeria's national income, he knew he would have to work out the practicalities of conducting the exercise carefully in such a sprawling and complicated country. That's when things can start to fall apart, to borrow from the title of a novel by Chinua Achebe, the Nigerian writer. Statistics are only as good as the quality of the data collected. Even in rich countries with ample budgets, efficient civil services, and a long history of data collection, getting hold of accurate numbers is not easy. You can't know everything about the economic activity of every single business, household, and individual. All you can do is collect a sample and cross-check results against as many pieces of real data as possible. In a country like Nigeria, with less money to spend and fewer series of existing data to work with, such problems are massively amplified.

Just for starters, it is hard to know something as basic as exactly how many people there are. Population censuses in Nigeria are even more controversial than surveys of GDP. That is because the population of an individual state or region can determine everything from its political influence to its entitlement to tax transfers from the federal government. Nigeria is a young country whose borders were drawn by British imperialists, who created a country predominantly Muslim in the north and predominantly Christian in the south. In 1967 it was nearly torn apart when Igbos in the east declared the independent republic of Biafra, triggering a civil war in which several million civilians starved to death. So knowing how many people live in each region is controversial to say the least.

There are also practical difficulties. The British used to count people only in Lagos, then the capital. An early national census was interrupted by swarms of locusts in the north and tax riots in the southeast.[13] Most demographers have never really trusted Nigeria's population figures, either the overall total or the breakdown between regions and ethnicities. Yet unless you know how many people there are, you cannot accurately calculate the size of the economy, which requires scaling up the results of surveys. "I don't use the census: the numbers don't make sense," says Kale bluntly.[14]

Kale had several other headaches. Nigeria is a huge country. Some parts are remote, reachable only after days of travel by car, motorbike, or even canoe. The people employed to fan out across the country collecting data could not always be trusted to perform their arduous task; there was a history of staff making up the numbers from the comfort of their own homes. Kale used GPS tracking to ensure that his operatives were where they said they were and made random calls to those surveyed to verify they had actually been interviewed.

Once, he says, he sent six of his 3,000 data collectors to a remote corner of Ekiti, a state in the southwest of the country. "They went into the village on their motorbikes and took out their gadgets and their iPads. The villagers weren't used to seeing that—six people in their shiny coats and boots," he recalls. "They rounded them up and took them to the chief and threatened to kill them. We had to call the local chief very quickly to intervene." Kuznets, as far as we know, never had such scrapes to contend with.

Kale had to be creative about survey questions. When people were queried about how much they earned, for example, they often underdeclared because they were suspicious of the tax authorities. Ask them how much they spent, however, and, chest puffed up, they often gave a more expansive account of their purchasing prowess. In surveys, says Kale, getting the question right matters.

There were big issues over other data too. He had to rely on figures from the notoriously corrupt petroleum industry and port authorities about the amount of oil produced and the volume of goods shipped. The suspicion was always that the official figures underestimated the real amount, creating the scope to skim off revenue at source. The informal economy was so vast and unknowable, Kale says, that even after the 89 percent jump, he suspected he was still underestimating it. Technically, Kale was being asked to conduct what national accountants call a rebasing exercise. When countries calculate their national income they do so in relation to a base year, which serves as a reference point. The reason they need to do so is to take account of changing prices. Let's say Nigerians produce 100 million bags of rice in the base year. (The figures are entirely fictitious and doubtless highly implausible.) The next year they produce 110 million bags. That makes it easy to compare one year with another. The increase is 10 percent. Conversely, if prices are taken into account, adjustments need to be made for an appropriate measure of inflation. It is far easier—and statistically cleaner—to compare volumes.

So far so good. The problem is that the base year quickly becomes out of date. Economies change in nature. Some industries grow, others shrink or disappear. Perhaps Nigerians don't grow rice anymore, but have switched to sorghum. Much of the country's textile industry has been wiped out by cheap Chinese imports. The UN Statistical Commission recommends changing the base year every five years, but in resource-scarce Africa it can be decades before statistical offices get around to this arduous—and expensive—task. That is another reason many of the statistics the UN produces are wildly inaccurate. When Liberia calculates inflation it uses a basket of items put together decades ago. I like to imagine Liberian statisticians scouring the markets to work out today's prices for bell-bottom jeans and vinyl records.[15]

In Nigeria's case the base year was 1990. By 2014, when the

National Bureau of Statistics released its new numbers, a lot had happened. Mobile phones were a case in point. In 1990 there were almost no such devices in the country. Instead, Nigeria had about 300,000 fixed lines, perhaps 100,000 of them in actual working order. There was not even a reliable phone book, and this reporter remembers having to send a driver through chaotic Lagos traffic to someone's house just to obtain his telephone number. By 2010 the situation had transformed: there were 80 million mobile phone subscribers, but because national statistics made reference to 1990, when telephony was a tiny fraction of the economy, this explosive growth was all but invisible.

Nigeria's economy had changed in other ways too. It now had a thriving movie industry, dubbed Nollywood, which churned out hundreds of films a year but which no one was bothering to measure. Films like *The Last Flight to Abuja* had gained an ardent following, not just in Nigeria but also across Africa and the African diaspora, yet to the compilers of national statistics, relying on the 1990 base year, Nollywood did not exist. Banking had grown exponentially too, driven by technology, rising wealth amid a certain stratum of society, and inflows of foreign money into Nigeria's oil-soaked economy. Again, this was not reflected in the weighting given to banking activities in the 1990 base year.

When Kale's bureau eventually released its new national income statistics, using 2010 as the base year, they showed that the structure of Nigeria's economy had radically altered. The new Nigeria had dramatically diversified. The share in the economy of oil and gas, assumed to be the country's economic mainstay, had more than halved from 32.4 percent of GDP to 14.4 percent. Agriculture was relatively more important and telecoms alone was contributing 8.6 percent to output as opposed to just 0.8 percent in 1990.

Even Nollywood, with its cheap production costs and massive piracy problems, was said to account for 1.4 percent of all economic activity. What had been blurred had come into some sort of focus.

Yet when we earnestly compare the size of economies and living standards across nations, we should remember what Terry Ryan says: much of it is rhubarb.

8
GROWTHMANSHIP

was twenty years old when I first traveled to India. I remember the aircraft door opening and wading down the rickety staircase into air so hot it felt like bathwater. It was 3 a.m. and outside the airport I became aware of the quietly snoring presence of hundreds of homeless people sleeping in the open air. With no better place to go they had chosen to make their beds outside Delhi's international airport.

The year was 1985 and India was an extraordinarily poor country. In dollar terms, according to the World Bank, its income per capita was around $300. Life expectancy was fifty-six. The most abject poverty was visible everywhere, with gangs of shoeless children roaming the streets and beggars jauntily waving deformities at passersby. Sickness, malnourishment, and destitution were in plain view, in the cities, in the towns and in the villages.

India today is still very poor. But it is another country. Its income per capita has quintupled to more than $1,500—or roughly $6,000 if you adjust for local prices—and life expectancy has improved by more than a decade to sixty-eight.* Infant mortality has

---

*So-called purchasing-power parity is a way of comparing income per capita— or GDP per capita—across nations by making adjustments for the fact that prices vary from country to country. A haircut in Mumbai is likely to cost less than a haircut in New York—partly because the hairdresser will earn less— which means that a dollar in India goes farther than a dollar in the US. The method makes it easier to compare incomes internationally but has many technical problems of its own.

fallen by almost two-thirds from one in ten live births in 1985 to thirty-seven per thousand today.[1] Though poverty is still endemic and India retains the capacity to shock, the trappings of modern life are everywhere: cars, motorbikes, flyovers, mobile phones, supermarkets, tall buildings, call centers, pace, energy. For all its litany of indignities and daily injustices, India feels like a country that, as one author puts it, is "becoming"—though quite what it is becoming is yet to become clear.[2]

It is important to state something unequivocally. Growth—and by that I mean even raw growth as measured imperfectly by GDP—has the power to transform poor people's lives. The economist Ha-Joon Chang recalls growing up in South Korea in the 1960s. Two years before he was born, in 1963, per-capita income was $82, compared with $179 in cocoa-producing Ghana, a newly independent west African country that was thought to have great potential. Chang remembers the redness of the soil in Seoul, South Korea's capital, where, he said, all the trees had been cut down for firewood. At that time relatively resource-rich North Korea was considered the wealthier half of the peninsula. Now South Korea's capital is a prosperous city of frenetic pace, wall-to-wall neon, and street upon street of chic shops, restaurants and nightclubs. People the world over use South Korean smartphones and drive South Korean cars. Since 1960 what is known as the Miracle on the Han River has changed South Korea from a country significantly poorer than Ghana to one as wealthy as most places in Europe. Today South Korea's per-capita income is approaching $30,000. The country has evolved into one of Asia's most rambunctious democracies, one that in 2017 had the confidence to impeach a president for abuse of office.

Certainly, modern-day South Korea has its problems, many of

them associated with the stress of advanced societies. Suicide rates are high. Social pressure to outperform and get rich is intense. Many youngsters come through the pressure-cooker education system with strings of qualifications but with little prospect of a fulfilling job or the status they crave. Yet it is important not to romanticize poverty. South Koreans today have immeasurably more opportunity to live the life they choose than their grandparents ever had. Collectively, they have done far better than Ghanaians, the majority of whom remain too poor to shape their own destinies. In 2017 South Koreans are more than eight times wealthier than their Ghanaian counterparts for one reason: the miracle of compound growth.[3]

This book has argued that growth is not all it is cracked up to be—often it does not mean what you think it means. But if you are poor, economic growth can be transformative. Fast growth can alleviate poverty both by generating jobs—digging roads, constructing office blocks, or manning call centers—and by providing the government with tax revenue that it can use to redistribute wealth and build the physical and institutional infrastructure needed for more and better growth.[4] Of course it can create other problems, pulling people from the countryside into urban slums or clogging up the roads with diesel-spewing vehicles. But unless you believe in the rural idyll, in very poor countries growth is the raw material from which better lives can be fashioned.

That sounds like little more than a statement of the obvious, yet for decades the idea that India should prioritize growth was far from commonly accepted. Mahatma Gandhi, leader of the independence movement against British colonialism, held a romantic idea of life in the Indian villages. Those views influenced post-independence thinking, insinuating into national discourse the idea that there was something almost noble about poverty. Jawaharlal Nehru, India's first prime minister and a towering intellectual figure, was much more in favor of development and modernization than Gandhi, but he had a strong socialist and distributionist streak. The problem was that there was so little to distribute.[5] Influenced by the Soviet Union, under Nehru, India became a centrally planned and protectionist state. Its leaders sought to build up heavy industry and blocked the import of many consumer goods in an effort to spur local production, a policy of nation-building that had the unintended consequence of producing shoddy—and overpriced—goods for all.

India's leaders were almost suspicious of growth, fearing that if some people benefited first it could lead to social unrest. In 1972 Prime Minister Indira Gandhi, Nehru's daughter, lashed out at what she called growthmanship. Giving "undivided attention to the maximization of GNP can be dangerous," she said in a speech, "for the results are almost always social and political unrest."[6]

If India's policy was to avoid excessive growth, it was working like a charm. The country became stuck in what became known derisively as the Hindu rate of growth. In the forty years following independence in 1947, annual GDP growth rose at around 3.5 percent. That doesn't sound too bad until you realize that the population was expanding at about 2 percent. What matters is income per capita. In those terms, India was growing at barely above 1 percent, nowhere near enough to make a dent in its grinding poverty. There was no Miracle on the Ganges.

In the late 1980s India's economy bounced from crisis to crisis and foreign exchange reserves dwindled to almost nothing. With its back to the wall, the government finally embraced economic reform. In 1991 Manmohan Singh, the finance minister, was empowered to implement a radical series of measures: he cut import tariffs, slashed taxes, and removed barriers to foreign investment. Most important, he dismantled what was known as the License Raj, the maddeningly bureaucratic system of permits, licenses, and regulations that controlled industry and had effectively restricted moneymaking opportunities to a coterie of crony capitalists. Through the 1990s growth began to pick up, rising steadily to above 7 percent, a rate at which an economy doubles in size every decade. Successive governments introduced policies to deepen the reforms, opening up more areas of the economy to market forces and foreign investment. By 2016 India was vying with China as the fastest-growing large economy on earth.[7]

In a 2010 speech to the Lok Sabha, India's lower house of parliament, Jagdish Bhagwati, a prominent and rambunctious Indian economist with a twinkle of mischief in his eye, praised the impact of growth on the life of ordinary Indians, some 200 million of whom he said had been lifted out of poverty. The architects of liberal reform, he said, had never intended to create growth for growth's sake. Rather growth was viewed as an enabler, a means of attacking poverty. He denied that such policies had anything to do with the discredited trickle-down economics popularized by Ronald Reagan with his aggressive tax cuts for the rich. Instead, he told parliament, growth was "a strategy for pulling the poor out of poverty through gainful employment, not as an end in itself."

Bhagwati's position was different from that of another prominent Indian economist, Amartya Sen, recipient of the 1998 Nobel Prize for economics and a contemporary of Bhagwati's at Cambridge back in the 1950s. (Manmohan Singh, the architect of India's reforms, also studied economics at Cambridge at the same time.) Sen has railed against "market fundamentalism" and stressed instead what he calls social capabilities, a term that boils down to an individual's freedom and capacity to achieve things: from the basics, such as accessing food, education and health, to the more ambitious, such as expressing a political opinion, participating in the democratic process, or choosing how to live one's life free from racial or gender prejudice.

When he was about ten years old, the young Sen was playing in the family garden in Dhaka, now the capital of Bangladesh but then a city in India before partition.[8] Suddenly a man came screaming into the garden with a knife wound in his back. Those were the days of communal violence between Hindus and Muslims. The knifed man, a laborer called Kader Mia, had come to work in a predominantly Hindu neighborhood and had been set upon by local thugs. The traumatized young Sen gave him water, and his father rushed the injured man to the hospital. On the way, Kader Mia explained that his wife had urged him not to come to the Hindu area in such troubled times, but that he had had no choice since he needed even the pittance he could earn as a day laborer to buy food for his family. Otherwise they would have had nothing to eat. "The penalty of his economic unfreedom," writes Sen, "turned out to be death, which occurred later on in the hospital." For the boy who would grow up to become a Nobel economist, the incident crystallized the connection between poverty and lack of freedom.

According to Sen, the purpose of development, a concept too often crudely reduced to an economic statistic, is "expanding the real freedoms that people enjoy."[9] Economic growth, he writes, can provide individuals with the wherewithal to escape "unfreedoms," the lack of choice to mold the contours of one's life. It so happens, Sen argues, that expanding people's freedom by, for example, ensuring they have access to basic rights such as health and literacy, is also good for growth. But in Sen's writing, liberty—freedom from unfreedoms—should be seen as a requisite of development, not a prerequisite for growth.

The positions of Bhagwati and Sen may seem like two sides of the same coin: one argues that growth can alleviate poverty, the other that poverty inhibits freedom. Yet the apparent compatibility of their arguments has not prevented a bad-tempered, not to say vicious, feud between the two. After Bhagwati's speech to parliament, Sen told the *Financial Times* that India's government was "stupid" for prioritizing double-digit growth when tens of millions of Indians were undernourished.[10]

Bhagwati, who mocks Sen as the "Mother Teresa of Economics," accused him of being a latecomer to the virtues of growth and antagonistic to necessary pro-growth reforms. "Significant redistribution in India could not have preceded growth as there were too few rich and too many poor," he wrote. If you want to cut up a pie evenly, you first have to have a pie. Sen, he writes in typically vituperative style, "puts the cart before the horse; and the cart is a dilapidated jalopy!"

The argument between the warring economists intensified during the 2013 election campaign. This pitted Rahul Gandhi, scion of the Nehru-Gandhi dynasty that had dominated Indian politics since independence, against Narendra Modi, an outsider and son of a tea seller. Modi had been the controversial governor of Gujarat province, praised by some for his pro-business, no-nonsense style, but excoriated by others for allegedly standing by during a 2002 massacre of nearly 800 Muslims. Modi was a polarizing figure, and Bhagwati and Sen were duly polarized. Bhagwati supported Modi and Sen did not.

More generally, Sen was among the many who wondered what

all the headline growth in India was for. He was appalled by both the continued misery of its poorest people, including what he alleged was widespread malnutrition,[11] and by the excesses of its wealthy. Rich Indians were known for extraordinary conspicuous consumption: one Indian mining tycoon invited 50,000 guests to his daughter's wedding at a mock-Tudor castle in Bangalore at a cost of $80 million.[12] The country boasted a growing number of billionaires, some of whom did not exactly wear their social consciences on their sleeves. In Mumbai, a city where millions live in squalid slums, Mukesh Ambani, the wealthiest man in India, built a twenty-seven-story house, a "vertical palace" reputed to have cost $1 billion. Sen pointed to Bangladesh, a poorer country than India but one where, he argued, the poor (especially women) enjoyed higher life expectancy, better immunization rates, and more control over reproduction than their Indian counterparts.[13] In other words, Sen argued, Bangladesh had achieved more development with less GDP.

Bhagwati disputes Sen's assumptions. Instead, he highlights what he says are reduced poverty numbers and the advances in social indicators achieved by Indian growth. Growth, he says, "is a necessary condition, not a sufficient condition. The more you have of GDP, the more capability you have—if you have a good intention—to indulge it."

The intellectual spat between the two men can seem petty. Boiled down to its essence, Bhagwati says you need growth to generate funds to spend on health and education, while Sen says you need decent health and education to create the necessary conditions for growth. Their dispute has more to do with the order in which things take place than with the desired outcome.

In the court of academia their argument rages on, but in

the court of public opinion the verdict was somewhat clearer. Narendra Modi won a thumping victory. I followed that election closely, visiting India several times in 2014, the year the drama unfolded. A couple of weeks before voting took place, when Modi's victory already looked certain, I wrote that the downfall of the long-serving Congress Party lay in not recognizing how much India had changed. Fifteen years of growth had not yet worked miracles, but it had reduced the number of people who were desperately poor. That had cut their reliance on Congress's patrician brand of politics.

"Most Indians," I wrote, "are no longer satisfied with the make-work schemes or food handouts in which Congress has increasingly specialized. Many have caught the whiff of a better life. Now they want jobs and opportunity. Even those who have not yet clawed their way on to the bottom rung of the aspirational ladder have seen what it looks like, courtesy of the satellite television channels that beam images of a middle-class life into even the most benighted corners of the country."[14]

Many Indians had graduated from what one economist called a "petitioning class" into an aspirational one.[15] India's elite had failed to grasp the changes that fifteen years of growth had wrought. It was Modi who saw how alluring and transformative economic growth could be.

Not too long before he died in February 2017, I discussed the issue of growth in poor countries with Hans Rosling, a Swedish academic. Rosling was that rarest of things, a pop-star statistician.[16] A master of the TED talk—in which he used dynamic bubble charts to present data, which he pointed to with a rubber hand attached to the end of a long stick—Rosling was a self-described "edutainer." Although he objected to the term, he was also an optimist.[17] He believed that poor countries were gradually closing the gap on rich Western ones, a trend that was most discernible in basic health data such as infant mortality. These were leading indicators, signs that countries had started on the road to development and would eventually make the transition from what he called lightbulbs to washing machines. Like me, Rosling thought this convergence of global living standards was something to celebrate wholeheartedly.

During our hour-long conversation he began with a defense of growth. "Here you are now talking to a professor in global health from a department of public health science in Sweden—Sweden, the most tax-loving country in the world," he said, pausing for comic effect and almost deliberately playing up his singsong Swedish accent. "And I say, 'I love money. I love GDP.' Because for me GDP was never an outcome measure; it was always an input measure. 'This is what you have, and now you can make something out of it.' "

Growth is not an end in itself. But managed sensibly it can be the magic dust to improve people's lives. "I did a study some years back where we compared GDP per capita and child survival. And GDP per capita explains 80 percent of child survival in the countries of the world."[18] There is, in other words, a pretty clear correlation between higher incomes and better health, in this case measured by child survival rates. But the correlation doesn't explain everything, nor settle the dispute as to whether the growth or the healthier population comes first.

Rosling's figures also show that in 20 percent of cases you can get your policies wrong. Angola in southern Africa is an example of a country that grew spectacularly fast in the first fifteen years of this century before oil prices crashed. Yet, in that time, it failed to translate double-digit growth into a better life for the majority of its people. That was largely because most of the wealth went to a narrow coterie connected to the government of José Eduardo dos Santos, who led the country for thirty-seven years until he finally stepped down in 2017. In that year, all that growth notwithstanding, Angola had an infant mortality rate of ninety-eight per thousand and a life expectancy of fifty-three, near the very bottom of all league tables and far worse than nominally poorer countries.

Part of the reason for Angola's failure—apart from bad policies and lousy distribution—is because its growth story is so recent. To translate economic growth into welfare takes time. (This suggests that growth might sometimes *precede* health gains, as Bhagwati contends.) "You cannot buy health at the supermarket. Look at Kuwait and Saudi Arabia and the United Arab Emirates. They've got the money, but it took them twenty-five years to convert that into social welfare and health." Still, the correlation between health and economic growth holds pretty firm. "There is not a country in the world with more than $20,000 per capita that has high child mortality, and there's not a country in the world that has less than $1,000 per capita that has low child mortality. So the capitalist hell doesn't exist and the communist paradise doesn't exist."[19]

The big advances in health come when a country moves from lower-middle-income status, like India and Indonesia, to upper-middle-income status, like China. That happens at around a nominal income of $4,000.[20] The big leap comes when you go from being India to being China. But, in health terms, going from China to Europe or North America doesn't make very much difference. Another way of putting this is that big health gains can be achieved at fairly low levels of income, around $4,000 per capita. Health returns begin to diminish after that. Because of advances in basic medicine, including vaccines and antibiotics, more health is available at lower cost. Vietnamese people today are at roughly the same economic level as Americans in the 1880s, but they have the same life expectancy as Americans had in the 1980s. In health terms Vietnam has stolen a march of a hundred years.[21]

Rosling had something to say about inequality too. In a poor country take-off is inevitably accompanied by widening inequality, since not everyone can escape poverty at once. He used the example of Ethiopia, a country of 100 million people that has been both growing rapidly and translating that growth into improvements in health. "They are doing it at the same time. But when you cut down the society in quintiles, you see that there are different parts of Ethiopia doing different things." In Ethiopia as a whole, for example, women are having far fewer babies, 4.6 in 2015 compared with 7 in the 1990s.[22] But that disguises huge differences. In remote parts of the country women are still having lots of children, but in Addis Ababa, the fast-growing capital, the fertility rate has dropped below two, lower than London.

If he is right, then prioritizing equality in poor countries, particularly during the initial stages of growth, may not always be wise. "Africa cannot reduce inequality in the population over the next decade. They have to forge forward, and the highly educated people in Africa must get even better health services and education, and then everyone else must follow," he said. In the long run you need policies to bridge the divide and to redistribute some of the wealth created. If not, you risk social friction or worse. "But the difference between the worst off and the best off doesn't have to diminish until one to two decades down the road." Deng Xiaoping made the same argument. The man who set China on the path to transformational growth also famously tweaked the egalitarian principles of communism with his dictum "Let some people get rich first."

Growth and social improvement can be self-reinforcing. "It's mutual. More money brings better social well-being, and better social well-being gets more money if you run your policies wisely," Rosling said. He offered a recipe for turning growth into development. "You keep your institutions improving. You keep peace between the ethnic groups and the regions. You invest in people with public money, in schools and basic health, in infectious disease control. And you put tax on cigarettes. And then you let your private sector thrive. And if you do that wisely, then you will take off, as we've seen South Korea doing, as we've seen many being able to do."

Does growth automatically follow basic improvements in health and education? "Never automatically. Never automatically," he replied. Cuba was an example of a country that, because of what he called "stupid economics," failed to translate its excellent social indicators into growth. "I lectured once at the ministry of health in Havana. I was invited there because I am neutral politically. And after my speech, the minister of education said, 'This professor shows that Cubans are the healthiest of the poor.' And everyone applauded," Rosling said, chuckling quietly at the minister's false logic. "On the way out, a very bright, brave young statistician whispered in my ear, 'We are not the healthiest of the poor,' he said. 'We are just the poorest of the healthy.'"

9

BLACK POWER, GREEN POWER

They called it the Airpocalypse. In November 2015 a suffocating blanket of poisonous smog rolled over Beijing, China's capital of 22 million people. Much of it was blown in from the surrounding provinces of Hebei and Shanxi, where coal-burning factories and coal-fired power stations were helping to power China's economic miracle. By December, as world leaders were gathering a continent away for the Paris climate talks, Beijing's netizens were in revolt.

The Chinese government acted, issuing its first-ever air-pollution red alert. That meant closing 3,200 schools and advising children to remain indoors. Private vehicles were banned on alternate days according to their license-plate numbers, pulling 2.5 million cars off the road at a stroke. When drivers did venture out, they put on their headlights to penetrate the blackness. Tiananmen Square was shrouded in darkness. Thick, sulfurous air hovered over the world's largest public gathering space, curling around the giant portrait of Mao Zedong and the ancient walls of the Forbidden City. Even the bulkiest of buildings, including the tangled steel exterior of the Bird's Nest stadium built for the 2008 Olympics, were barely visible in the filthy air. Barbecues were banned. So were fireworks, a favorite Chinese pastime. Factories were shut, construction halted.

Still, many Beijing residents struggled on, performing aerobics to blasted music in the ghostly parks or braving the gloom to trudge to work. One foreign reporter took to Twitter after witnessing a small scene of defiance—or madness. In an improvized "Beijing haiku"[1] he wrote,

A man on a bench in code red smog
pulls down his mask
to drag on a cigarette

I have had plenty of experience of Beijing's hazardous air. An enchanting city on those rare occasions when the skies are a crisp eggshell blue, on the days the air turns vile China's ancient capital is a vision of hell. Skin smarts in the chemical-laden air. Eyes water. Lungs heave with phlegm and dust. On a bad day in Beijing the air-quality index tops 200. We know this because the American embassy started taking measurements from its rooftop, releasing data on social media in an effort to embarrass the Chinese authorities. According to US standards, if the air-quality index drifts above 50, you are at the upper limit of safety, though Beijing residents treat anything below 100 as reassuring. A typical tweet from the embassy, this one from Tuesday, February 25, 2014, went, "440. Hazardous. Health alert: everyone may experience more serious health effects, please avoid physical exertion and outdoor activities." A US official once described a reading above 500 as "crazy bad." During the worst of the Airpocalypse, it edged above 1,000.

Chinese air pollutants include sulphates, ozone, black carbon, desert dust, mercury, and acid rain. The carbon-laced soot particles produced by cars, cooking stoves, and factories have a diameter of less than 2.5 micrometers, penetrating deep into lung tissue and making it easier for other toxins to be absorbed. This can cause asthma, bronchitis, shortness of breath, and chronic respiratory problems. The *Lancet* estimated that in 2010 air pollution in China contributed to the premature deaths of 1.2 million people, 40 percent of the world total of those dying of similar causes.[2]

From a health point of view, the data being streamed from the American embassy's rooftop were more important than the level of growth, a number over which the Chinese government—and to a great extent the Chinese people—had been obsessing for years. But until recently information on particulates was actively suppressed.

By 2017 everyone in China, from President Xi Jinping on down, had become more conscious about the environment. Even then old obsessions were hard to let go. That year many viewers expressed deep admiration for a character in a hit television show, *In the Name of the People*, a fifty-five-episode series sometimes described as China's *House of Cards*. One of the characters, a local party chief named Li Dakang, exhibits a single-minded devotion to economic growth. "There is nothing wrong with demolishing the old China," Li says, explaining why the country must push on with development even in the face of public protests. "There will not be a new one without demolishing the old one."

According to the *New York Times*, Li "sometimes neglects the negative effects of a headlong pursuit of growth. He does want to protect the environment, but it is his obsession with gross domestic product that has won him wide admiration among viewers and inspired Internet memes." One read, "Don't bow your head. The GDP will drop if you do."[3]

...

Six months before the Airpocalypse, on a humid day in April 2015, I head out by taxi through the congested streets of Beijing. The sky is a uniformly gray veil over the city, but the air is good by the capital's lamentable standards. Our battered car rattles along the second ring road (there are now seven) and past the Lama Temple, a Tibetan place of worship that began life as a residence for court eunuchs in the seventeenth century. We head farther toward the outskirts of the vast city, where futuristically shaped skyscrapers give way to less imposing architecture, ending up at a slabby sand-colored building occupied by the Chinese Academy of Sciences.

I've come to see Niu Wenyuan, a small man in his mid-seventies who ushers me into his office and proceeds to smile and nod encouragingly at everything I say during our ninety-minute encounter. Niu's face, like that of many Chinese of his generation, is etched with a rugged dignity. He is a renowned economist, an adviser to the state council (China's cabinet), and the recipient of a 2011 award from the Chinese government for his work on environmental protection and sustainable growth. He is also the inventor of China's "green GDP."

In the office are photographs of Niu with various Chinese leaders, including Hu Jintao and Wen Jiabao, the former president and premier respectively, who ran the country for the decade before Xi Jinping took over in 2013. When Niu is making a point, he moves his hands extravagantly through the air. When his thought is complete, he crosses his arms and smiles benevolently. Throughout our discussion he drinks aromatic tea from a modest silver flask, which his secretary periodically refills with piping-hot water.

Calculating economic output, he tells me with lavish understatement, is "interesting and complicated." China officially began to measure GDP only in 1992, he says. Before then it had used the Soviet system of national accounts known as the Material Product System. That method, which reflected the Soviet Union's emphasis on heavy industry, barely measured services, which were considered more or less irrelevant. It was only in China's seventh five-year plan, 1986–90, that the Communist Party, which in all but name had abandoned communism several years earlier, altered its methodology. It wanted to reconcile its own measures of economic performance with those of the non-communist world.

Since those early days, China has embraced GDP with the passion of a convert. For the Communist Party, delivering year after year of rapid economic growth has become its principal source of legitimacy. A poem recited by a father to his son and subsequently to his grandson in *To Live*, a film by Zhang Yimou set against the backdrop of China's transition from serfdom through communism to state capitalism, sums up the idea of material progress.

Our family is like a little chicken.
When it grows up it becomes a goose
And it'll turn into a sheep.
The sheep will turn into an ox
And after the ox is communism
And there'll be dumplings and meat every day.

The Communist Party has justified its monopoly on power by its track record of bringing ever-greater abundance to what had been a desperately poor peasantry. For party officials progress through the communist ranks has—as with the fictional Li Dakang—been determined by the ability to conjure economic growth at a local level. For years before the recent slowdown, it was almost an article of faith that growth must never be allowed to dip below 8 percent lest that unleash a fury of social protest. In the jostling for supreme power, only those party officials whose provinces expanded fast enough could hope to scale the Communist Party's top echelons.

Niu is skeptical about growth at all costs. Yet, like many free thinkers in his country, he has learned how to couch his observations in language that does not openly challenge Communist Party doctrine. He starts not by burying growth, but by praising it. "GDP is a very important instrument to measure a nation's wealth. So far there is no alternative method to rival it," he says, beaming. "As you know, GDP has been called one of the greatest inventions of the twentieth century. Although the current method of calculating GDP has its defects, no better way has yet been invented."

When China began to study the United Nations System of National Accounts in 1986, it reconstructed its national income accounts right back to 1952, just three years after the communists took over in 1949. For nearly a quarter of a century Mao Zedong, founding father of the People's Republic, had led a ruinous experiment in collectivization and would-be economic liftoff. Mao's Great Leap Forward (1958–62) was an emblematic, if still mostly hushed-up, catastrophe. In order to catch up with industrial nations, Mao had ordered the collectivization of farming into supposedly more efficient units and the establishment of what turned out to be useless backyard furnaces producing steel from pots and pans. Though crop levels fell as a result of the misguided experiment, local governments misstated their harvests in order to comply with centrally mandated targets. They handed over pretend surpluses and China continued to export grain to earn foreign currency. With only the crudest of measurements at their disposal, many central planners had little idea of what was really going on. The result of industrialization-at-any-cost was wholesale famine in which as many as 46 million people perished.[4]

Historical data, calculated by the new growth metric, showed that China's performance during the communist years had been extremely erratic, with growth above 10 percent in some years, followed by periods of catastrophic recession. In 1961, at the height of Mao's Great Leap Forward, the economy shrank by an astonishing 27 percent. But from the early 1990s, by which time the new accounting practices had been fully adopted, the picture changed. With a consistency that has often been called into question, China registered growth of around 10 percent in virtually every year from 1992 to 2010.[5] In the process, it catapulted itself from poor peasant economy to modern powerhouse.

The results were astonishing. In 1979 income per capita was a miserable $272. That was the year when Deng embraced market-driven policies by allowing farmers to sell surpluses and by establishing free-trade manufacturing zones to attract foreign investment. By 2015 income per capita had surged to $8,000, pushing China comfortably into middle-income status. Because of its huge population, China was also becoming a power to be reckoned with on the world stage. In 2000 its economy surpassed that of Italy, one of the world's so-called Group of Seven. In 2005 it overhauled France, in 2006 Britain, in 2007 Germany, and in 2010— the sweetest moment of all—it supplanted bitter rival Japan as the world's second-largest economy. Only the US stood in the way. Spending on the military tracked this newfound wealth.

All this growth, though, came at a cost, says Niu, turning more serious. As in the days of Mao's Great Leap Forward, it was a cost—in disrupted lives, poisoned air and rivers, and unsustainable exploitation of natural resources—that the Chinese Communist Party either could not or would not recognize. People knew there had to be a better measurement, he says, one that would track both the good and the bad aspects of such explosive growth. And so he set about inventing one.

"My research team and I were the first to publish an article proposing the concept of green GDP," he says. Conventional GDP can only count things you exchange in the market, he says. It can't measure "the forces that can be used to maintain stability nor the forces of morality," he adds in what sounds like a version of Robert Kennedy's famous dictum that GDP measures everything "except that which makes life worthwhile."

"The method we use is pretty raw," he concedes about his alternative measurement. "We take the current GDP figure and we scrape away the parts that we believe are wrong or miscalculated. And in this way we arrive at something that is closer to the real GDP."

Niu says there are three elements to his method. The first starts with the assumption that you should not "overconsume" the environment. If you need "one pile of coal and a hundred units of electricity" but instead use three piles of coal and three hundred units of electricity then the "wasted" part of that process should not be counted. The excess part should be "scraped away."

Second is when you produce growth "by mistake." "I'll give you an example," he says, a twinkle in his eye. "In a particular county you have a party secretary named Zhang. He decides that you need to dig this field. During that digging process you create GDP. Then Party Secretary Li comes along and says, 'You should not be digging that field. Please fill up the hole.'" Niu shakes his head sorrowfully as though disagreements of this type between

Comrade Zhang and Comrade Li are all too common—and presumably on a larger scale. "These kinds of management mistakes can be avoided. They should not be counted," he says.

Incidentally, before we mock the Chinese for digging holes, filling them up again, and calling it economic activity, we should recognize that in the West we are not immune to such sleights of statistics. My favorite example of this is digging gold out of the ground and then storing it in a bank. In the words of one famous economist, "Men mine gold from the bowels of the earth only to have it go back to the earth in the vaults at Fort Knox."[6]

Number three on Niu's list is what he calls the "cost to society." If social relations are harmonious and levels of crime and social protest low, he says, you don't need to spend much money on keeping order. "If there is a higher rate of disorder, you need a bigger police force to keep the peace," he says, sounding like a Chinese Simon Kuznets. "That also creates GDP, but you shouldn't count it because it is unnecessary. Is that the kind of growth we want?"

Niu's proposal for green GDP was designed to account for what economists call externalities. Negative externalities are the unrecorded side effects of economic output. A factory producing steel or plastic may, for example, be causing serious damage to the rivers and air by pouring out toxic chemicals or particle dust. While it makes products and profits—duly recorded as economic activity—everyone suffers in the form of poorer health and higher taxes to pay for the cleanup. These are the invisible costs that a producer can quietly offload onto society. Not only do conventional growth measures fail to register these costs as a negative, all too often they log them as a positive: dredging a poisoned river, treating cancer patients, and giving victims of early death a good funeral all count as economic activity. One commentator describes our measurement of growth as a "statistical laundromat" to make social evils magically disappear.[7] There are also positive externalities, the unmeasured benefits of an activity or asset. Creating a green space in a city might look like a drag on the economy—think of the steel plant you could build there instead—but a park brings economically invisible benefits in the form of leisure, stress relief and mental well-being that are likely to save money on health care.

The aim of Niu's new method was to expose the hidden costs of negative externalities. But his modest, somewhat eclectic, proposal was highly subversive in a one-party state whose raison d'être was to maximize growth. Not only was China doing untold damage to the environment; its political system was also causing hidden social costs. One of the engines of China's growth, for example, has been converting agricultural land into industrial land, which has a higher productive capacity. Officials of local municipalities, struggling to meet centrally mandated growth targets—and to enrich themselves while they're at it—have got this down to a fine art. They forcibly remove peasants from the land, providing inadequate compensation or no compensation at all. The land is then sold on to industry or property developers, and at a stroke money and growth have been spirited out of thin air.

Much of China's growth—indeed the transformation of any pre-industrial economy into a modern one—results from converting one thing into another: young peasant women into factory workers, coal in the ground into energy and pollution, and communal land into private property. Often growth is an act of monetizing what was already there. As anywhere, there are hidden costs: environmental destruction, social dislocation, inequality and, in China's case, the spiraling debt—250 percent of GDP by 2017—needed to keep the show on the road.[8] That is not a criticism of China's growth model in particular. Nor is it to say that these trade-offs are not worth it. They may just be the price of progress. But the problem with our obsession with growth is that we do not count the negatives. You cannot call it a trade-off if you only measure one side of the equation.

For Niu, suppressing one's own people is not a positive that should count toward growth, but rather a negative that should be scraped away. Similarly, to count a mistakenly dug hole—for which read white-elephant dams, roads to nowhere, and redundant steel mills—is to put what should be a negative on the positive side of the ledger. And it is wrong, he says, to count environmental destruction as growth when future generations will have to pay to clean it up. "If you make mistakes, the GDP you create is not real," he says.

"In 2006 we wanted to publish green GDP but we had no success," Niu once told another interviewer.[9] "Political pressure was one reason; local government officials felt green GDP damaged their promotion prospects. The other was that it was overcomplicated and the public did not understand it." Unperturbed, five years later he returned with his GDP quality index, a simplified version of the original. Provincial leaders were still upset, and Niu's index has remained more of an academic exercise than a driver of official policy.

Still, Niu's small team has produced numbers on China's "real" growth rate—adjusted for waste, environmental destruction, and social disharmony. They are controversial, inconvenient—and more or less secret. "We have a rough calculation but we don't announce it," he says cryptically. Pressed, he concedes that, according to his calculations, "about a third of China's stated GDP is not real."

"We shouldn't worship GDP and we shouldn't abandon GDP," he said on another occasion. "Our aim is to have a GDP that consumes fewer natural resources, is less harmful to the environment and has a low social management cost. We want rational, genuine GDP."[10]

Niu is an idealist. He is after something that no economist—perhaps no social scientist—has yet discovered: how to quantify what he calls a green mentality. His ultimate goal, he says, one that sounds naively out of sync with a frenetically modernizing China, is to discover "the green in people's hearts." Only then, he says, "when people get wiser can GDP be green."

In March 2013 residents of Shanghai awoke to find the carcasses of thousands of pigs floating down a suburban river. A few years before, as China prepared to host the summer Olympics of 2008, mysterious algae began to spread—like the protagonist of some horror movie—off the coast, threatening the sailing events in the port city of Qingdao. By the time the authorities began to bring it under control, the algae had spread several hundred miles along the eastern seaboard. State media played it down, quoting scientists saying the outbreak was a natural phenomenon. Chinese environmentalists begged to differ, blaming the visitation on industrial pollutants and fish farming. "The natural ecosystem of the ocean has been destroyed, which is why strange events such as this can happen," said Wen Bo, coordinator of Save China's Seas Network.[11]

Two-fifths of China's river water is undrinkable and one-sixth is so polluted it is unfit for any use. The *baiji*, or Goddess of the Yangtze, one of only four types of exclusively freshwater dol-

phins, has been driven to extinction, ending its 20 million years
on earth. Though air pollution has grabbed most of the headlines,
soil erosion is just as catastrophic.[12] Soil accounts for just a few
inches—or at best a few feet—of the earth's surface. Once eroded
by overcultivation, blown away or washed into the rivers and
oceans, it is replaced only over geological time. According to one
estimate, soil is eroding in China thirty to forty times faster than it
can be replaced naturally. China is also scattered with "cancer villages" such as Xinglong in Yunnan province, where a local chemical plant has dumped thousands of tons of waste chromium—a
known carcinogen—into the nearby hills and river.

To be fair—something that people writing about the negative
impacts of economic expansion not always are—China's growth
brings many benefits too. Air pollution may cause as many as 1.2
million premature deaths a year, but it is equally true that China's
remarkable economic progress has contributed to a leap in life expectancy, which has more than doubled from thirty-five in 1949
to seventy-five today. That outpaces gains in most other countries
and reflects a dramatic rise in the standard of living of most people,
bringing better food, better hospitals, and better housing.

Whether or not China's growth threatens the planet—as well
as its own sustainability—is a matter of conjecture. Ever since
Thomas Malthus, a cleric and scholar who wrote his famous *An
Essay on the Principle of Population* in 1798, people have been predicting that the earth is reaching its natural limits. Malthus thought
that population growth would always outpace improvements in
agricultural production, ensuring that living standards would stall
and eventually catastrophe would strike. Malthus has been much
pilloried. Like a stock market analyst forever predicting a crash,
his ghost has had to watch on as the world has forged ahead into

bull market territory.[13] Certainly, there have been famines, war and pestilence, but the human population has grown exponentially and despite all the poverty that still remains, has grown immeasurably richer.

One of the patterns of industrial growth has been that, in the early stages of development, countries pollute. Then, as they grow richer and more technologically advanced, they clean up. Take London, which as late as 1952 had "pea souper" pollution days. So foul was the air on some occasions that the greyhound races at White City were abandoned because the dogs could not see the mechanical hare they were meant to be chasing.

London in 1952 sounds like Beijing in 2015. Yet some think China's industrialization may be the final straw for the planet. That is because of China's scale. Other countries, as they have grown richer, have managed to push polluting industries to other, poorer countries, like a game of pass the parcel. Much of the pollution that goes to make American and European goods has simply been outsourced to China. The question is, when China finally gets rich enough, will it be able to pass the parcel to someone else, say Africa? Or is the collective parcel of global production now simply too large to be palmed off? As it closes the wealth gap on America, might China's emission of CO_2 alone lead to an unsustainable rise in temperatures, triggering catastrophic changes in global weather patterns? If China is unable to repeat the trick that other nations managed as they climbed up the industrial ladder, Malthus might just have been a couple of hundred years early in his prediction.

Of course China may be able to clean up by applying technology, shifting from manufacturing to services, and gradually repairing some of the damage already done. But to do so it will first have to recognize the problem. In some ways that is already happening. In 2015 Chai Jing, a former journalist for state broadcaster China Central Television, uploaded to the Internet a documentary she had made and financed herself. It was called *Under the Dome* and it dealt with the environmental catastrophe in the coal-mining province of Shanxi. In the film's most poignant moment Chai asks a six-year-old girl if she has ever seen the stars. She has not.

The reaction to the film was nothing short of breathtaking (excuse the pun). It was downloaded more than 150 million times even though it was quickly removed by China's censors. Nevertheless, the environment minister at the time praised the film, comparing it favorably with *Silent Spring*, a 1962 book by Rachel Carson that attacked the chemical industry and is credited with sparking the modern environmental movement. Even before the film came out, in 2014, Li Keqiang, the Chinese premier, had declared a "war on pollution," and called smog "nature's red-light warning against the model of inefficient and blind development."

We should be cautious of the rhetoric of China's leaders. But we also need to acknowledge that much has changed. As one report argues, Beijing "has become a green energy juggernaut after designating renewables as a strategic industry. China has more than a third of the world's wind power capacity; a quarter of its solar power; six of the top ten solar-panel makers; four of the top ten wind-turbine makers and more battery-only electric car sales last year than the rest of the world combined."[14]

Beijing's switch to renewable energy—including nuclear—is hampered by the fact that the country still has a lot of catching up to do if it wants to match Western standards of living. That will mean years of fast growth, even though Beijing's leaders have been gradually lowering expectations about what is possible, from the double digits of just a few years ago to below 7 percent. And although the share of non-fossil fuel energy is increasing, absolute levels of dirty energy are continuing to grow. In 2016 a Chinese official said coal power generation could increase by one-fifth over the following five years alone.[15]

Some of the improvements China is making, including in the quality of air, involve a domestic pass-the-parcel. In the first three months of 2016 Beijing's average concentration of $PM_{2.5}$ (fine particulate matter) was down 28 percent, year on year, reflecting the results of a concerted crackdown. Shanghai's air was 12 percent better, according to data collected by Greenpeace. But while coal-fired plants were being closed in northern Hebei province, a neighbor of Beijing, they were being built in central and western provinces, where regulations are laxer. Of the cities surveyed there, ninety-one reported an increase in air pollution.[16]

Still, a study in 2016 conducted by the London School of Economics found that Chinese carbon emissions would peak in 2025, and might even have already done so. It maintained that projections were too bleak because China's economy was already shifting from heavy industry to less carbon-intensive technology and services. Xie Zhenhua, China's top climate negotiator, said his country's CO_2 emissions had not peaked and were still climbing because of the construction and vehicle ownership that came with urbanization. But, he said, they might stabilize soon because of China's policy shift. "In reality, our CO_2 emissions are still increasing, but the efforts we are making are very big."[17]

Things were beginning to change politically as well. Niu's green GDP was beginning to catch on. In 2015 China's environment ministry again floated the idea that the performance of provincial officials should be judged partly by progress on improving the environment. In 2014 more than seventy smaller cities and counties jettisoned GDP as a performance metric for government officials, prioritizing environmental protection and poverty reduction instead. That summer President Xi had told party officials, "We need to look at obvious achievements as well as hidden achievements. We can no longer simply use GDP growth rates to decide who the [party] heroes are."[18]

Internationally too, Beijing had gone from laggard to putative world leader. Even as Donald Trump was pulling America out of the Paris Climate Agreement, Beijing agreed with the European Union to accelerate what was called a historic shift away from fossil fuels. Wang Hui at the University of International Relations in Beijing said Washington's withdrawal had given China the opportunity to lead. "Trump is a businessman who emphasizes America's own interests rather than common interests. China and Europe must now step up and assume our international responsibilities together."[19]

As green technology advances, the arguments about a trade-off between growth and pollution may prove a red herring. Some of that apparent trade-off is simply because we are not measuring things correctly. Are the parts of "growth" that make people's life miserable and kill them off prematurely really worthy of the name? Admiration for Li Dakang, the go-for-growth local official in *In the Name of the People*, suggests not all Chinese people see it that way. Perhaps if you are escaping from poverty, you want growth in whatever form and at whatever cost. But even Li might agree that it would be better to have the data so one could judge more precisely what the trade-offs are.

As Jonathan Watts, a reporter and keen observer of China's environment, was leaving China in 2012, he gave a memorable speech. In it he said that Beijing had made almost no political reforms during his nine years in the country but had achieved vast leaps in terms of environmental reform. He listed anti-desertification campaigns, tree planting, an environmental transparency law, adoption of carbon targets, eco-services compensation, eco accounting, caps on water use, lower economic growth targets, the Twelfth Five-Year Plan, debate and increased monitoring of $PM_{2.5}$, and investments in renewables and clean tech.

Of course that didn't mean China was any cleaner. During the same nine years the size of China's economy had quadrupled, there were five times as many cars on the roads, and carbon emissions had doubled and surpassed those of the US. The country now accounted for almost half the coal burned on the planet. China, said Watts, was both a "black superpower" and a "green superpower." It could kill the world, but it could also save it.

PART THREE

BEYOND GROWTH

10
WEALTH

Imagine for a moment two people, Bill and Ben. Bill is a banker and earns $200,000 a year at Goldman Sachs. OK, he's miserably paid by banking standards, but bear with me. Ben is a gardener and earns $20,000 pruning roses and trimming hedges. Who is better off? If you measure the income each receives, then Bill is clearly richer, in fact precisely ten times richer. This measurement is the equivalent of GDP; it tells you about the "flow" of income each receives in a particular year. But, just like GDP, these numbers don't reveal much about the true wealth of Bill and Ben.

To discover more, you'd need to know about their stock of assets. Did I forget to mention that Ben the gardener recently inherited a huge country estate in Long Island worth $100 million? In truth, he works in his own vast garden as a bit of a hobby on Tuesday afternoons and pays himself a token wage. But he plans to sell off the estate next year, move into somewhere more modest in Manhattan, and live off the interest from investing the $95 million or so he'll have left over.

Poor Bill, meanwhile, is up to his neck in debt. He has to fork out half his salary each month on his mortgage, which has another ten years to run. He has car payments on his (scratched-up) Porsche and a troubling bank overdraft that he's acquired to maintain his highfalutin lifestyle. Unfortunately, he's also pushing fifty (Ben is nineteen by the way) and the bank is going to have to let him go.

Now who looks better off, Bill or Ben?

Our standard growth measurement tells us everything about income and nothing about wealth. This is one of its fundamental shortcomings. That goes for nations as well as individuals. Growth numbers for Saudi Arabia are virtually meaningless. Why? Because they are predicated on flows of oil, which will one day run out. At that point, unless Saudi Arabia has discovered another method of producing today's level of income, its economy will shrivel.[1] Saudi Arabia would then become the Bill-the-banker of nations.

Measuring wealth—the stock of assets—is indispensable if we are to get a true picture of the world. And yet, when it comes to national accounts, we have limited tools at our disposal. National accounts contain huge amounts of information, but these are rarely brought to light by growth-obsessed policymakers who home in on only one of the numbers—GDP—at their disposal.

That is extraordinary if you stop to think about it. When investors are sizing up a company, they look not only at its profits and losses, but also at its balance sheet. The profit and loss account, sometimes known as the income statement, shows the flow of revenues and expenditure over a set period. Broadly speaking, if revenues exceed expenditure, the company is in profit. If not, it is in loss. The balance sheet is different. Rather than measuring the flow of incomings and outgoings, it takes a snapshot. It lists assets, liabilities, and shareholder equity. It shows what the company owns and what it owes. In the process it reveals what a company is actually "worth" rather than merely showing the profits it is able to generate this year—but not necessarily in the years ahead.[2]

Politicians and policymakers rely on only a threadbare set of accounts by comparison. We call it GDP. It is the equivalent of an income statement. Beyond a few experimental satellite accounts, there has been no systematic attempt to measure a nation's stock of assets, or what we might call its wealth.[3] "There's been no innovation in national accounts. It's totally stuck," says Umair Haque, a leather-jacket-wearing economist. He regards this as a shocking failure. It is urgent, he argues, for the so-called great economic minds, including those at multilateral bodies like the IMF and World Bank, to come up with wealth measures to match all the countless revisions and updates that have gone into perfecting measurements of growth. "Why isn't there innovation in national accounts that lets us have a more accurate picture of the economy? Without a measure of national wealth we have no idea," he fumes (literally), cigarette in one hand and espresso in the other. "Without a picture of the stocks, we can't say with any accuracy how wealthy we really are."

Partha Dasgupta is the Frank Ramsey professor emeritus at Cambridge University and a pioneer of environmental economics. He has spent much of his career looking at how we might think differently about our economies. I went to Cambridge to talk to him. He met me outside the imposing Great Gate of St. John's College, dressed in a suit jacket, trousers, and white trainers. For a man of seventy-four, he looked trim and agile. He walked me to his book-lined study near the River Cam, where he offered me sherry, a throwback to a more genteel age. I readily accepted. It was, after all, already 11 a.m.

Like many people who have made their home in a new country—Dasgupta was born in what is now Bangladesh but came to England in the early 1960s to do a PhD in economics at Trinity

College, Cambridge—he is more English than the English. He has a gentle, refined way about him. Dasgupta is not so much a critic of growth as convinced that it is measuring the wrong thing. Whatever unit we are studying—households, nations, or the planet as a whole—we ought to be interested not in income but in wealth, he argues. By wealth he means "the social worth of an economy's stock of capital assets, comprising manufactured capital (roads, ports, machinery, and so on), human capital (population size and composition, education, health), knowledge (the arts, humanities, and sciences), and natural capital (ecosystems, sources of water, the atmosphere, land, sub-soil resources)."[4]

That seems like a tall order. How on earth, for example, could we put a numerical value on knowledge or culture? Dasgupta is not oblivious to the conceptual difficulties, but he has two responses. One is that since the 1940s humans have invested huge intellectual capital and tens of billions of dollars in creating, revising, and refining growth measurements. In comparison, the effort to produce a balance-sheet version of national accounts has been minuscule. "Never mind how difficult it is to estimate. The fact that it's very difficult to estimate is not an argument for running away from it," he says firmly. "Because GDP is also very difficult to estimate."

Second, he says, the best intellectual approach to any problem is to push a hypothesis to its limit and then retreat if things turn out to be too hard. Conceptually, we ought to have a balance sheet of our national economies, a snapshot of what we own and what we owe. So we should not shrink from the task; instead we should put our collective brains into creating one.

Stock and flow measures are intimately related, much as they are in a set of corporate accounts. A company has machinery and a skilled workforce that help it produce goods and services to generate an income this year and in future years. It can run down its assets to generate more profits now, or build up assets, suppressing today's income in order to make more money down the road. For example, it could stop replacing machinery to maximize profits today. At some point though the machines would grind to a halt. Alternatively, it could invest in next-generation robots or send its workers on expensive training courses to upgrade their skills. Both would maximize competitiveness (and profits) tomorrow, but at the cost of lower profits today.

Take a household. In a rich country a person's assets might include her house, her investments, and an estimate of her likely future lifetime earnings and pension adjusted to today's prices. "That's a stock, and it's what enables you to have a plan of life. You could eat into it if you wish—say, to educate yourself. You might be disinvesting some of your assets in order to acquire some other asset, namely human capital." In a poor country a person's assets might include land, livestock, or the right to fish in communal waters off the coast. In hard times you might sell your cow to buy food to maintain your own human capital (in this case physical strength) and to pay for transport to the city to find salaried work. "You are converting one form of capital into another."

The assets of a household or a nation go beyond physical assets, whether natural or industrial. They include skills, counted for example in trained carpenters and the number of professionals with PhDs. You can stretch the idea as far as cultural capital. Take two identical islands. On the first households have absolutely no trust in one another, and on the other they have absolute trust. On the island with trust trade across households is possible because people trust one another to fulfill their side of the bargain, say providing milk for a year in return for two blankets. But in the other there's no trust and thus no prospect of exchanging goods between households. The futures of the two islands are going to be entirely different, even if they start with exactly the same asset base.[5]

Let's stick for the moment to natural capital. "Contemporary models of economic growth and development regard nature to be a fixed, indestructible factor of production. The problem with the assumption is that it is wrong," Dasgupta writes. "Nature is a mosaic of degradable assets. Agricultural land, forests, watersheds, fisheries, freshwater sources, estuaries, wetlands, the atmosphere—more generally, ecosystems—are assets that are self-regenerative, but can suffer from deterioration or depletion through human use."[6]

In gross domestic product, Dasgupta says, "the rogue word is 'gross.'" That is because it does not count the depreciation of assets. "If a wetland is drained to make way for a shopping mall, the construction of the latter contributes to GDP, but the destruction of the former goes unrecorded." If the social worth of the mall was less than the social value of the wetland, "the economy would have become poorer—wealth would have declined—and potential well-being across the present and future generations would mimic that decline. But GDP would signal otherwise."

There are three interlocking reasons why we should think about the stock of wealth in addition to the flow on which "growth" is based.

First, to do so helps societies make better decisions about the interplay between stock and flow, between the present and the future. For an individual, if you know how much money you have in the bank, you know how much you can afford to spend on, say, a master's degree that may eventually bring rewards (in addition to the pleasure of learning) in the form of higher earnings. At the level of a nation, there are myriad occasions when it would be useful to weigh the advantages of using income to build up capital stock or sweating assets to generate more growth. Free university education, for example, might seem like an unaffordable economic sacrifice, but if you were measuring the stock of wealth rather than the flow, all those additional educated people might look like an increase in your nation's wealth, not a diminishment of its growth. The same goes for investing in infrastructure, say high-speed rail, in anticipation of future returns on investment. How one accounts for these things matters. In the US independent senator Bernie Sanders and in the UK Jeremy Corbyn, the opposition Labour leader, both want to increase public funding and scrap student fees. Their policies look less radical—and therefore more plausible—from a wealth-accounting perspective.

The second reason for counting assets is that today's actions have an impact on future generations. Recording today's national income offers no help whatsoever when making intergenerational decisions. The signal it sends is to maximize growth today no matter what the impact tomorrow. At the extreme, one generation might use up all a nation's forest cover and all its oil reserves in the interests of double-digit growth and in the expectation that future generations will somehow sort things out. Today a government pushing such policies would point to rapid growth as a justification for its actions. But a wealth measure would show a sharp fall. That would at least give voters pause, by offering a clearer picture of the trade-off. WEALTH FALLS 5 PERCENT does not make quite as good a headline as ECONOMY GROWS 3 PERCENT. Getting a handle on wealth would give present generations the chance to see more clearly what sort of future they were leaving their children and grandchildren.

The third, closely related, reason for considering wealth is sustainability. Put starkly, measuring wealth could help societies avoid collapse. Easter Island, 2,000 miles off the coast of South America, is a well-known example of a once-flourishing civilization that imploded. It is famous for its mysterious stone-head carvings, which now lie abandoned and desecrated.[7] When the island was "discovered" by Dutch explorer Jacob Roggeveen on Easter day in 1722 it was already a barren grassland without a single tree or bush over ten feet tall. Though it was inhabited by Polynesians, once famous for their seafaring skills, the islanders had been reduced to paddling about in decrepit canoes. Many lived in caves and scratched out a miserable living. Yet once Easter Island had looked very different. When it was first settled, in about AD 400, it was covered in trees and bushes and had abundant wildlife, offering its inhabitants a rich diet. By AD 1200 the islanders had started to carve the big heads from stone found in one part of the island and transport them using logs and ropes several miles to the coast to be displayed on giant plinths.

They had felled the trees not only for the purpose of transporting the stone heads, but also for firewood and for building homes and canoes. What could have possibly induced the islanders to cut down the last tree on which the whole civilization depended? In reality the destruction would not have come about this way. Instead, it would have happened gradually, like the proverbial frog being boiled alive in an imperceptibly warming bath. Easter Island's civilization collapsed not with a bang—or the strike of the last ax on the last tree trunk—but with a resigned croak. By the time Roggeveen arrived, its population had fallen to between a quarter and a tenth of its peak, the flora and fauna had been all but destroyed, and the civilization mangled. The islanders, who once feasted on a rich diet of porpoises, shellfish, and seafood, had apparently sunk into cannibalism. Their most "inflammatory taunt" was "The flesh of your mother sticks between my teeth."[8]

Easter Island is the earth writ small, a parable of what can happen to societies if they neglect the wealth on which their livelihood depends. Pointing to a refrain of loggers in northwest America "Jobs over trees"—Jared Diamond, an American geographer and polymath, says that modern societies are not immune from sudden collapse. Far from it. "If we continue to follow our present course, we shall have exhausted the world's major fisheries, tropical rainforests, fossil fuels, and much of our soil" in a few generations, he says. "Perhaps someday New York's skyscrapers will stand derelict and overgrown with vegetation, like the temples at Angkor Wat and Tikal."

Keeping an accurate record of a society's wealth is not enough in itself to stave off catastrophe. Scientists have been warning for years about the dangers of global warming, providing strong evidence of the link between carbon emissions, raised temperatures, and observable and possible future environmental changes. Yet, without the acceptance of the science or the political will to act, all the data in the world is not enough to make societies adjust. Who knows whether the Easter Islanders, had they been in possession of sophisticated wealth accounts showing their practices were unsustainable, would have changed course and saved themselves? And yet measuring must be the starting point. Without that, as a species we may be doomed to repeat the Easter Islanders' collective suicide.

Dasgupta thinks of it like fish in a giant pond. "If the size of the fish population is low, then there is plenty of food in the pond and the fish population grows. If there are too many fish, then they can't manage on the food supply and so the stock declines." Without the intervention of humans, the fish stock would reach a natural equilibrium based on a given supply of food and nutrients. "Now come some fishermen. They can catch fish and of course the stock declines. But that doesn't mean that they're necessarily ruining the fishery because if the stock declines, then the net output of fish, the reproductive rate, could rise because there are fewer of them. They are eating up less of the food, so they reproduce at a faster rate. But, if you constantly take more, then eventually it collapses." Managing a fishery efficiently thus means taking out just the right amount of fish so stocks can regenerate.

"Think of the biosphere as being like the fishery in a stable state. Then, as we grow, we are living off more of the biosphere's output and changing the state of the output. And you ask the question, the amount of biomass we are converting for our purposes, how does that compare with the biomass that's being produced by the biosphere? The footprint is really the ratio of the demand and the supply."

The methodologies for measuring natural wealth all have their difficulties, but the problem of underpricing natural resources—or treating them as free—demands some sort of response from economists. Why should putting a price on nature help us to see what we are doing and maybe stop us from doing it? "Suppose you're an entrepreneur and you are trying to develop a new technology for producing honey or whatever, or a new type of car," says Dasgupta. "Are you going to economize in your design on the expensive stuff or are you going to economize on the cheap stuff? Well, you want to economize on the expensive stuff. Now, if natural capital is underpriced, the direction of technological change is inevitably going to be toward more rapacious types of discoveries.

It's very natural. Air is free. Water is free. We know that oil is un-derpriced because it is not dictated by the fact that there's this huge externality [carbon] every time you burn a gallon of petrol. And if it's underpriced, then there will be a tendency for technological change to be slow. In other words, technological innovations are biased against nature."[9]

As with the Easter Islanders, catastrophe could creep up on us rather than coming all at once. The gradual destruction of species and biodiversity is one worrying sign. "I'm not talking about kan-garoos and tigers. I'm talking about the ones you don't see: all the bugs and the birds, the pollinators and the decomposers. You have a variety of statistics—markets, if you like—which suggest that we are stretching and we have been stretching for some time now." It's all too easy to be optimistic about human progress. "We live longer, we eat better, we are taller, we are better educated, we are enjoying goods and services, we travel. But are we short-changing the future in doing that? Are we borrowing from the future? Bor-rowing from the future by, for example, dumping so much carbon that we are going to be in trouble. The answer, in all likelihood, is yes. We are going to be in trouble."

A MODERN DOMESDAY

The Domesday Book, completed in 1086 on the orders of King William the Conqueror, was a survey of land in England and much of Wales. Its purpose was to catalog what people owned and therefore what taxes were due, as well as to establish the extent of lands controlled by the Crown following the upheavals of the Norman Conquest. As with Oliver Cromwell's mapping of conquered lands in Ireland and the early days of GDP itself, the impulse to measure what we now know as the economy often stirred as a consequence of war.

According to the *Anglo-Saxon Chronicle*, a medieval annal, William the Conqueror's voluminous text sought to record "what, or how much, each man had, who was an occupier of land in England, either in land or in stock, and how much money it were worth." Because its findings were final, it came to be known as the Domesday Book after the Day of Judgment, though the manuscript refers to itself more prosaically as a *descriptio*, or survey. So detailed are some sections that individual heads of livestock are recorded in its all-knowing pages. "Not even an ox, nor a cow, nor a swine was there left, that was not set down."[1]

The Domesday Book was the Google Maps of its age. It was also a balance-sheet view of the world that, more than 900 years later, our modern statistical agencies—for all their survey techniques, computers, and satellites—have failed to match. A modern Domes-day would fill a gaping hole in the way that we think about our economy by creating a balance sheet of our assets, both natural and physical. "It would not be a pretty sight," says one proponent, who argues that it would show humans are unsustainably running down their resources in the interests of growth. But "dressing up economic performance in the brighter colors of GDP does not alter the reality."[2]

Let's start with natural capital. Or to give it its more colloquial name, nature. If we were to put a dollar amount on it, what would nature be worth? We know from the Bible that it was created in just six days. Not that big a deal, then. So what do you reckon? How about $33 trillion?

That figure is not actually made up. Or at least not made up by me. It is the work of Robert Costanza, a famous "ecological econ-omist."[3] His $33 trillion was presented in a breakthrough—and extremely controversial—paper published in 1997 by *Nature*, a scientific journal, under the headline PRICING THE PLANET. It was attacked both by economists, who thought it was ridiculous to put a price on "ecosystem services" (in the hideous jargon), as well as by environmentalists, who objected to the very idea of attaching a cash value to something as precious as a rain forest or a meadow. Lord Darlington in Oscar Wilde's *Lady Windermere's Fan* quips that a cynic is "a man who knows the price of everything and the value of nothing." Instead of cynic, perhaps he ought to have said economist.

Still, if you don't put a monetary value on something, people tend not to value it at all. Unless governments can make an economically rational case for saving this beachfront or for preserving that wetland, nature almost always loses out to the imperatives of growth. Economic textbooks look at the world through inputs of labor, capital, and knowhow and through the mediums of production, exchange, and consumption. More often than not, nature doesn't get a look-in.[4]

If we hold our noses for a moment and try to put a price tag on nature, where on earth do we start, given that air and water, let alone complex ecosystems, are rarely traded? Rain falls free of charge and trees push up toward the light of their own accord. Nutrients are silently recycled. Ecosystems are so complex and delicately balanced, we often have only the loosest grasp of how they perform their regenerative miracles. So how can we possibly put a price on these activities? The answer is that we can't. But economists have managed to develop some—admittedly extremely crude—methods to work out what they call a shadow price for goods or services where no market exists. This involves either working out proxies for what people are willing to pay (revealed preference), or by asking them directly (stated preference). One proxy method is to figure how much it would cost to build a man-made equivalent. New York City worked out that the ecosystem services delivered by the Catskill Mountains, which provide a natural purification service for New York's drinking water, would cost $8 to $10 billion to replicate with a man-made water-treatment plant.

Many of the calculations in Costanza's landmark paper were a synthesis of similar research conducted in more than a hundred separate studies. He and his co-authors supplemented these findings with calculations of their own. The paper divides the natural world into sixteen biomes, such as oceans, forests, wetlands, lakes and rivers, and seventeen ecosystem services, including water supply, pollination, food production, cycling of nutrients, soil formation, genetic resources, recreation, and culture. It then produces a matrix estimating what, if anything, each biome contributes to each service. The ocean, for example, contributes nothing to pollination or soil formation, but plenty to food production and "cultural services."

But what is the price of things as subjective as the ocean's aesthetic, artistic, educational, spiritual, and scientific benefits? The proxy that Costanza uses is the price premium commanded by coastal properties over non-coastal properties. This shows what people are willing to pay to be near the sea, a revealed preference. Costanza uses the figure of $76 a hectare. Extrapolating for the entirety of the world's oceans, that works out at $2.5 trillion for the whole lot. I warned you this was crude.

In each calculation the methodology employed establishes a quasi-market price by discovering what people are willing to pay for the natural asset under consideration. Although not included in Costanza's paper, for example, how much are the 1,000 or so mountain gorillas that inhabit the rain forests of Rwanda, Uganda, and the Democratic Republic of Congo worth? One method might be to find out how much people are willing to spend to see them. That includes airfares to central Africa, the cost of hotels and gorilla-viewing permits, which in Rwanda cost $1,500 per hour and are rationed like gold dust. (Remember this is an entirely *Homo sapiens* view of the world.) These magnificent—and incredibly gentle—animals, which this author was fortunate enough to see in the bamboo forests of Uganda, are also deemed to have what economists call an existence value. That is determined by the amount that people would be willing to pay to have them exist, even if they had no means or intention of actually visiting them.

Valuing nature is no walk in the park. In fact it is more like a hack through the Congolese jungle. Still, a summary of Costanza's findings goes as follows:

Figure 2

SERVICE BY BIOME	TRILLIONS OF 1994 US $
Open ocean	8.4
Coastal areas	12.6
Total marine	*21.0*
Forests	4.7
Grass and rangelands	0.9
Wetlands	4.9
Lakes and rivers	1.7
Croplands	0.1
Total terrestrial	*12.3*
Total	*33.3*

BY ECOSYSTEM SERVICES	TRILLIONS OF 1994 US $
Gas regulation	1.3
Disturbance regulation	1.8
Water regulation	1.1
Water supply	1.7
Nutrient cycling	17.1
Waste treatment	2.3
Food production	1.4
Cultural services	3.0
Other	3.6
Total	*33.3*

To call such methodology a back-of-the-envelope calculation would be to do a disservice to envelopes. (Or should I call them envelope services?) One response to such numbers is that they are gobbledygook. Why, for example, should nature's cultural services, at $3 trillion, be worth almost twice its food production services, when presumably without the latter we wouldn't be around to enjoy the former? But Costanza has been undaunted by the criticism that his exercise in intellectual bravado has stirred. Answering one critic, he wrote, "We do not believe that there is any one right way to value ecosystem services. But there is a wrong way, and that is not to do it at all."[5]

In 2012 the British government formed the Natural Capital Committee, said to be the first of its kind in the world. The committee describes its work as "advising the government on natural capital, such as forests, rivers, minerals and oceans." By 2020 the government wants the Office of National Statistics to incorporate a measure of natural capital into Britain's national accounts. The committee will help develop "suitable metrics" to track the state of the environment and to benchmark the English countryside against the rest of the world. It will also draw up a "risk register" of endangered habitats and advise the government on its twenty-five-year environmental plan.

The seven-member committee is chaired by Dieter Helm, a professor at the University of Oxford and an expert in environmental accounting. Helm has formulated an iron law in his academic work that he hopes will steer the committee in the real world. The law sounds disarmingly simple, but it has complex implications. It goes like this: "The aggregate level of natural capital should not decline."[6]

Helm starts with a standard definition of sustainable development: "Humanity has the ability to make development sustainable to ensure that it meets the needs of the present without compromising the ability of future generations to meet their own needs."[7] He goes on to describe what he calls a "chain letter between generations" in which the people of one generation sign an unwritten contract to leave the next generation with the resources to prosper. When it comes to natural capital, each generation is obliged to leave the stock of wealth as it found it. That's what "The aggregate level of natural capital should not decline" means, he says.[8]

Clearly that does not imply that we cannot touch nature. No society, not even a pre-industrial one, could commit to that. Humans interact with their environment. They chop down trees and they plow fields. They siphon off non-renewable resources, such as oil and gas. They adapt, change or destroy renewable resources. They might transform part of a river by building a dam to produce hydroelectric power. Or they may, over generations, cut down primeval forest and replace it with the modern English countryside, with its hedgerows and pasture and cropland, or transform bison-rich prairies into wheat fields. It is unrealistic to expect one generation to leave the ecosystem exactly as it found it. The point is, says Helm, it should leave the *aggregate* amount of natural capital intact.

But how? And almost as important, how would we know? Peter Drucker, a management guru, is said to have reasoned, "If you can't measure it, you can't manage it." That could have been a subtitle for this book. If nature is transformed from forest to sheep pen or from river to electricity, we need some kind of accounting tools to figure out how much of a net loss that is to the stock of natural capital and how much we need to do to compensate.

On one level the whole exercise is flawed. Economists are

precisely not the type of people you want to start messing about with nature. As soon as they get their hands on our lakes and our forests, the danger is these will be commoditized and bought and sold into oblivion. In the end economists can't answer questions like "Should we build on the greenbelt to relieve the housing shortage?" Some trade-offs are ethical and not susceptible to number-crunching. In theory an economist may decide that it is "worth" driving a river dolphin to extinction if the result is a hydroelectric plant producing so many megawatts of power for so many hundreds of thousands of people. Yet that is a question for a moralist as much as an economist. King Solomon is no less qualified to answer it than Mervyn King, governor of the Bank of England from 2003 to 2013. That doesn't mean, however, that economists have nothing to contribute to the debate. It is at least worth hearing what they have to say.

In his quest to measure the unmeasurable, Helm first divides natural capital into two categories: renewable and non-renewable. There has traditionally been a lot of focus on non-renewable resources. Have we reached "peak oil"? How are we to manage when there's no more coal or copper? But non-renewable resources are the easy part. They are relatively simple to value using market prices. If a government knows it has fifty years' worth of natural gas, it can work out the value at today's prices and decide how much it wants to "spend" today and how much to save for tomorrow.

Renewable resources are trickier. Take the example of wild salmon.[9] We may know the value of salmon per pound, but since the fish reproduce indefinitely, it is impossible to quantify present and future revenue streams. They are infinite, which makes salmon effectively free. That is of course unless we drive them to extinction, in which case they become priceless—the word economists use for extinct. More important than valuing salmon, then, becomes working out where the threshold for their survival is. We need to know how much salmon we can safely take from a given location without endangering future supplies. Just as important, we also need to work out the thresholds for the ecosystem in which they flourish.[10] We should err on the side of caution. Once we have identified a point beyond which we should not go, common sense dictates that we should stop well before reaching it.

One approach would be to draw up a natural capital balance sheet—especially of ecosystems that are at risk—in order to track aggregate levels of natural capital. Helm's rule would require that damage to one bit of the ecosystem be offset by repair or improvement of another bit. If a wetland is destroyed to build a shopping mall, then the government (or private company) concerned would be obliged to offset that destruction by, say, improving the quality of soil or returning farmland to wilderness. If trees are chopped down, you must plant them elsewhere. Divert a river and you're required to protect a wetland somewhere else. In the case of non-renewable resources like oil, you could simply compensate for its use either by building up other forms of capital, including savings for future generations, or by making repairs to renewable natural capital.

This may all sound abstruse. On one level it is. After all, humans can't even agree on reducing carbon emissions, though science tells us pretty definitively that global warming could have—indeed already is having—brutal environmental consequences. Just ask any African farmer about the sudden unpredictability of rainfall patterns that had been constant for generations.[11] The carbon-trading scheme meant to put a price on pollution has, by most accounts, been a miserable flop. People are extremely resistant to the idea of a carbon tax, usually on the grounds that it would harm growth. That makes it hard to believe we could do better in the task of measuring other assaults on nature—from destroying rain forests to creating rubbish landfills—and then actually doing something about it.

Difficult or not, Helm's rule has become official British policy. If you squint closely enough at the governing Conservative Party's 2015 and 2017 manifestos, you'll find a variation of: "We pledge to be the first generation to leave the environment in a better state than we inherited it." Of course it is easy for a political party to make such an open-ended commitment. Today's political leaders will be long gone by the time their promise is tested. But that is precisely why, environmental economists argue, we need robust accounting methods to keep politicians honest.

Although Helm talks as much about thresholds as he does about pricing nature, his committee did come up with valuations for trees and wetlands. In a report to the government, in which it determined that England's natural capital was in "long-term decline," the committee listed several priorities. Among its recommendations here are three, taken more or less at random.

- Woodland planting of up to 250,000 additional hectares. Located near towns and cities, such areas can generate net societal benefits in excess of £500 million per annum.
- Peatland restoration on around 140,000 hectares in upland areas. This would deliver net benefits of £570 million over 40 years in carbon values alone.
- Wetland creation on around 100,000 hectares, particularly in areas of suitable hydrology, upstream of major towns and cities, and avoiding areas of high grade agricultural land. Benefit: cost ratios of 3:1 would be typical, with 9:1 possible in some cases.

It is easy to scoff at such recommendations. That's why people do. Written in the uninspiring language of official reports and with numbers that appear plucked from thin air, putting a price on nature seems crass at best. For a start, why should the units of measurement be monetary? We don't measure weight or height in dollars or euros. Yet kilograms and meters provide meaningful signals that we can act upon. For example, doctors can recommend that a patient go on a diet if his weight:height ratio creeps over a certain level. We know a runway has to be so long for an Airbus A380 to land. For safety purposes, we don't need to know it costs $700 million to build. (Would we build a shorter one if it cost half the price?) So why, as one author puts it, has money become "the moral lingua franca"?[12] We need to get away from the idea, dominant since the invention of GDP, that the only measurements worth a candle have $ or £ in front of them.

Money *is* a strange unit to apply to nature. We can print money at will—as our central banks have demonstrated with gay abandon. The whole point of trying to value the environment is surely to highlight finite constraints. By putting a price on carbon, one plausible conclusion is that we are free to pollute indefinitely so long as it is paid for in endlessly printable, potentially worthless, currency.[13] Instead of pounds, dollars or euros, we could perhaps measure carbon in *momme*, a unit of mass for measuring pearls in Japan in which 1 *momme* = 10 *fun*. Alternatively, one author suggested, we could use Cat, an old American measure of the minimum fatal drug dose per kilo of cat.[14] Personally, I would love to see Cat replace GDP as our principal measure for economic activity just so I could write the headline LAST QUARTER THE ECONOMY GREW BY A WHISKER.

Pricing nature might not only be meaningless, it could also be reckless. It suggests nature is fungible and can be safely traded; moreover, that it is only valuable to the extent that it performs a service for human beings. "The paradox of environmental economics is that we feel compeled to price nature to make its loss visible on the balance sheet, but in doing so we legitimize its commodification and validate its critical overconsumption"[15] is how one author puts it. At its worst, "biodiversity offsetting" might mean that one piece of nature, with its beauty and wonder and millennia of history, could be mechanically substituted by another. A "hunched and fissured coppiced oak," in the words of another author, becomes replaceable by a "sapling planted beside a slip-road with a rabbit guard around it."[16] To frame the debate using monetary values is to cede the moral high ground to economists with their ruthlessly utilitarian world view.

It is precisely to get around such dilemmas that some economists have taken a different, non-monetary approach. One such is that developed by the Global Footprint Network (GFN), a California-based research organization that has gone so far as to invent a new holiday. Just in case you missed it, August 2, 2017, was Earth Overshoot Day. If you're American, it was the holiday wedged between Independence Day and Thanksgiving. It may not have been celebrated in your neighborhood and Hallmark has not yet produced cheesy cards in its honor, so don't worry if it passed you by. Earth Overshoot Day marks the date on which humans have used up all of the ecosystem's regenerative capacity for that year. From that day onward in 2017 we were running down the earth's ecological gas tank to fuel our consumption.

Earth Overshoot Day seeks to highlight the issue of sustainability by drawing attention to the ratio between our ecological footprint and the earth's biocapacity—its capacity to absorb that activity and regenerate itself. It is an attempt to account for the environment in a currency other than dollars and cents. The GFN purports to provide a way of comparing what the earth is able to supply against the demands put upon it. Its founder and president, Mathis Wackernagel, insists that the methodology is scientifically rigorous, though many argue it is more useful as a tool of publicity than of policy.

Biocapacity is the earth's capacity to provide humans and other animals with food and resources—wood for building houses, water for our crops, wildebeest for a lion's breakfast—and to absorb the waste produced. That waste includes human pollution, such as nitrate runoff from farms and carbon emissions from industry. The demand is the footprint. GFN divides the earth into five broad categories: cropland, grazing land, forests, fisheries, and built-up land. Cropland provides food to eat, forests provide building materials, firewood and CO_2 sequestration. Areas deemed mostly unproductive, such as deserts, are not counted.[17] The basic unit of measurement is the global hectare. This is calculated by multiplying the physical area, say of cropland, by the yield, which varies from country to country, and by something called the equivalence factor, which accounts for the difference in productivity, say, between cropland and less productive grazing land. The methodology, though rough-and-ready, allows all land to be expressed in terms of a single unit—the global hectare.

GFN calculated that the total amount of productive land and water amounts to 12 billion global hectares. With roughly 7 billion people on earth, this equates to 1.72 global hectares per person.[18] (A hectare is roughly the same size as a soccer pitch.) According to GFN, we have only relatively recently started exceeding the earth's capacity to regenerate itself. In 1961 human demand accounted for 0.7 planet's worth of biocapacity. That meant we were in the black. By the mid-1980s humanity had tipped into the red, and by 2008 the picture had changed dramatically. In that year, GFN said, we needed 1.5 planets to sustain us, something that is clearly unsustainable. It is enough to make Thomas Malthus stir from his grave to say, "I told you so."

Wealth is a measure not only of the present but also of the future. That is because today's wealth—the balance sheet of all our assets, natural, physical and institutional—is tomorrow's income. That contrasts with our standard economic gauge—GDP—which is essentially a backward-looking measure, a way of recording what has already been produced, say in the past year. But trying to peer into the future raises important conceptual problems.

First, the value of today's assets is essentially unknowable. That is largely because of changes in technology. Cobalt mined in Congo is today in high demand because it is an essential element for electric car batteries, but perhaps tomorrow some presently less valuable mineral will take its place. Depending on technological advances, we may be able to produce more with less in the future. Perhaps we'll develop new techniques to extract previously unreachable oil and gas. That has already happened with the shale revolution. Perhaps we won't need oil and gas at all; we'll have new forms of energy, currently undiscovered or underutilized.

Some economists view attempts to measure natural capital as essentially bogus, a tool of environmentalists who want to impose unnecessary constraints on growth. Larry Summers, a US economist, goes so far as to suggest it is a way for people who are already rich to tell those who are poor that they're dreadfully sorry, but the planet just can't take any more growth.

"In my view, it's all a political doom and gloom operation," he practically growled down the phone when I raised the subject of how to measure natural wealth.[19] "In any theory where depleting your oil constitutes a loss of GDP, finding new oil should constitute an increment to GDP. But they [environmental economists] never take account of anything positive. They're quick to call it a depletion of capital if you deplete your oil. But they're never honest enough to acknowledge that, when fracking technology is discovered, that is an augmentation to your resources," he said.

"When we discover video conferencing technology and fewer people travel and put carbon in the air, we should be giving ourselves credit for that. But for the people who do this, it's all a one-eyed operation in favor of everybody staying home. Everybody staying home and knitting." Pushing aside the image of clacking needles and shapeless stripy sweaters, I pressed on. Surely it wouldn't be hard to come up with a rigorous theoretical framework that went beyond environmentalist propaganda? "If you did the conceptually appropriate corrections, you might well conclude that GDP was growing faster. You have to do it both ways. You have to recognize bad things and you have to recognize good things. If it was done right, it might be interesting," he said. "But I think the correct posture toward the people who are doing it now is disparagement."

Adding as well as subtracting ought not to be beyond the wit of anyone—least of all economists. But there is another, more philosophical, problem with the future. Why should we care about it? After all, in the end not only are we going to die, but our universe is going to die too. It will turn into a zero-energy soup. In the very long run our current assets are worth precisely nothing.[20] Put a different way, one can love one's children and one's children's children, even if they have not yet been born. But what about their children and their children after that, indefinitely into the future? Humans can happily go about their business while wars and famine rage a few thousand miles away. Can we really expect them to act now to avoid something in another time dimension for the benefit of the as-yet-unborn, even if they are ever-so-distantly related to us? Philosophically, let alone economically, it is a practically unanswerable question.

So far we have talked mainly about natural capital. But there have been attempts by no less august a body than the World Bank to come up with what it calls the "comprehensive wealth" of nations, a measure not only of natural capital but also of physical and institutional capital. Since the mid-1990s the Washington-based organization has had a small team (to be fair a very small team) dedicated to the task. The team's guiding principle appears in the foreword of one of its big reports: "How we measure development will drive how we do development."[21]

One of the report's findings is that as countries become richer, the importance of natural capital diminishes. That is because nations convert the income stream they gain from exploiting natural resources—say by selling bananas or oil or uranium—into other types of capital, say roads or universities or robots to produce cars. At least that's the idea. Nigeria, sub-Saharan Africa's most important oil exporter, started attracting serious investor attention from the mid-1990s, when its oil exports were earning it handsome rewards. As the World Bank report points out, from a growth perspective Nigeria was doing brilliantly. But from a wealth perspective, it was going backward. Its elites were stealing or squandering its future by failing to convert income into physical or human capital. The way we measure things cannot stop unscrupulous leaders from selling off a nation's patrimony. But it can shine a clearer light on what is happening. If headlines about Nigeria had read NIGERIA'S WEALTH PLUMMETS and not NIGERIA'S GROWTH SOARS, the government might have come under pressure to change course.

For produced—or physical—capital, the World Bank uses, where able, numbers collected by national statistics agencies. Some thirty national governments compile comprehensive data on capital stock: factories, roads, sewerage systems, and so on. These are given virtually no publicity, but the numbers do exist. For the rest, the bank relies on data compiled for 150 countries by a group at the University of Groningen in the Netherlands.[22]

When it comes to natural capital, the World Bank takes a more down-to-earth approach than Costanza. Instead of trying to value whole ecosystems, it confines itself to valuing agricultural land, forest land, and subsoil resources such as oil, coal, bauxite, and gold. Very broadly, it calculates the value of farmland at a commercial rate: how much would it cost to buy a wheat farm in Australia or an orange grove in Spain? For subsoil assets, it restricts its valuation to four energy sources and ten major minerals for which there is comprehensive market data on price and reserves.[23] Forest land is valued not for its beauty or capacity to absorb carbon, but, more prosaically, according to the amount it would fetch if all the trees were chopped down and sold as timber.[24]

The services that nature provides—for example, the value of

pollinators such as bees—are assumed to be counted in the cost of the land. Even important minerals such as diamonds, uranium, and lithium, and marine resources such as fish, are not counted because of a lack of definitive data. Water is not counted as an energy source, even though hydropower is hugely important from China to Ethiopia. Protected areas such as Yellowstone National Park or Tanzania's Serengeti are not valued according to their natural beauty or genetic diversity, but rather by the cash they would fetch if they were sold off as farmland. The bank's estimates are a gross underestimate of the true "value" of nature.

An interesting aspect of the bank's wealth report is the very high value it attaches to "intangible capital" such as an educated workforce and functioning institutions. In rich countries, for example, it finds that natural capital contributes only 2 percent to total wealth, compared with a whopping 81 percent for intangible capital. Produced capital makes up the remaining 17 percent.[25]

So how, exactly, is intangible capital calculated? Frustratingly, the answer is that it isn't. It appears as a "residual," which in layman's terms means an error. One can't help raising a skeptical eyebrow when 81 percent of what we're trying to measure turns out to be a mistake. Without going into detail, the World Bank basically works backward by calculating how much capital we must have to produce so much income. Having taken into account natural capital and physical capital, the missing amount must be institutional capital. It is a little like the assumptions scientists make about dark matter.

If you remember the parable of the two islands, one where people trust each other (and trade) and one where they don't (and don't), then attributing a large portion of income to institutional capacity is not ridiculous. Still, the bank's numbers seem implausibly high in comparison to natural capital. For the record, here are the numbers for total wealth in trillions of dollars, with the breakdown expressed in percentages.[26]

Figure 3

COUNTRY INCOME GROUP	TOTAL WEALTH (TRILLION $)	INTANGIBLE CAPITAL (%)	PRODUCED CAPITAL (%)	NATURAL CAPITAL (%)
Low	3.6	57	13	30
Lower middle	58	51	24	25
Upper middle	47	69	16	15
High	552	81	17	2
World	674	77	18	5

This chart provokes a few observations. As noted above, the contribution of natural capital to total wealth in rich countries is just 2 percent. Even in poor countries, many of which have little manufacturing, it accounts for only 30 percent of total wealth. Of the world's total wealth of $674 trillion, just 5 percent is attributed to natural capital, while 77 percent is supposedly made up of the intangible elements of human, institutional, and social capital.

Second, each percentage in the chart carries the same weight. Thus theoretically any country would do well by converting its natural capital into other forms of capital: oil and gas into roads; and schools and wheat and salmon into universities and well-run courtrooms. And that is exactly what the bank says a country should do on its journey from underdeveloped to developed status. But there is an obvious problem. If every country took this advice literally, there would be no nature left. The planet would be denuded of natural capital and everything on it would be dead.

A country could pollute itself out of existence and drive its animal and plant life to extinction without its actions showing up as a problem in these wealth accounts. The bank acknowledges the problem, which stems from the fact that it assumes one form of capital converts seamlessly into another, something it calls substitutability. (In economics as in other disciplines, long words are more often than not a cause for alarm.) But this fails to highlight the "possible irreversibilities and catastrophic events" that might ensue. For a measure that is supposed to emphasize sustainability, this is more than a minor kink in the methodology.

The third point is more of a curiosity. The World Bank's method of counting natural capital is based on the market price of minerals, farmland, and so on. It is entirely different from the way Robert Costanza set about the same problem in his *Nature* paper. He tried to price entire ecosystems right down to the value to humans of a landscape's recreational and spiritual benefits. The bank sticks to oil and gold and cows and potatoes but still finds that natural capital makes up 5 percent of the world's total wealth of $674 trillion. That puts natural capital at $33.7 trillion, within a whisker of Costanza's $33.3 trillion. It is pure coincidence. But for such wildly different approaches, you've got to admit, it's a bit spooky.

Clearly wealth accounting has some way to go. There are many conceptual and ideological problems. Besides, economists have only so much to say on such matters. In fact, they have already gained too much authority over our decision-making processes. It has become a given that nothing can be done if it harms the economy—something that only a priesthood of economists can determine. If "taking back control" has become a mantra of our times, then wresting back public policy from the sole oversight of economists must be part of the solution. Paradoxically, sometimes when you put theory to one side and actually take practical measures to deal with some of these issues, things can become clearer. Take the example of Norway.

Knut Ole Viken is a Norwegian tree counter.[27] He has been counting trees for nearly three decades, first as a child with his father in remote woodlands close to the Arctic Circle and now as part of a long-term assessment of the country's forests by the Norwegian Institute of Bioeconomy Research. In what is a five-year cycle, a team of forest experts including Viken sets out to examine trees the breadth and considerable length of Norway at 15,000 separate locations. Forests and wooded land cover nearly 40 percent of Norway's territory, including the wintry north of the country.[28] When the five-year exercise ends, it is time to start again. Counting Norwegian trees is a never-ending task.

The business of tree counting began nearly a hundred years ago, in 1919. It was then that the Norwegian government decided it had to take action. For much of the previous century the country's once-ubiquitous forests had been rampantly exploited. Much of the old-growth forest had been logged and shipped off to Europe. "Locally, farmers were using firewood to warm their houses and the grazing from their animals prevented forests from recovering," Viken told the BBC. "There was no program for planting or regeneration."

The plan to conduct a complete inventory of Norway's forests was the first of its kind in the world. Other European countries had done piecemeal assessments but none had attempted what Norway was proposing. Norway's National Forest Inventory proved a turning point. It enabled the government to gain a clear picture of which forest areas had been denuded, which were still thriving, and where the greatest biodiversity still existed. From there it could begin to make sensible decisions about which areas could be safely logged and which needed protecting to ensure wildlife habitat and the preservation of at least some old-growth areas.

Today Norway has nearly three times the amount of standing wood it had a hundred years ago. To be precise it has 823 million cubed meters of growing forest, of which 8 to 11 million cubed meters is logged each year. Since the forest is growing at about twice that rate, Norway is adding to its stock of forest land all the time. It has enough trees to absorb nearly 60 percent of its greenhouse emissions. Of course things are not perfect. Only 4 percent of its forests are pristine, with much of the rest consisting of relatively new-growth trees planted for commercial logging. In the nineteenth century swaths of the country's ancient forests were destroyed, shrinking biodiversity. Still, Norway's forest inventory was a pioneering idea. It is the kind of thinking that has made the country more effective at guarding its natural resources than almost anywhere else on earth.

Just two days before Christmas 1969 Phillips Petroleum informed the Norwegian government that it had discovered a huge oil field on the country's North Sea continental shelf. This was the first of several big finds that was to make Norway one of the world's top oil producers for decades to come. For the first twenty years, Oslo reinvested its growing oil revenues back into the oil industry itself and spent money on developing the country. But by the early 1990s, with oil revenues surpassing all expectations and forecast to continue for decades more, the government started planning for the future. It set up the Petroleum Fund of Norway, a sovereign wealth fund to hold savings for future generations.

In 1996 the first oil money was transferred to the fund. Just twenty years later, what is more commonly known as the Oil Fund has become the biggest of its kind in the world, with holdings of around $875 billion.[29] It invests what it likes to call "the people's money" in three classes of assets—equity, bonds, and property, all outside Norway. Today the fund has stakes in some 8,000 international companies from Apple to Nestlé and controls around 1 percent of all shares listed on global stock markets. It also invests tens of billions in government debt and has built up a large real-estate portfolio. Among its dozens of property holdings are part of Regent Street in London and buildings on New York's Fifth Avenue and in Times Square. In Partha Dasgupta's terms, Norway has run down one form of capital (oil beneath the seabed) and converted it into another form (money in the bank for future generations).

It all sounds so easy. But Norway is an exception. Many countries, especially ones in the developing world with weak institutions, fall prey to the so-called resource curse. Instead of using revenue to build the country's future, they scramble to spend it as fast as possible. What should be a once-in-a-lifetime chance to improve a country's prospects becomes what economists call a rent-seeking opportunity, with those in power and their hangers-on scrambling to make a quick buck.

This applies not only to developing countries. Even the UK, a nation with generally well-functioning institutions, can be accused of squandering its oil revenues. Like Norway, Britain benefited from the vast quantities of petroleum discovered in the North Sea. But unlike Norway, it simply spent the money. From the 1970s to today, oil companies paid around £330 billion in taxes to the UK Treasury. Existing generations benefited from these windfall revenues in the form of current expenditure, higher investment—some of it at least presumably on lasting and beneficial assets—and lower taxes. But no explicit provision was made for future generations. There is no UK Oil Fund. Indeed, as oil reserves began to run down from around 2010, it became clear that the industry would become a drain on the Treasury. Instead of receiving money, the government has promised to subsidize companies to decommission exhausted oil fields.

If oil is money in nature's savings vault, the Bank of the North Sea is about to go bust.

12

THE LORD OF HAPPINESS

A common way economists determine how much something is worth is by applying what is known as the willingness to pay principle. How much would someone be willing to pay for a tangible thing, such as a plastic Pez dispenser, or an intangible one, say an unpolluted bay or more time off work? How much, for example, is the head of Jeremy Bentham, the great English philosopher who died in 1832, worth? This book is chock-full of skepticism about the value we attach to certain things and about the difficulty of pricing things we really should be measuring, like pollution, housework, and nature. Here, at last, is a simple question with a simple answer. Jeremy Bentham's head is worth ten pounds.[1]

We know this for a fact because, when students took his head hostage in 1975, University College London, to whom it belonged, agreed to pay ten pounds for its return. The offer was accepted. In economics that's about as near to a slam dunk as you're ever likely to get.

How Bentham's head ended up in the possession of UCL is a curious tale. Toward the end of his life, Bentham, who devoted much of his career to writing about what made people happy, got it into his ten-pound head that his body needed to be preserved after death. So gripped was he by this notion that for the last decade of his life he apparently carried two glass eyes with him in his pocket at all times so that embalmers would have something to fix in his eye sockets if the need suddenly arose. In his will he asked that his skeleton be mummified, then dressed in a black suit and preserved as an "auto-icon," sitting upright in a glass case. For a philosopher closely associated with the idea of what makes you happy, I suppose the only appropriate response to his final wish is "Whatever floats your boat."

Bentham's body is indeed kept today in a glass-fronted case in a hall in the South Cloisters of UCL. In line with his wishes, he is occasionally taken, sans case, to attend meetings, such as the one he presided over in 2013 for the final council meeting of the then provost.[2] (The minutes note that he was in attendance but did not vote.) Unfortunately for Bentham, his head is no longer with him. When he died, aged eighty-four, the embalming was botched and the head replaced with a wax replica. The original was kept in the cabinet, from where it was stolen in 1975 by prankster students raising money for charity. It is now stored separately for safekeeping.

In truth, this chapter has less to do with how much Bentham's head is worth than what was inside his cranium. Was he happy or was he sad? How should we interpret his ideas on human happiness today? More precisely, the subject at hand is the feasibility of measuring happiness at all and whether it is a worthwhile enterprise.

In economics the happiness discussion has been unhelpfully hijacked by Bhutan and that small, mountainous country's promotion of what it calls gross national happiness. Mention measuring happiness to some people and they'll look at you with a slightly knowing look and say, "What, like Bhutan?" I'll deal with Bhutan later, but the more interesting discussion on happiness has to do with attempts in the great universities of America and Europe to measure it.

Ever since 1974, when Richard Easterlin, an economics professor at the University of Pennsylvania, wrote his landmark paper "Does Economic Growth Improve the Human Lot?," researchers have drawn on psychology, neuroscience, economics, and sociology to probe the mysteries of happiness. Easterlin set the ball rolling by questioning the link between income and happiness, arguing that, once a certain level of prosperity had been achieved, additional income furnished no further joy. That was a radical idea because it undermined the notion that the maximization of growth—which had become the overriding policy goal of governments—was the best way to improve well-being.

Since then economists have become increasingly interested in defining and measuring happiness and in determining what conditions and policies might bring it about. By one account more than 10,000 academic papers have been written on the subject, and Western governments have conducted regular surveys on the levels of happiness reported by individuals. Happiness, in short, has become a deadly serious business. And no discussion of the subject can begin without Jeremy Bentham.

Bentham was a British philosopher and social critic born in 1748 in Houndsditch, London. The son of a wealthy lawyer, he was a child prodigy. By the age of three he was said to be learning Latin declensions and he attended Oxford University at twelve. Graduating with a master's degree at the ripe old age of eighteen, he quickly gave up the practice of law, which he detested, and devoted his life to writing and pressing for social change.

Bentham was an eccentric. Just in case the story about his mummified head hasn't convinced you of that, he once wrote to the Home Office to suggest that its various departments be linked by a web of "conversation tubes" to aid communication. You could call him the father of the Internet. He also drew up plans for a panopticon prison, which would allow a single guard to observe every prisoner simultaneously. Bentham was a social reformer, who wrote in trenchant prose about everything from equality of the sexes to state punishment. The "fundamental axiom" of his philosophy was the principle that "it is the greatest happiness of the greatest number that is the measure of right and wrong."

That sounds enormously progressive for a man writing 200 years ago, but in the story of economics, at least as told by me, Bentham can appear as both hero and villain. Bentham is usually regarded as the founder of a doctrine called utilitarianism, which states that an action is right if it promotes overall happiness. Writing about the concept, Bentham said, "nature has placed mankind under the governance of two sovereign masters, pain and pleasure. It is for them alone to point out what we ought to do."[3]

Bentham's ideas are governed by the idea of utility, by which he means not what is useful but rather "that property in any object, whereby it tends to produce benefit, advantage, pleasure, good, or happiness." His ideas can be summed up as happiness maximization, and he expressly stated that the goal of society should be to maximize total happiness, not just happiness for a particular individual.

Bentham's notion of utility, later taken up by John Stuart Mill, has become foundational in modern economics. It is predicated on the idea that economics is an almost mechanical science in which utility-maximizing agents—people to you and me—pursue their own rational interests. If markets are functioning properly, this benefits not only themselves but also society at large. This interpretation borrows heavily from the physical sciences. The victory of mechanism over moralism, it takes as a starting point the notion that markets function best when individuals are left alone. In this Bentham's utility merges with Adam Smith's invisible hand to form a view of the world in which rational actors produce the best possible outcome under given constraints. "It is not from the benevolence of the butcher, the brewer or the baker that we expect our dinner," wrote Smith, "but from their regard to their own interest."

Bentham's utility is the mechanism by which individual decisions add up to a greater whole. Neoliberals argue that the market is "a vast sensory device, capturing millions of individual desires, opinions and values, and converting these into prices."[4] Bentham was an enemy of abstract philosophical concepts such as goodness, duty, wrong, and right. They were all right for the likes of Plato and Aristotle, but what did such terms really mean? Far better, thought Bentham, to reject such "fictitious" concepts and to root one's inquiry in things we know to be real, such as pleasure and pain.

His can be a very Gradgrindian view of the world. Indeed Charles Dickens's Thomas Gradgrind, the school superintendent and industrialist in *Hard Times*, was modeled after the Victorian utilitarians of his day. Gradgrind was, Dickens wrote, "a man of facts and calculations. A man who proceeds upon the principle that two and two are four, and nothing over . . . With a rule and a pair of scales, and the multiplication table always in his pocket, sir, ready to weigh and measure any parcel of human nature, and tell you exactly what it comes to."

This may be a caricature of Bentham's thinking, but the notion that utility can be measured—usually in terms of price—has come to dominate modern economics. Rational-choice theory says that if everyone is left to their own devices they produce the best possible outcome for the maximum number of people. That is the origin of *Homo economicus*, "a somewhat miserable vision of a human being who is constantly calculating, putting prices on things, neurotically pursuing his own personal interests at every turn."[5] That makes Bentham "the inventor of what has since come to be known as 'evidence-based policymaking,' the idea that government interventions can be cleansed of any moral or ideological principles, and be guided purely by facts and figures. Whenever a policy is evaluated for its measurable outcomes, or assessed for its efficiency using cost-benefit analysis, Bentham's influence is present."[6]

It also makes Bentham an important figure in the business of measuring economic growth, which seeks to attach a single number to the sum of human activity. The adoption of Bentham's thinking can be seen as sending the whole discipline of economics off track about 150 years ago. Bentham's narrow definition of happiness— the experience of pleasure and the absence of pain—put economics on a Gradgrindian path of weights and measures. In this view of the world there is no room for the broader, more uplifting Aristotelian concept of happiness—eudaemonia—which centers on virtue, friendship, and the formation of character. All these were unmeasurable fictions of little use to the Great Utilitarian.[7]

By this account, Bentham's ideas are a forerunner of the bloodless, utility-maximizing version of humanity that today we call economics, but there is another, kinder, version of Bentham lurking in his writing. A happier version, as it were. To discover that, we need to go to the London School of Economics, where "happiness economics" has found one of its greatest prophets.

...

For a lord, Peter Richard Grenville Layard is an unassuming type. The man who comes to greet me in the nondescript hall of the university building is silver-haired and quietly spoken. He has none of the pomposity of some successful people, rather the air of someone comfortable in his own skin. There's a twinkle in his eye and, at eighty-two, a spring in his soft-footed step. He's been a member of the House of Lords since he was made a life peer in 2000, but he remains every inch the rumpled academic in casual trousers and comfortable shoes. One small detail stands out. On his jacket lapel is a round white badge bearing the words ACTION FOR HAPPINESS.

For more than forty years Layard has championed the cause of well-being. Originally a labor economist whose research focused on unemployment and inequality, in the 1970s he became curious about the emerging discipline of happiness. As well as happiness itself, Layard developed a strong interest in mental health and mental suffering. A disciple of Bentham, he believes that the logic of happiness maximization is not calculating mean-spiritedness at all. Rather, it promotes a caring, progressive society, he says, in which it is more important to relieve the suffering of those who are unhappy than to add a bit of extra happiness to those who are already content. For Layard, a true interpretation of Bentham carries a profoundly humanistic message, pointing us toward a society in which cooperation is as important as competition. The goal of society, he says, should be to "create as much happiness as you can in the world. The mark of a civilized society is that people are enjoying their lives."

Layard has bought sandwiches for our lunch. Brown paper bag in hand, he ushers me into his tiny office. At various stages of the conversation he springs up from his seat to take down a book from a shelf, opening it to a table on comparative happiness across countries or to data showing an individual's level of happiness during a particular day. According to one table, which awarded a numerical score to favored activities, researchers had discovered that people very much enjoy sex and very much dislike commuting. *I could have told you that*, I thought to myself, *for half the funding.*

Layard takes a slightly narrower view of happiness than your average Greek philosopher. "Aristotle didn't get it quite right, but Bentham got it pretty much right," he says. Like Bentham, he regards happiness as a real thing that can be measured. Like him too, he believes that the goal of any society should be the maximum happiness of the maximum number of people. "The amount of unhappiness is extraordinary at the moment," he says, shaking his head at the perceived misery all around him, the result of such diverse phenomena as family breakup, chronic pain, long-term unemployment, and what he sees as the often-pointless pursuit of money and material possessions.

He uses the terms "well-being" and "life satisfaction" interchangeably, though he clearly has a soft spot for the more intuitive "happiness." But policymakers are uncomfortable with the idea of happiness even though it is a concept to which they attach great importance in their daily lives. "Probably an awful lot of them make key decisions based on whether they think it will make them happy. Who to marry or what job to do? Is your child happy at school? There could hardly be a more important question," he says with the frustration of someone who has been banging the same drum for decades. "But it doesn't seem to them something the state should be doing. When they talk about happiness, they think, *Oh, it's ridiculous. Happiness is a fleeting thing.*"

He has adapted his terminology. "What could you say to get

policymakers to take you seriously? That has always been my approach. And most policymakers have very little difficulty with 'life satisfaction.' They're used to asking people, 'Are you satisfied with your garbage collection or with your hospital?'" From there it's not such a leap to ask them whether they are satisfied with their lives.

For politicians there may be expedient reasons to pay attention to life satisfaction. Bill Clinton's conviction that the state of the economy always determines the result of an election turns out to be questionable. In fact, politicians who tracked happiness would have a better grasp of their re-election prospects. One paper written at the London School of Economics compared data from a twice-yearly Eurobarometer survey conducted since 1973 against election results across Europe. In the survey, which covers a random sample of more than one million respondents, people are asked, "On the whole, are you i) very satisfied, ii) fairly satisfied, iii) not very satisfied or iv) not at all satisfied with the life you lead?" The paper found that answers to that question were a "robust predictor of election results" and a better guide to voting intention than any other measure including GDP.[8] To Bill Clinton, Layard says, "It's happiness, stupid."

In the new "science" of happiness there are several ways of measuring what researchers call "subjective well-being." One is to rely on fast-advancing neuroscience. Richard Davidson at the University of Wisconsin has developed ways to measure people's mood by attaching electrodes to the scalp. When people are shown an amusing video clip, the left side of their brain—associated with happiness—becomes more active. A frightening sequence provokes the opposite reaction. Left-siders, the left side of whose brains is naturally more active, are generally happier. Right-siders tend to smile less and are assessed by their friends as less happy. For Layard, the science confirms the basic premise that happiness is real and measurable and that "there is a direct connection between brain activity and mood."

Most of the work in happiness economics, however, rests on the same basic technique as those used to compile growth statistics: collecting survey data. Numerous methods have been developed for assessing people's happiness by asking them how they feel. Here one must distinguish between different types of happiness. Some surveys concentrate on what might be called mood—asking people how they feel right now or how they felt at various times on the previous day. The UK's Office for National Statistics asks, "Overall, how happy did you feel yesterday?"

The surveys that tend to be favored by economists seeking to capture national well-being concentrate more on what might be called life satisfaction. In the most comprehensive, which covers 150 countries, people are asked to evaluate the quality of their lives on an eleven-point scale known as the Cantril Ladder. They are asked to imagine a ladder and to place their life satisfaction on the appropriate rung, with the best possible life for them being 10 and the worst 0. Another question, in the European Social Survey, asks, "Taking all things together, how happy would you say you are?" with answers ranked from 0 to 10. Yet another—the World Values Survey—poses a similar question but orders answers on a scale of 0 to 3. "Taking all things together, would you say you are: Very happy, Quite happy, Not very happy, or Not at all happy?" These types of questions are the ones that Layard says produce the most useful results.

The good news for happiness economics is that the results of different surveys tend to match. Happiness as measured by asking people how they feel and by testing them are broadly similar, as are results of surveys using different types of questions with different scales. Layard argues that happiness measures are robust enough to make public policy decisions based on their findings. In his book—no prizes for guessing that the title is *Happiness*—he states his case in commendably straightforward language. "Happiness should become the goal of policy and the progress of national happiness should be measured and analyzed as closely as the growth" of the economy. To me he says, "GDP isn't going to tell us anything that we want to know about welfare."

I can't resist asking him if he would call himself happy. His work presumably gives him a sense of purpose, one of the keys to satisfaction. His eyes flicker at the mischievousness (and doubtless predictability) of the question and he responds with what I assume is a joke. "If you think about your happiness too much you become miserable." The only way of knowing if he means it would be to strap electrodes to his head.

What, you might ask, are they putting in the water in northern Europe? In each of the years since the World Happiness Report first came out in 2012 Nordic countries have dominated the list of the happiest countries on earth.[9] The 2016 report was no exception, with all five Nordic countries in the top ten. That's not bad for a group of nations associated with darkness—quite literally during the winter months, when the sun rarely surfaces. Think Nordic noir, the ludicrously bleak drama of August Strindberg, and the troubling art of Edvard Munch, who painted the face of a screaming figure set against a shifting orange sky. And that's not to mention some of the highest taxes on the planet. Hardly a recipe for happiness, you might think. Yet the Scandinavians are among the most contented people you can meet. If you add the Netherlands and Switzerland, as well as Canada, which probably qualifies as the Scandinavia of the Americas, it is virtually a clean sweep. The other two countries to make up the top ten are Australia and New Zealand, henceforth to be known as the Nordic antipodes.

These are the rankings for the top and bottom countries in the world, according to the Cantril Ladder, which scores from 0 to 10.[10] There is a large four-point gap between the top-ranked countries and the bottom ones, which are mostly in sub-Saharan Africa, a result replicated in other surveys. Denmark is the happiest country on earth, Burundi the saddest.

Figure 4

TOP 10 (SCORE OUT OF 10)	BOTTOM 10 (SCORE OUT OF 10)
1. Denmark (7.526)	148. Madagascar (3.695)
2. Switzerland (7.509)	149. Tanzania (3.666)
3. Iceland (7.501)	150. Liberia (3.622)
4. Norway (7.498)	151. Guinea (3.607)
5. Finland (7.413)	152. Rwanda (3.515)
6. Canada (7.404)	153. Benin (3.484)
7. Netherlands (7.339)	154. Afghanistan (3.360)
8. New Zealand (7.344)	155. Togo (3.03)
9. Australia (7.313)	156. Syria (3.069)
10. Sweden (7.291)	157. Burundi (2.905)

The happy countries are all rich and the unhappy ones are all poor. Higher income does bring happiness then, at least up to a certain point. The results support the conviction that happiness is a measure of something real. If you thought happiness was purely a matter of a person's mood or personality, you might expect people to adapt to whatever conditions they lived in and to exhibit similar levels of happiness around the world. That is decidedly not the case. In countries where conditions are objectively bleak, people assess themselves as unhappy.

But the differences cannot be explained by income alone. In fact, of the top ten countries by per-capita GDP, only Norway and Switzerland make the list of the ten happiest.[11] Eight of the top ten countries by income—including the likes of Luxembourg, Qatar, and Singapore—do not make the super-happy cut. If a certain amount of material comfort brings happiness, there is also strong evidence that happiness is about more than income alone. One of the happiest countries in the world (coming in at number 14) is Costa Rica. That's despite the fact that it is only the 77th wealthiest, with a per-capita income of $15,000.[12]

Three other middle-income countries in Latin America—Brazil (17th happiest), Mexico (21st), and Chile (24th)—all come high relative to much richer countries. Latin countries are better at converting modest levels of income into happiness. The UK, which is ranked 23rd, virtually ties with Chile, even though its average income is nearly twice as high. France, in 32nd place, and Italy, in 50th, do worse still. The Italians—noticeably miserable relative to their income—rank below several far poorer countries, including Algeria, Guatemala, and Thailand. So much for *la dolce vita*.

The US ranks 13th, roughly in line with its income per head, but probably below where many Americans would expect it to be. The Declaration of Independence, after all, enshrines the pursuit of happiness as one of its citizens' inalienable rights. Israel ranks surprisingly high at 11th, despite its near-permanent state of high alert, versus the Palestinian Territories, which is more predictably at an unhappy 108th. China, for all its economic strides, is only 83rd in the world merriment rankings.

In the bottom ten are Syria and Afghanistan, which have both suffered terrible civil wars. The others are all in sub-Saharan Africa. One that sticks out is Rwanda, a darling of development agencies because of its progress in tackling poverty under Paul Kagame, its formidable president. But Rwanda is also authoritarian and still living with the memories of a 1994 genocide in which some one million people were butchered in one hundred days. It is perhaps understandable that Rwanda is not as happy a place as its recent material advances might suggest.

According to the authors of the report, three-quarters of the variation between happy and less happy nations can be explained by six variables. These are income (GDP per capita), healthy years of life expectancy, having people to turn to, trust in others (roughly equated to lack of corruption), perceived freedom to make life decisions (what is sometimes called agency), and generosity (the propensity to donate to charity).

Layard's work focuses less on cross-country comparisons and more on what dictates levels of happiness within countries. Using data from the World Values Survey, which has been carried out since 1981, he singles out seven main determinants of happiness.[13] These are: family relationships, financial situation, work, friends, health, personal freedom, and personal values. He lists these in a table, showing the negative impact of various events on total happiness as measured on a scale of 10 to 100, with 100 being perfect happiness:[14]

Figure 5

EVENT	FALL IN HAPPINESS POINTS
Family income down by one-third	2
Divorced (rather than married)	5
Separated (rather than married)	8
Widowed (rather than married)	4
Never married	4.5
Cohabiting (rather than married)	2
Unemployed	6
Job insecure	3
Unemployment rate up 10 percentage points	3
Health (subjective health down 20 percent)	6
No religion	3.5

The table highlights a number of patterns. Finding a stable partner to live with brings happiness, but being married is better still. When married couples break up, levels of happiness plummet. Once they are divorced, presumably after some time has elapsed since separation, happiness levels recover somewhat, though not fully. Family breakup has become more prevalent. In 1950 divorce was still uncommon in the US, but today only one-half of American fifteen-year-olds live with their biological father. Divorce has been identified as the biggest reason behind rising youth suicide in the US.[15]

Unemployment is a double blow because it affects not only income but, more important, also self-esteem and sense of purpose. Even the unemployment of others has a negative impact, presumably because it makes everyone feel less secure in their own job and impinges on social harmony. A fall in income by a third has a negative impact on happiness (minus 2), but not nearly as much as other factors, such as family breakup (minus 8). Religious belief also seems to be a source of happiness, a more comforting finding in the US than in more secular Europe. People who answer no to the statement "God is important in my life" are 3.5 points less happy on average than those who answer yes.

Finally, health is important. People do adapt to some health problems, but chronic pain and mental illness are both big and—according to Layard—largely preventable sources of misery. For people with mental health problems, he advocates cognitive therapy, which he argues produces better self-healing results than Freudian rummaging around in one's childhood. In some circumstances he also recommends the use of drugs such as Prozac, and urges more research into better medicines with fewer side effects. Layard is certainly not the only promoter of medication to relieve mental suffering. Carrie Fisher, the actress who played Princess Leia in the *Star Wars* films and who was an outspoken advocate for mental health patients, had her ashes interred in an urn shaped like a Prozac pill.[16]

Layard is so convinced the data are robust, he thinks government policy should be aimed at happiness maximization, not growth maximization. "We know that the really big factors that influence happiness are mental health, which is hugely important, and the quality of relationships in the family, at work, and in the community," Layard says.

"We should put much more effort into teaching parents how to be good parents, how to stop them breaking up if they didn't want to break up, help them with problems of child behavior and so on. All of these things would be top priorities for public expenditure. And getting from London to Liverpool faster would just be not quite so important. You'll never see any difference in national happiness because of how long it takes to get from London to Liverpool."[17]

Several other interesting, sometimes surprising, policy recommendations emerge from our discussion. All stem from Layard's conviction that happiness is as important as income.[18] Some of Layard's ideas are deeply unfashionable because they put less emphasis on individualism and more on the collective, such as teaching ethics at school. He is aware he can come across as an old fuddy-duddy harking back to a supposedly kinder, pre-television age. His ideas are also counterintuitive because, instead of pandering to what makes us happy, he often argues for public policies that counteract what he sees as our self-destructive urges. Layard's state sometimes knows best.

One counteractable human foible, he argues, is the search for status, something that research tells us is wired into our genes. Status makes us happy. But the problem, says Layard, is that there is only so much status to go around. So if I am top dog, then you cannot be. If you are promoted, then I must necessarily lose my former status. He compares the phenomenon to people in a seated football stadium who stand up to get a better view. Once I stand up, you have to stand up, and soon everyone is standing up. Then everyone's view is exactly the same as it was before, only we have the inconvenience of having to stand on our feet to obtain it. This zero-sum status game fails the Benthamite test of a society's maximum happiness. Left unattended, it condemns us to a status-seeking rat race and an erosion of overall happiness.

How could public policy address so inherent a human desire? Layard would use tax. One of the ways in which people seek status, he argues, is through salary. Happiness research shows that higher salaries for the already wealthy confer little extra happiness on the beneficiaries, but they do bring more unhappiness for those whose salaries become smaller by comparison. Layard's solution is to tax higher incomes more heavily, not only for the usual reasons of redistribution, but also because this acts as a disincentive against what he sees as the addictive but ultimately futile pursuit of higher earnings. We quickly get used to a higher income—and hence are no happier—yet we make everybody else more miserable in the process. The seeking of status through salary means we work harder than we otherwise would. In the process, we neglect something that research shows us is important for happiness: time spent with friends and family. Addictively seeking status and income is like smoking. "We usually deal with addictive expenditures by taxing them. We tax cigarettes heavily and rightly so . . . We should not hesitate to tax other unhealthy addictive expenditures as well."[19]

He would tax or regulate anything that reduced overall levels of happiness, like smoking or pollution. He would, for example, follow Sweden's example of banning advertising directed at under-twelve-year-olds on the grounds that it inculcates consumerist—and ultimately fruitless—desires in the young and impressionable. The French right-to-disconnect-from-the-Internet policy, which stipulates that companies can no longer expect out-of-office employees to respond to after-hours emails, fits roughly into the same philosophy of legislation to promote happiness.

Won't all this taxing of hard work affect growth? So what, says Layard. The object of life is happiness, not some abstract notion of the size of a national economy. He favors redistribution even if it shrinks the economic pie, until such a point that aggregate happiness itself is damaged.

Layard argues that stability is more important to humans than economists think. He cites research showing that people hate loss more than they like potential gain by roughly two to one. If you ask someone how much, on the toss of a coin, they would require in winnings to compensate for the potential loss of £100, a typical answer is around £200. Whereas an economist might put this down to irrational risk aversion, Layard believes that humans don't like loss and abrupt change. He would fashion public policy accordingly.

"Happiness not dynamism should be the goal of public policy," he says. Continual reorganizations of the public sector in a supposed search for efficiency tend to bring more misery than productivity gains. Economists are too enamored of supposedly efficiency-enhancing labor mobility and blind to the invisible costs of social disruption, alienation and higher crime in areas with large transient populations. "A good predictor of low crime rates is how many friends people have within fifteen minutes' walk."[20] Mobility, like pollution, has hidden costs. Governments should take all this into account either through tax or incentivising local jobs.

Despite its tendency toward redistributive or socialist policies, happiness economics can push in less predictable directions. Because health, particularly mental health, plays such an important role in people's happiness, Layard argues that trying to fix that is more important than seeking to end poverty. He cites research suggesting that it would be sixteen times cheaper for a government to increase happiness by investing in better mental health services than it would to produce the same impact through relieving poverty. "To say mental health is a bigger issue than poverty makes some people very angry. But the evidence is so glaring, you have to say it."

Much of what Layard describes has a familiar ring. Higher

taxes, an emphasis on social trust, and a state that is not afraid to intervene. You might call it a nanny state. You might call it Scandinavia. Layard does not blush at either suggestion. Indeed, he says, Scandinavia has done a much better job of promoting what he sees as healthier, happiness-enhancing values. These are not founded excessively on Darwin's survival of the fittest or on Smith's invisible hand, what Layard calls the two doctrines underpinning Anglo-Saxon societies. Rather they are based on a feeling of common purpose and shared endeavor.

He cites a study in which 77 percent of Swedish children aged eleven to fifteen supported the assertion "Most of the students in my class are kind and helpful." In the US only 53 percent agreed with the statement, and in the UK that view was shared by only 43 percent. Britain, it seems, is good at teaching children how to get ahead. Sweden is better at teaching them how to get along.

Who could be against happiness? If measuring it helps the government design better policies, then surely we should embrace it. A happiness index could even become a standard complement to our standard growth measure, if not an outright replacement. Yet before we hug happiness economics too closely, we should consider some reasons for skepticism.

One problem about the way happiness is measured is that it is on a finite scale. In one of the commonly used survey methods participants are asked to rate their happiness between "not happy at all" for zero points and "very happy" for three points. Income, however, is measured on an open-ended scale, as in theory it can rise indefinitely. So comparing one against the other makes little sense. "In the United States people are no happier, although living standards have more than doubled," writes Layard of the period since 1950. But happiness levels could not have doubled because of the way it is measured.

It makes sense to measure happiness this way. Happiness is likely to be a finite thing, not something you can add to indefinitely. But that fact may limit its usefulness as a policy tool. In the US happiness surveys following the three-category method typically yield a result of about 2.2. For that to improve substantially, tens of millions of people would suddenly need to move from "not very happy" to "happy" or from "happy" to "very happy," something that is hardly likely. That makes it hard to correlate happiness with anything, not just income. Public spending in the US, for example, almost doubled between 1973 and 2004 even allowing for inflation. In Britain, it rose 60 percent over the same period. "Yet in both countries, recorded happiness increased by a mere 2 percent," writes Paul Ormerod, a happiness skeptic.[21] "If we were to rely on happiness data as a basis for policy, what is the point, one might reasonably ask, of all those schools and hospitals?" Only data that can be easily interpreted are worth collecting. A data set that doesn't budge in forty years would not seem to fit the bill. "It is one thing to value happiness; quite another to expect the happiness of society as a whole to be measurable or to respond to policy intervention in understandable ways."

Layard counters that this is too simplistic. Break down the data and you'll see a more subtle picture: higher incomes and social spending have improved happiness to some extent, but these have been offset by other phenomena, including declining social trust, the stress of the rat race, and increased crime. Happiness may be an imperfect measure. But then simply abandoning it in favor of measuring growth—also far from perfect—is to take the easy, but illogical, option, "like looking for the keys under the lamp post because it is easier to look there." Instead, "We should be looking for what we want, wherever it is to be found."[22]

Second, an element of social engineering can quickly creep into happiness economics. The virtue of income is that you can do with it what you like. But once we start trying to figure out what makes people happy, you don't have to stretch things too far to imagine a "brave new world" in which governments continually probe into people's minds and ply them with drugs to make sure they are happy—and docile. Indeed, Layard writes that, while Aldous Huxley's novel was meant to make his modern dystopia seem "revolting and threatening," drugs that make people feel better are not bad in themselves. "If someone finds a happiness drug without side effects, I have no doubt that most of us will sometimes use it."

But do we really want the state openly leading us all in the direction of inner bliss? Almost worse than that, do we want it nudging us through invisible incentives—a ban on advertising here, a tax on moving to a new city to find work there—toward "happier" or "more sensible" behavior? You don't need to be a libertarian to see in this more than a tinge of Big Brother.

Moreover, happiness research—though often promoted by left-leaning economists—sometimes points to a rather paternalistic, conservative view of the world. Stable married relationships and religious faith are two important contributors to well-being. Should we tax divorce and subsidize church attendance? One can even read the literature as encouraging people to be satisfied with their lot, including their social position, since continually striving for a better standard of living is seen as a happiness-destroying fool's errand. That sounds both paternalistic and blunting of ambition. As Donald Trump might say, "Happiness? Sad."

You could even regard the pursuit of happiness as an argument against modernization or economic development altogether. This is where Bhutan, a tiny country of just 800,000 people wedged between India and China, comes in. In 1972 the fourth king of Bhutan, Jigme Singye Wangchuck, still a teenage monarch, made his country the first in the world to declare gross national happiness and not gross domestic product the prime orientation of policy. His decree, hailed as enlightened by many development economists, drew on a long national tradition of emphasizing happiness. Bhutan's legal code, dating from unification in 1729, states, "If the government cannot create happiness (*dekid*) for its people, there is no purpose for the government to exist."[23]

Gross national happiness (GNH) is different from the type of happiness studied by most Western academics. Unlike the sort of work Layard does, GNH is not focused primarily on subjective well-being or self-reported happiness. Instead, it conceives of an "objective" view of happiness with Buddhist overtones, categorized in the nine domains that form the basis of the GNH index (listed below). It is also different from Bentham's version of happiness, a phenomenon that can be detected primarily through an individual's sense of pleasure and pain.

In 2008 Jigme Thinley, Bhutan's first elected prime minister, put it thus. "We have now clearly distinguished the happiness . . . in GNH from the fleeting pleasurable feel-good moods so often associated with that term. We know that true abiding happiness cannot exist while others suffer, and comes only from serving others, living in harmony with nature, and realising our innate wisdom and the true and brilliant nature of our own minds."

The Bhutanese government's "National Human Development Report" describes the goal in these terms: "Bhutan seeks to establish a happy society, where people are safe, where everyone is guaranteed a decent livelihood, and where people enjoy universal access to good education and health care. It is a society where there is no pollution or violation of the environment, where there is no aggression and war, where inequalities do not exist, and where cultural values get strengthened every day."

Too good to be true? The components of the index are as follows:

1. Psychological well-being
2. Health
3. Time use
4. Education
5. Cultural diversity and resilience
6. Good governance
7. Community vitality
8. Ecological diversity and resilience
9. Living standards

The idea of grounding Bhutan's priorities in these domains is to avoid the fate of poor countries that have lunged headlong into development. While rapid development has sometimes brought higher growth and bigger economies, too often the side effects have included urban slums, social alienation, rampant inequality, destruction of forests and rivers, and pollution of the air, as well as loss of cultural heritage and even identity. GNH is supposed to provide a different compass, pointing toward a kinder, gentler form of development. Planning policies—including building dams or developing the capital, Thimphu—must pass a sort of GNH-impact review, much as proposals elsewhere are subjected to environmental-impact studies.

Development is indeed a messy business. Until 1999 Bhutan banned television. After it was legalized, the Bhutanese became exposed to what Layard calls the "usual mix of football, violence, sexual betrayal, consumer advertising, wrestling and the like." Next thing you know, the poor defenseless Bhutanese will be getting the Internet! The results of getting television are predictable: family breakup, crime, drug-taking, and violence in school playgrounds. Yet it is hard to know what to do with this information. It is undoubtedly true that exposure to the modern world, with all its temptations, is not always a recipe for contentment. Even if we too often idealize the pre-modern world—playing down the downsides of illiteracy, male domination, and ill health—we must at least acknowledge the possibility that ignorance can sometimes mean bliss. But elevated to public policy, there are real dangers of paternalism or outright authoritarianism.

Is it working? Bhutan is, after all, undergoing a wrenching transformation dramatic even by the standards of places like India and China, which have seen huge increases in wealth. As recently as 1953 Bhutan was still a feudal country. Its first paved road was built in 1962. Now it is a parliamentary democracy of sorts, with an elected prime minister and a constitutional monarch. Rapid development has inevitably been accompanied by some of the usual trade-offs, as roads and dams sully previously untouched beauty and as people once content with subsistence living become unhappy city dwellers striving for a modern (and probably unattainable) lifestyle.

"Who wants to do subsistence farming and get up at four in

the morning and carry water if you don't have to?" Paljor Dorji, a member of the royal family and a longtime close adviser to the former king, told one journalist. "Once you educate the people, nobody is going to live the same miserable life their parents did."[24]

Thimphu's development is being strictly controlled, and the government has sought to ensure adequate provision of roads, sewers, and schools. One can't compare tiny Thimphu with a sprawling megalopolis like Mumbai, a city with twenty times the entire population of Bhutan, but as any visitor to the less well-planned cities of India, Indonesia, or the Philippines knows, the uncontrolled influx of people can present ghastly urban problems of squalor, pollution, gridlock, and disease.

By contrast, Bhutan's modernization is planned and contained. If you want to build in Thimphu, you can't just put up a tin shack and filch electricity from a nearby pylon. Constructions must incorporate designs from traditional Bhutanese architecture, including pitched roofs and distinctive windows. People are strongly encouraged to wear national dress in public. Bhutan limits tourist numbers and, through minimum spending requirements, ensures that only upmarket tourists can visit. "Thimphu is a pleasant walking city, with none of the chaotic warrens present in many Indian cities. Its people are cheerful, its merchants show none of the pushiness common in south Asia, and even its stray dogs seem benign. There are no slums," writes one reporter.[25]

Still, Bhutan is no Shangri-la. It is a lower-middle-income country with an income per capita of just over $8,000 adjusted for local prices.[26] It has low literacy levels, despite the government's association of happiness with good education; only 55 percent of Bhutanese women can read and write. In much poorer Bangladesh 58 percent of women are literate, while the Philippines, no richer than Bhutan, does even better, with female literacy at 97 percent.[27] Nor is Bhutan's health provision particularly outstanding, again notwithstanding the attention given to health in the National Human Development Report. Life expectancy is just below 70, which places Bhutan 114th in the world. That compares with a life expectancy of 79 (32nd place) for Cuba, a country dedicated to communism not happiness, and 81 for Chile (28th place), a state whose initial take-off under authoritarian rule was engineered by Chicago School economists. Neither Fidel Castro nor Milton Friedman were known as Mr. Happy.

Bhutan's dedication to cultural preservation is often praised. Culture is seen both as a source of identity and as protection against the more corrosive aspects of modernization. In the domain of "cultural diversity and resilience," GNH measures fluency in one of a dozen dialects, people's knowledge and interest in thirteen artisanal skills, including blacksmithing and embroidery, and their adherence to something called Driglam Namzha, or the Way of Harmony. Bhutanese people are expected to participate in six to twelve days of "socio-cultural" activities each year. In 2010 only one-third of the population reached the desired threshold of six days. (About 15 percent spent thirteen days or more in such activities, though whether this is seen as overdoing it is not mentioned.)

Yet the idea of preserving culture covers a multitude of sins. Not all cultures are equally attractive. Culture could mean that women should know their place or get on with their embroidery instead of learning to read. In parts of Africa an index that rewarded cultural preservation would award points for female genital mutilation. In Bhutan culture has sometimes meant ethnic purity. In the 1990s the government cracked down on ethnic Nepalese, driving tens of thousands out of the country in what some human rights groups have called an act of ethnic cleansing.[28]

Using Bhutan's own yardstick, 91.2 percent of the population was happy in 2015, a 1.8 percent improvement on results when the exercise was carried out in 2010.[29] A breakdown showed that 8.4 percent of Bhutanese were "deeply happy," 35 percent "extensively happy," and 47.9 percent "narrowly happy," leaving under 9 percent categorized as "unhappy." Both the result and the improvement appear to be a victory for the Bhutanese government, but one's interpretation of the result depends entirely on one's agreement or otherwise with what is being measured. The fact that Bhutan is measuring not happiness as reported by respondents, but a potpourri of bureaucratically determined indicators, might give pause.

Interestingly, when it comes to subjective well-being, as formulated in the 2016 World Happiness Report, Bhutan scores 5.196 out of a possible 10. That puts it in 84th place in the world, just behind China and ahead of Kyrgyzstan. Call me a cynic, but for a country whose public policy is dedicated to delivering happiness that does not strike me as unalloyed success. Bhutan, then, has become symbolic of the happiness debate, but it may be a distraction rather than the useful campaign tool some of its proponents seem to imagine.

It is entirely sensible for Bhutan to try to handle development cautiously and responsibly. Left purely to market forces and the vagaries of globalization, poor countries seeking to overcome poverty can indeed experience violent dislocations. But we should recognize the limitations of Bhutan's approach.

Happiness economics may have more to say about rich countries, for which the accumulation of ever-greater income cannot be the answer to everything. Layard is surely right that happiness measures point to some important things like the futility of endlessly seeking status and money, the importance of community, and a sense of security and stability. One does not need to treat happiness measures as sacrosanct to see that they can throw an important light on neglected areas of policy, such as depression and overwork.

When it comes to self-reported happiness, though, one thing is certain: the Scandinavians are doing something right. If it is subjective well-being that you're after, then, objectively speaking, you'd rather be in Tromsø than in Thimphu.

13
GDP 2.0

f Simon Kuznets could choose where to be reborn, he might well choose Maryland. The inventor of GDP had serious reservations about his own measure of economic activity, which counted many "bads" and which ignored so much of what makes life worthwhile. Kuznets thought it was crazy to count pollution, commuting, and military defense as pluses. Likewise, he favored a measure that better captured some of the intangible contributions to well-being. But GDP, born in recession and war, took on a life of its own. By the time of Kuznets's death in 1985 it had become precisely what he had warned against—a proxy for well-being and the distillation of everything we are supposed to aspire to as consumers, producers, politicians, voters, and citizens.

If our obsession with growth as charted by GDP is the accidental fruit of Kuznets's labor, Maryland's alternative, the Genuine Progress Index, is much closer to the great man's spirit. You could call it GDP 2.0. The GPI was adopted by Maryland in 2010. It was not invented there; its history goes back at least to the 1970s, when economists William Nordhaus and James Tobin began to think about what they called "measure of economic welfare."[1] Using GDP as a base measure, they added previously invisible "goods" such as leisure time and unpaid housework, and subtracted what they quaintly called regrettables, including commuting time, pollution, and spending on crime prevention.

Variations on the same theme were developed over the years by academics and practitioners. The GPI, which came out of work begun by Herman Daly, an ecological economist, is one of the most enduring of an alphabet soup of attempts to go beyond GDP. One way of thinking about these measurements is as net domestic product. Remember the G in gross domestic product stands for "gross," with little account taken of depreciation of assets, especially natural ones, nor the side effects of production. By subtracting the bads, the various alternative indexes use GDP as a starting point and then attempt to come up with a more reasonable net figure. Like Niu Wenyuan, the father of green GDP in China, they hoped to scrape away at the outer form of the twentieth century's favorite economic statistic and uncover something more authentic within.

Martin O'Malley had been mayor of Baltimore for eight years until 2007, when he was elected the 61st governor of Maryland. During his time running the city, "he was very much into data," says Sean McGuire, whom O'Malley hired to change the way Maryland measured progress. "He really thought data could drive decisions. Having the metric, having specific data sets and making sure that those data sets depict what's really happening—versus what we think is happening—that's really crucial."

McGuire had been interested in alternative economic measures since his student days at the University of Maryland, when he had studied ecological economics under Herman Daly. When Governor O'Malley asked McGuire to come up with a new metric, he was tapping into something McGuire had been thinking about for years. McGuire's first thought was to suggest his favorite measure of all. It was called the Happy Planet Index. "It's very elegant, it's very clean," McGuire enthuses. "It's your happiness, multiplied by how many years you're on earth, divided by the ecological footprint."

There were two big problems with the Happy Planet Index. One was that Maryland didn't measure either happiness or its ecological footprint, which left McGuire pitifully short of relevant data. The second problem was more fundamental still. "I have never come across an elected leader," says McGuire, "who could say 'Happy Planet Index' without laughing." In the real world that matters. No index can be useful without political and popular credibility. Measurements need to be taken seriously. If the Happy Planet Index goes down, it should make grim headlines on the evening news and flash up on your Twitter feed. Heads should roll and voters should consider throwing out their elected leaders. That was never going to happen. McGuire gave it five minutes' thought—and jettisoned the idea.

At that point he turned to the GPI, a measurement with a forty-year track record, which had been tried out in various forms in countries from Japan to Finland. The GPI, says McGuire, is not that radical. It is really a refined version of GDP. Maryland's Department of Natural Resources, which compiles the index, says the GPI is drawn up according to three basic principles. It adjusts for income inequality, which is regarded as bad. It includes non-market benefits from the environment (such as wetlands) and from society (such as volunteer work), and it deducts such things as the costs of environmental degradation, spending on things like crime prevention or health insurance, and loss of leisure time. Altogether, it uses twenty-six indicators, each expressed in dollars, to produce a single number akin to GDP. The indicators are divided into economic, environmental, and social categories as follows:

Figure 6

ECONOMIC INDICATORS	ENVIRONMENTAL INDICATORS	SOCIAL INDICATORS
Personal consumption expenditures	Cost of water pollution	Value of housework
Income inequality	Cost of air pollution	Cost of family changes
	Cost of noise pollution	Cost of crime
Adjusted personal consumption	Cost of net wetlands change	Cost of personal pollution abatement
Services of consumer durables	Cost of net farmland change	Value of volunteer work
Cost of consumer durables	Cost of net forest cover change	Cost of lost leisure time
Cost of underemployment	Cost of climate change	Value of higher education
Net capital investment	Cost of ozone depletion	Services of highways and streets
	Cost of non-renewable energy resource depletion	Cost of commuting
		Cost of motor-vehicle crashes

McGuire says one attraction of the GPI was that Maryland could compile it without collecting any new information. "This is all data straight from federal sources or data we were already collecting," he says. "It is total acres of forest, total acres of wetlands, debt, roads. Every single thing in the twenty-six indicators we already had, we were already tracking. So that was another big sell. There's nothing new here, kids. It's just taking what we are already collecting and reformatting it slightly."

McGuire got some grant funding, hired an intern from the University of Maryland, and set about producing the first official state-level GPI in US history. The two of them started work in February 2009. By October they had crunched all the numbers and were ready to release their findings, together with a fancy new website. Because of a lag in the data, the most recent year for which they had a GPI was 2008. What did they learn about 2008 from all that work? I ask McGuire. "That's a great question," he replies. "We learned nothing."

Like GDP, he explains, the GPI is a single number. So on its own it doesn't tell you a whole hell of a lot. The trick is to compare the GPI from year to year. Fortunately McGuire had been able to plot Maryland's GPI right back to 1960, and that revealed rather more. One thing the half-century of data showed clearly was something that had cropped up before: while GDP had continued to grow, the GPI had stalled. Put another way, after a certain level of income, simply adding to economic activity produced diminishing returns—or no returns at all. There was a reason for that. You could increase GDP, say by building on greenfield sites or getting people to work longer hours, but in GPI terms the positive of higher economic output was offset by the negatives of natural destruction or the loss of leisure time.

In explaining the GPI's rationale, the department's website gives the example of economic expansion resulting from the "explosive growth of urban sprawl." All that activity in construction, new sewerage systems, new roads, and new cars counts toward growth, but sprawl is also associated with several costs such as longer commutes, loss of community, destruction of natural land, as well as water and air pollution. "Just because we are exchanging money within an economy does not necessarily mean that we are sustainable or prosperous." It is pure Kuznets.

McGuire has since moved to Oregon, where he is helping that

Figure 7

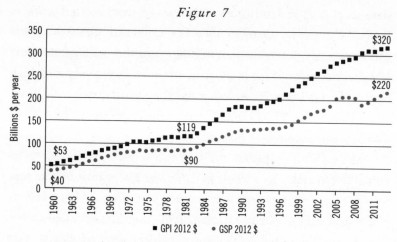

GPI vs. the Gross State Product (GSP) of Maryland since 1960.

state go through a similar exercise. So I called Elliott Campbell, who has succeeded him as the keeper of Maryland's GPI. I start by asking for a few more details about how the GPI is actually compiled. First, he says, start with consumption. The GPI counts as positive all the things we pay for that we actually want, things like the food we eat, the house we live in, our holidays and leisure activities. "If you want to spend your money on something that contributes to your satisfaction, to your economic utility," he says, invoking Jeremy Bentham, "we include that as a positive in the ledger of GPI calculations."

But "if you would rather not spend your money on something, which is what we term a defensive expenditure, that's counted on the negative side of the ledger." So health insurance, locks for your doors, legal services, the costs of alimony and child support (remember the impact of separation or divorce on happiness), food waste, energy waste, and tobacco are all subtracted. So is "pollution abatement," the money households and government are deemed to spend on dealing with noise pollution by for example fitting double glazing, or on mitigating water pollution, say by installing filtration systems. For normal growth measures, which make no distinction between spending money on a movie or on anti-cholesterol tablets or on a burglar alarm, all such items would be added indiscriminately.

The GPI has evolved even in the few short years Maryland has been compiling it. These days Maryland is able to use big data to reflect real state consumption patterns rather than, as before, estimates extrapolated from national data. Similarly, it uses satellite imagery to work out more accurately the extent of Maryland's forest and wetland reserves. We may have known for decades that growth was a poor measurement of well-being, or even of market activity, but new technology and big data provide the chance to improve our metrics. "Kuznets certainly recognized the limitations of gross domestic product," says Campbell. "I think if he had the sort of data that we have available today, he would have developed the GPI."

The fact that Maryland does not have to conduct special surveys to calculate the GPI highlights something important. It is not that we don't already possess tons of valuable information in our national income statements about what makes our societies tick and what makes them sick. The problem is that we don't choose to emphasize much of it. One of the reasons for that is GDP's extraordinary rise to become the *sine qua non* of economic success, so important that it obscures most of the numbers in the hierarchy beneath it. A lot of important data remains hidden, squirreled away in official reports or buried in a jumble of numbers on electronic spreadsheets.

If our goal as societies is to maximize growth, says McGuire, then the question will always be, what do we need to give up to achieve that: free time, green space, job security, fire or environmental regulations, public services? "Essentially, we always ask the question: 'How much can we sacrifice for economic gain?'" says McGuire. "We never ask the question: 'How much economic gain are we willing to sacrifice to ensure that our environment and our health are at ultimate highs?'"

McGuire remembers that when he first came up with the idea of GPI for Maryland someone in the state—a person he cheerfully describes as a "right-wing nut job"—accused him of simply throwing his favorite measurements into a pot. "He called the GPI 'a Ouija board and Yahtzee dice.' Just a random collection of numbers. That always stuck with me." McGuire strongly disputes that characterization. He took the GPI exactly as he found it, he says, making only the tiniest adjustments to fit Maryland's circumstances. For McGuire the GPI is an off-the-shelf index with a venerable history. Yet the right-wing nut job made a valid point. It is one we need to consider carefully when weighing up the pluses and minuses of indexes. Because the thing about an index is that you can put in it almost anything that takes your fancy. It is what Hans Rosling, the Swedish statistician, calls "GDP in the age of Excel."

Almost everything in the GPI is a value judgment. Booze is an example. Alcohol in moderation is counted as a positive expenditure. Who doesn't like a glass of red wine or a beer after work? But anything above what is considered reasonable consumption is deducted from the GPI, which subtracts money spent on "binge drinking." Academic research apparently puts binge drinking at 25 percent of all alcohol consumption, so this portion is subtracted from the GPI rather than added. Depending on your politics, you might consider the underlying value judgments of the GPI eminently sensible. Cigarettes and wetland destruction: bad. Home ownership, work life balance, and clean air: good. But we must recognize that these are subjective. The GPI, for example, counts time spent in your car as wasted because you could be at home playing with your children. I might, however, adore driving and hate spending time with snotty-nosed kids—even my own.

The GPI says that if you drink yourself silly you are detracting from the well-being of society. I might find solace in the bottle and think it is none of the government's business what I spend my money on, even if that happens to be copious quantities of vodka. The GPI says that inequality is bad because research shows unequal societies are less happy. But you could—as many people do—defend inequality as necessary in order to penalize laziness and reward people for hard work and new ideas. You might find the GPI's emphasis on preserving the environment perfectly rational. You could, though, regard the extinction of an obscure beetle or the lesser-spotted throat warbler as a perfectly acceptable price to pay for a larger TV screen and more money in your children's university trust fund.

The point is that indexes are self-referential. They send the signals you want them to send. You load them up with what you think is important and the index tells you how you are doing. Scandinavian countries, for example, regularly come in at the top of the Human Development Index. That, says one critic, is "because the HDI is basically a measure of how Scandinavian your country is."

In the search for a replacement for—or useful addition to—GDP, it is important to acknowledge this basic problem with composite indexes.

The man who came up with the Scandinavian put-down is Bryan Caplan, a professor of economics at George Mason University in Virginia. He was having a go not at the twenty-six-component GPI, but at the far simpler three-component Human Development Index. The HDI was one of the first serious attempts to invent an alternative to GDP. It is the brainchild of Pakistani development economist Mahbub ul Haq, who once wrote of GDP, "Any measure that values a gun several hundred times more than a bottle of milk is bound to raise serious questions about its relevance to human progress." Haq's index, drawn up in conjunction with Amartya Sen, was launched in 1990. It was simplicity itself, combining three elements: income, literacy, and longevity. Though it has been tweaked since to include a measure of inequality, the basic premise remains the same. Income is measured by GDP per capita adjusted for the cost of living; longevity is life expectancy at birth; and education is a combination of literacy and enrollment at school and university.

The following is a list of the top countries, according to the HDI, compared with the top by GDP per capita. Note that this is a snapshot for 2015. Countries and numbers vary quite substantially from year to year, especially for GDP per capita.

Of the countries that do well on conventional GDP, only three—Norway, Ireland, and Switzerland—are in the top ten of the HDI. The other seven GDP stars don't do as well at converting income into health and education. The US on the other hand doesn't quite make the top ten in GDP per capita, but it does make the HDI top ten.

Figure 8

RANK	BY HDI	BY GDP PER CAPITA
1	Norway	Qatar
2	Australia	Luxembourg
3	Switzerland	Singapore
4	Denmark	Brunei
5	Netherlands	Kuwait
6	Germany	Norway
7	Ireland	UAE
8	United States	Ireland
9	Canada	San Marino
10	New Zealand	Switzerland

On the face of it, there is not much to object to in the HDI. This author quite likes it as a more rounded measure than our traditional growth gauge. Yet Caplan's criticism is both considered and trenchant. Scores on each of its three measures—income, life expectancy, and education—are awarded between 0 and 1, he notes, with 1 being the maximum score. "This effectively means that a country of immortals with infinite per-capita GDP would get a score of 0.666 (lower than South Africa and Tajikistan) if its population were illiterate and never went to school," he says drily. Moreover, to get a score of 1 on education, a country would need to turn everyone into a permanent student, not necessarily a desired outcome. (Who would teach them?) Income, on the other hand, could theoretically keep on rising; yet in wealthy countries it is already close to its upper limit of 1, leaving almost no room for improvement. That is because Huq and his fellow creators did not think income was important above a certain level. So HDI, like other indexes, tells you what you want to hear. "The ultimate problem with the HDI," writes Caplan, "is lack of ambition. It effectively proclaims an 'end of history' where Scandinavia is the pinnacle of human achievement."[2]

Yet indexes have their place. Measurements are powerful tools. If we measure something we consider positive, politicians will come up with policies designed to maximize that particular variable, whatever it is: higher income, cleaner air, or more doughnut consumption. This is very powerful. It means that "better" measurements have the power to produce "better" societies. If you want to look like Scandinavia—and measures of happiness suggest there are worse role models—then designing an index of how Scandinavian you are may be about the best place to start.

Of course, not every country wants to be like Norway or Sweden. If Barbados measured hours on the ski slopes it might come up short. But every country, presumably, wants to be a better version of itself. We should not forget either that GDP too has a hidden value system. It measures an economy's ability to maximize activity no matter what the cost in environmental destruction or social disruption. We might call GDP a measure of how Chinese your economy is.

Equally, you could see the GPI as attempting to mold a country as envisaged by ecological economist Herman Daly, who advocates what he calls a "steady state" economy, which downplays or even eliminates growth as conventionally measured. McGuire prefers to see the GPI as a tool for illuminating trade-offs. "When you destroy a wetland for a minimart there is a cost to that," he says. "I don't hang my hat on the GPI itself, but it is a way of saying, if we value something, what are we willing to do to preserve it? And if that means only 1.5 percent growth in GDP to keep all the things that we care about, are we willing to accept that?" There is, he says, "no system in the world that can grow at 3 percent into infinity."

The GPI subtracts negative externalities: air pollution, water pollution, and loss of forest, farmland and wetland. Likewise it adds positive externalities such as the hidden benefits of an investment, say a community's better mental and physical health resulting from the installation of a public swimming pool. At one point Governor O'Malley was pushing a policy to double the number of passengers using public transport. "I ran the numbers through the GPI meat grinder," recalls McGuire. "I could do a policy analysis with the actual numbers and show that, yes, taxpayers are actually benefiting in aggregate. There might be a little bit more spending on public buses, that kind of stuff, but when you count the benefits in terms of the cost of commuting, leisure time, car pollution, and use of non-renewable resources . . . it becomes an easy sell."

As well as being a useful policymaking tool, McGuire says, the GPI has shown itself to be more sensitive than GDP to real economic conditions. He cites figures for 2009, the year in which the impact of the financial crisis rippled with devastating effect through the US economy. Yet in that year the gross state product for Maryland (the state equivalent of GDP) actually rose 3.8 percent. In a memo to his boss at the department McGuire wrote that this was "almost implausible" given the real economic hardship people in the state were suffering. By contrast, the GPI for that year was down 6.3 percent. That made a yawning gap of 10 percentage points with GDP. One of the reasons the GPI was a "more accurate" reflection of what was really going on, he says, is because it picked up on the fact that net capital investment crashed from $9 billion in 2008 to minus $1 billion in 2009 as the state massively reined in spending.[3] The GPI was also more sensitive to unemployment and underemployment, including as it did people who had part-time jobs when they wanted to work full time and those who had given up looking for work altogether because job prospects were so lousy.

Weighting and value judgments are not the only potential problems with an index like the GPI. Because it is expressed in dollars, it runs into the same difficulties we encountered in the chapter on natural capital. "I hate this putting a monetary value on air pollution so that we can see a sunset or see the mountains," says McGuire. "It's soul crushing." When he first started costing Maryland's wetlands, forests, and green spaces, he says, "I'm like, this is not cool." But, he has concluded, in the real world of policymaking "numbers matter and money matters more. People say, 'How do you put a price on the priceless?' But if you don't do that, this is what you get, what we're doing right now: sacrificing our health and our environment for economic gain."

McGuire likens the GPI to a budgetary reality check in which the budget is clean air, clean water, and leisure time as well as dollars and cents. "I'm a county employee. I can't go out and buy a Ferrari every day. I am not making the dollars," he says by way of illustrating budgetary limits. "If we want to have economic growth, that's awesome. Just make sure we can afford it."

If the disadvantage of an index is that you can put in it anything you like, that is also its advantage. Canada has taken this idea to its extreme by asking—wait for it—Canadians themselves what they want to measure. The Canadian Index of Wellbeing has its origins in focus groups carried out across the country in the early 2000s. Bryan Smale, a professor at the University of Waterloo in Ontario

and the director of the index, says, "The focus groups were organized around a fairly simple question: 'What matters to you? What
makes your life good?'"[4] The index was not about how to make
Canada more Scandinavian. It was about taking Canadian values
and improving on what the country already had: in short, making
it more Canadian.

In the focus groups, which targeted a sample of society across
generations and political affiliations, Canadians were remarkably
consistent about what they valued: primary and secondary education, health care access, a healthy environment, clean air and water,
social programs, responsible taxation (whatever that means), public safety and security, job security, employment opportunities,
a living wage, work-life balance, and civic participation. These
formed the basis of the eight "domains" measured in the index,
which are: Community Vitality, Democratic Engagement, Education, Environment, Healthy Populations, Leisure and Culture,
Living Standards, and Time Use.

From there the index's administrators identified robust data
sets—Smale calls them "canaries in the mineshaft"—for each
domain. In all there are sixty-four indicators designed to measure
progress and raise the alarm if the quality of life in a particular area
is slipping. "The real issue was: can we find data that was valid and
reliable, consistently gathered over time that we could track to see
whether or not we were making progress?" he says. "For example,
we monitor incidence of diabetes within the Healthy Populations
domain. The reason for that is that, depending on how widespread
and severe the incidence of diabetes is, it is a marker for other sorts
of health conditions such as heart illness, obesity, and so on."

Attaching a weight to each of the sixty-four indicators is
"something we've struggled with," Smale admits. How could you

possibly weigh public debt levels against, say, the number of hours that children spend watching TV?[5] Clearly you can't, but what you can do is pick indicators that are "actionable." By that he means indicators that measure "the kinds of things that people can sink their teeth into and say, 'Here's what's happening with respect to, for example, greenhouse gas emissions. Here's what's happening with respect to people's time spent with friends.'"

As much as providing robust data, he says, the index has been a "great conversation starter. People are stepping back and going, 'How is our well-being? What aren't we doing that we should be doing?' How does this compare to progress in the economy?'" People, he says, keep hearing that the economy is recovering nicely from recession, but see that well-being is not. That prompts them to say, "What's going on there?"

In 2016 the Canadian Index of Wellbeing found that the gap between well-being and GDP, already large, had widened after the 2008 financial crisis. "In 2007 the gap between GDP and the Canadian Index of Wellbeing was 22 percent. By 2010 the gap had risen to 24.5 percent, and by 2014 it had jumped to 28.1 percent." Why? One reason was that, as in Maryland, recovery from the 2008 recession brought growth but not good jobs. So measures of job security fell, while those of inequality rose. The quality of "Leisure and Culture" also fell sharply as Canadians worked harder to make ends meet, took less time off work, participated less in volunteer activities and the arts, and took fewer vacations. On the plus side, the quality of education was keeping pace with economic activity and communities remained strong. In the official growth numbers all of these details were masked by the simple fact of economic recovery.[6]

The whole exercise, says Smale, has raised awareness about

public policy. While GDP is a "rearview mirror" which tells you what went on last year, the Index of Wellbeing is a measure of what sort of society Canada wants to be. "It looks at what people have said is important to them. If we want to be aspirational about where we want to go as a society, as a country, it asks where do we want to place our emphasis and increase well-being in a myriad of different areas?"

Smale does not claim that the index, despite its popularity, has had a discernible impact on national policy. "I think, naively, a few years ago I would have thought, *Hey, when we release this we're going to really have some influence on change in the country.* I've now come to realize that that's the long game," he says. "Some people have suggested that we're trying to replace GDP. We're not. We're just trying to broaden the conversation."

14

THE GROWTH CONCLUSION

The genius of GDP is that it somehow manages to squeeze all human activity into a single number. You could think of it as like pushing a large frog into a small matchbox. Still, at its best, GDP is a brilliant and useful insight. It provides a snapshot of one version of reality, a number that policymakers can act upon. But if the beauty of GDP is aggregation, that is also its biggest flaw. No single number can capture all that is worth knowing in life—even if you're an economist.

Think of it like a car dashboard. There's a fuel gauge that tells you how much petrol you have left in the tank and a speedometer indicating how fast you're going. Perhaps there's another display that tells you what music is playing. All three give you valuable bits of information. You cannot, however, combine them into a single number that tells you anything meaningful. They are in different dimensions.[1]

To create a single number requires measuring everything in the same unit, which in economics means converting everything into dollars and cents. When it comes to something hard to price—say volunteer work, life expectancy, clean air, or a sense of community—you must either figure out a way of attaching a dollar amount to it or just forget all about it. The idea that all things can be priced stems partly from the work of Jeremy Bentham, the man whose missing

241

head, you'll recall, is worth ten pounds. The theory of marginal utility, a foundation of modern economics, states that the price of a good or a service reflects the additional satisfaction gained from consuming an extra unit of that product. It is this reductionism that allows economists to convert everything into those complicated mathematical models that occasionally cause your eyes to glaze over.

But prices cannot be a proxy for everything. That means much of what we care about as human beings is either left out of our economic calculations or converted, using some jiggery-pokery, into a dollar amount that can be included. What about the other dimensions? One solution, instead of aggregating everything, is to go the other way—by disaggregating.[2] That might seem like a retrograde step, like uninventing the wheel. If GDP was a brilliant invention—which it was—then why on earth would we start taking it apart? If you don't like the idea of scrapping the wheel, think of it like this: how about liberating that frog from the matchbox?

The problem with growth as measured by GDP is that it has become the overlord of measures. It is *the* number we use to define success. Of course economists and policymakers look at dozens of data points—unemployment, inflation, net exports, retail sales, house prices, and wages—to arrive at their models and predictions; Alan Greenspan, the former chairman of the Federal Reserve, used to examine men's underwear sales as a proxy for economic activity. But in popular discourse GDP is king. Remember, economic growth is synonymous with GDP. To test out the supremacy of GDP, all you need to do is imagine a politician saying the following: "I propose shrinking our economy in return for X." No one angling for elected office would say such a thing, no matter what X is: flame-retardant public housing, a fairer society, a two-day working week, free pizza.

The idea of not maximizing growth has become almost unthinkable in modern political discourse. That is because growth has—almost without us knowing it—become all we care about.

This book does not argue—as some do—for GDP to be scrapped. However flawed, it is a powerful measure and a useful policy tool. As many rightly point out, economic growth often correlates with the things we do care about—education, health, freedom to choose how we live—because higher incomes and a higher tax base can provide the resources to pay for these things. Richer countries generally serve their citizens better than poor ones, as long as they are properly organized and have strong democratic institutions pushing for fairness and equality before the law.[3]

But this book does argue strongly for two things. The first is easy and quite within reach of any reader. Let's call it skepticism. Anyone who has read this book—and if you've made it this far, thank you—should have a better understanding of what our growth statistics capture and what they don't. What is in there that arguably should not be: pollution, crime, long commutes, missiles, long working hours. And what is not in there that arguably should be: good jobs, green space, decent health care, any measure of sustainability. So next time you hear the economy has grown by such-and-such, it is worth quietly chuckling to yourself and reflecting on the limited nature of that information, as well as the abstract nature of the economy being described.

I would argue that skepticism is valuable in itself. After all, as a journalist I've pretty much made a career out of it. But it gets you only so far. To say simply "I don't believe in this number" is a nihilistic way of looking at the world. Which brings me on to the second argument of this book and the question that always comes up in any discussion of growth and GDP: "What would you replace it with?" None of the alternatives are robust enough or broad enough to supplant GDP altogether, so the answer is this. Rather than replace GDP, we should add to it, so that we can flesh out a more nuanced view of our world.

Being of the TV generation, I think of it like this. If I switch on the evening news and the newscaster is putting on a grave voice and headlining five or six numbers, which numbers should we select? Or, if you get economic news alerts on your phone, which are the numbers you really couldn't live without? The idea is that the measurements in question should tell us something important. We the public should be invested in them, much as we are in growth as measured by GDP. Which numbers make the grade?

Here are a few suggestions.

GDP PER CAPITA

This is so obvious it feels almost embarrassingly late in the day to mention it. A startlingly easy adjustment to make to GDP is to turn it into a per-capita figure by dividing it by the number of people in the country. Yet this is rarely done—at least not in normal public discourse. All too often growth is expressed in absolute terms, with no account taken of population expansion.

If your growth rate is 2 percent but your population is also growing at 2 percent then, on a per-capita basis, you are going precisely nowhere. Investors often get excited about the growth rates of some developing countries, forgetting that much of it is simply the result of high birth rates. The easiest way of increasing the size of an economy is simply to add people. If Donald Trump wants 3 percent growth, it is very easy to achieve: all he has to do is knock down that unbuilt wall and invite in 10 million new people to America each year. What he really wants, however, is 3 percent *per-capita* growth, which is quite another thing—and much harder to achieve.

Figure 9

Top 10 Countries by GDP
(Purchasing Power Parity) per Capita in 2015,
Published by IMF

COUNTRY	GDP (PPP) PER CAPITA ($)
Qatar	132,870
Luxembourg	99,506
Singapore	85,382
Brunei	79,508
Kuwait	70,542
Norway	68,591
United Arab Emirates	67,217
Ireland	65,806
San Marino	62,938
Switzerland	58,647

Bottom 10 Countries

COUNTRY	GDP (PPP) PER CAPITA ($)
Eritrea	1,300
Guinea	1,238
Mozambique	1,192
Malawi	1,126
Niger	1,077
Liberia	875
Burundi	831
Democratic Republic of the Congo	767
Central African Republic	628

Economists struggle to imagine how a country can possibly progress if it is not forever adding people to its workforce. That's why so many talk about Japan, with its mildly shrinking population and positive per-capita growth rates, as being in a "demographic death spiral."[4] Economists are so wedded to the idea that the economy must always be expanding that they find it hard to break the logic of "just add people." If Thomas Malthus thought more and more people would be the death of human civilization, modern economists think the reverse.

Yet unless we imagine the world's population increasing indefinitely, we really must begin to imagine a world where the economy eventually stops expanding—in rich, mature economies at least.[5] That does not mean that income per capita necessarily needs to stop rising. And that is what ultimately counts. Reporting growth on a per-capita basis is a small but important step in putting people—rather than some abstract notion of the economy—at the center of our policymaking.

MEDIAN INCOME

This goes one better than GDP per capita. It has one big advantage and one little one. The big advantage is that it is a median and not a mean. The mean is the average, but people often misunderstand what this implies. In a society with a total income of 100 consisting of four people, if one person earns all the income and the others earn absolutely nothing, then the average income is 25. The chief statistician of the *Financial Times*, Keith Fray, tells a joke at his staff presentations. "Bill Gates walks into a bar. On average, everyone in the room is a billionaire." I laughed out loud when I heard it, but then that's me. The "humor" (oh those statisticians!) stems from the fact that the average is merely the sum total divided by the number of people, in this case those in the bar. It can give a distorted picture of what we think of as typical. That's because it doesn't tell you anything about how income is distributed. As our societies grow more unequal, this is a bigger and bigger problem.[6]

In contrast to the mean, the median lines everybody up—which sounds ominous, I know—and picks out the person in the middle. The median gives you a rough-and-ready idea about how the typical person lives. You could call it a number for the precarious middle class. In this age, when the middle class feels forgotten and misrepresented, that's a big advantage.

The little advantage of median income is that it deals with income rather than production. Income is a more intuitive concept for most people: what do I have to live on rather than how many forklift trucks were produced this year? In national income theory, production and income should be the same, since we buy what is produced and produce only what can be paid for, but it doesn't always feel like that.

Steve Landefeld, the man in charge of US GDP for twenty years, is also a fan of medians. But, he says, they tell a story that might make some politicians uncomfortable. "Given the political sensitivity of those numbers, that could be something a statistical agency would be a little nervous getting into," he told me. "But I think there is a rising consensus in the US and other countries that it's something we need to do."

INEQUALITY

Even the notion of median income has its limits. In addition to finding out how the typical person or household is doing, it is right to shine a light on those left behind. There are several ways of doing this. After all, it took clever academic sleuthing to uncover the shocking fact that less-well-educated, middle-aged white Americans have shortening lifespans. One basic measure of inequality is the Gini coefficient, which is often expressed on a scale of 0 to 100.[7] Invented by Italian statistician Corrado Gini in 1912, at one end of the scale 0 represents a society of perfect equality in which everyone earns the same; at the other 100 is an economy in which one person earns everything. Relatively equal societies, such as those in Scandinavia, have a Gini coefficient of below 30, with the most unequal society in the world, South Africa, at 63.[8] The US has a Gini coefficient of 41, the UK 33, and Germany 30.[9] One could perform the same exercise for wealth or assets—which generally reveals greater inequality still.

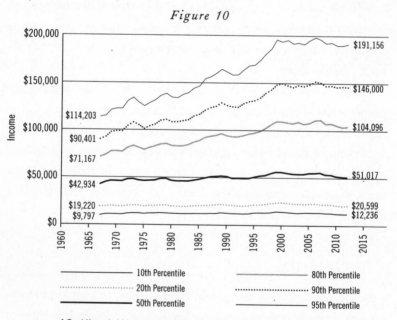

Figure 10

A Real Household Income at Selected Percentiles, 1967–2012 (reported in 2012 dollars).[10]

Another way is to disaggregate income according to percentiles of the population. This reveals how income is shared and how
the median fares against rich and poor. Figure 10 tells the story of
what has happened to US wages from 1980, for those at the top, in
the middle, and on the bottom strata of society. It also highlights
just how far the typical wage is from the average.

Yet another way of encapsulating inequality in a single number
is to compare one segment of the population with another, say the
top 10 percent by income against the bottom 10 percent. Here's how
a select number of wealthy countries look according to that ratio,
with the most equal at the top. For example, in relatively egalitarian Iceland, the top 10 percent of the population earns 20.6 percent
of total income against 4.1 percent by the bottom 10 percent—for
a ratio of 5 to 1. Meanwhile in Mexico, where the top 10 percent
earns a whopping 36.4 percent and the bottom 10 percent a paltry
1.7 percent, the same is 21.4 to 1.

Figure 11

Iceland	5.0
Germany	6.7
France	6.9
Canada	9.3
Japan	10.4
UK	10.6
Turkey	13.1
US	18.3
Chile	20.6
Mexico	21.4

OECD[11]

NET DOMESTIC PRODUCT

GDP measures the flow of income, but we also need to know about the stock of national wealth. Otherwise we'll get Bill, the banker, mixed up with Ben, the gardener. In the US the Bureau of Economic Analysis has been compiling net domestic product numbers for years, though these receive a fraction of the attention—to put it mildly—of GDP. Net domestic product (NDP) is calculated by subtracting the depreciation of capital goods such as roads, airports, and housing from GDP. If a nation is adding to its capital stock, the NDP will rise. If not, it will fall. The gap between NDP and GDP gives you an idea of whether a country is running down its capital to achieve an unsustainable boost to current production.

Brent Moulton, who served for many years as the number two at the Bureau of Economic Analysis, thinks there is a strong case for putting greater emphasis on NDP. "One of the fundamental questions about a nation is: is its wealth growing or shrinking?" he told me when we met at G Street Food in Washington, a sandwich joint that, confusingly, was not to be found anywhere near G Street.[12] (Directions as well as measurements can be misleading.) Figuring out wealth, he said, is particularly important in countries that are dependent on natural resources.

But even a country like the United States, if it is to prosper, needs to nurture its stock of assets, whether its infrastructure, its universities, or its natural resources. Whether or not countries are adding to their wealth should be a key question of national accounting.[13] Only countries with a strong net domestic product can raise their standard of living over the long term.

WELL-BEING

No serious advocate of GDP would claim it is a measure of well-being, yet few would deny that in public discourse it has morphed into a proxy of just that. What constitutes well-being is an intensely subjective judgment and thus impossible to measure objectively. But the attempt is worthwhile. That is because going through the exercise of trying to define and measure what well-being means helps societies prioritize. Trying to measure the unmeasurable—whether happiness or some broader measure of societal well-being—focuses the mind.

If Maryland's Genuine Progress Indicator were given the oxygen of publicity and political backing, it would become the subject of noisy public debate. Imagine if the governor said he was going to change policy dramatically because the GPI had fallen. Some people would celebrate the indicator's values, cheer when it went up, and worry when it went down. Others would argue that the GPI measures the wrong things and should be jettisoned for something better. Either way, seeking to get a handle on well-being would spark debate about what, as societies, we are striving for, and provide a benchmark against which those goals can be measured.

CO₂ EMISSIONS

I leave the most controversial to last. CO_2 levels are the simplest way of monitoring natural capital because measuring carbon does not rely on trying to put a price on a forest or a watershed, an exercise that is fraught with difficulty. CO_2 acts as a proxy for pollution. "If we're frying our planet," says Joseph Stiglitz, "you want to know that we're frying the planet."[14]

This suggestion highlights something that should have become glaringly obvious over the course of this book. Statistics are not neutral. Nor are they boring. They are hugely political. If we bother to measure something, it is because we think it is important and want to influence it. For those who accept that high levels of CO_2 are bad, the objective is to control or reduce it. But for those who don't accept that there is any correlation between human activity and climate change, trying to limit CO_2 emissions is a waste of time and money. More, it is destructive of what really counts: growth. That is essentially the argument Donald Trump made in pulling out of the Paris Climate Agreement.

The majority of scientists disagree with that assessment, saying that human activity is having a discernible impact on global temperatures. My position is this. I have no particular knowledge of climate-change science, just as I have no great understanding of aeronautical engineering. But when I board a plane, I trust that the engineers have got the business of keeping the plane in the air more or less down to a fine art. That's also my conclusion for the overwhelming number of scientists who warn about the dangers of climate change. I don't know, but I trust them. And if they're right, it seems eminently sensible to track the level of CO_2 and then do something about it.[15] What's the worst that could happen? More breathable air?

These are my suggestions. But they might not be yours. You may want to measure happiness or the regional distribution of income, or emphasize broader measures of unemployment.[16] You may like Alan Greenspan's underpants.

Whatever your preferences, there is always a trade-off between too much information and too little. As soon as you disaggregate numbers or come up with new things to measure, you have to weigh their importance. Many of the outcomes we might seek—a clean environment, healthy lives, safe streets, higher income, job security—are on different dimensions. Whenever you form an aggregate you lose information. On the other hand, if you don't form an aggregate you can't process or handle all the information that you do possess.[17]

One solution to this problem is the dashboard. Using the analogy of a car dashboard, or better yet one in an airplane cockpit, the idea is to monitor multiple things at once. Perhaps the ultimate dashboard concept is the OECD's Better Life Index, which was launched in 2011 after a decade of work.[18] This compares thirty-eight countries across eleven different "topics" from housing and environment to security and income. The beauty of the index is that you can personalize it, giving whatever weight you like to each category. It is a sort of studio mixing deck of well-being. Say you value work-life balance above all else, simply turn that dial up to maximum and see which countries come out best. (Answer: the Netherlands.)[19] The index is less of a policymaking tool and more of a way of illustrating the trade-offs between different desirable outcomes.

Another strong recommendation of this book is to improve how we measure public services. We tend to undervalue state provision of education, health care, and roads. That is because they are provided free of charge. The UK's Delivery Unit, which benchmarked everything from train delays to school exam results, was an imperfect but valuable step in the right direction. We should build on it. If we don't measure the contribution of the public sector properly, the likelihood is that we will privatize it into oblivion, although that is precisely what many countries—steered by the invisible incentives of growth—are seeking to do.

In poorer countries many years of fast growth may be necessary to bring living standards up to acceptable levels. But growth is the means to achieve desired goals, not the end in itself. In the richer world the whole idea of growth—at least as conventionally measured—may need to be overhauled. In economies where services dominate, goods and services tailored to our individual needs will be what determine the advance of our societies. These could be anything from genome-specific medicines to personalized care or tailored suits. That is different from more and more stuff, an arms race of growth. Instead, it means improvements in quality, something that GDP is ill equipped to measure. Some fifty years ago one US economist contrasted what he called the "cowboy" economy, bent on production, exploitation of resources, and pollution, with the "spaceman" economy, in which quality and complexity replaced "throughput" as the measure of success. The move from manufacturing to services and from analog to digital is the shift from cowboy to spaceman. But we are still measuring the size of the lasso.[20]

The quality issue also answers some of the underlying concerns about our seeming compulsion to acquire more and more material possessions, whatever the costs to our personal lives or the environment. The story of the Eurostar with free Chateau Petrus hints at how wealthy societies might "grow" in future by improving the quality of the experience. Quality—whether well prepared, locally grown food, personalized medical care, more cultural and outdoor activities, individually tailored products, or better design—is lower-carbon than quantity. Standard growth accounting leads us inexorably down the garden path marked MORE.

Some of the measures we might hope to emphasize—whether net domestic product or a broad definition of unemployment—already exist. Others, such as measures of natural capital, quality, or well-being, are very much works in progress. We need to put more money and more clever people onto the task if we are to invent killer measurements to match the ingenuity of GDP. Accountants are only messengers. (Of course, if the accountant works for PwC and hands Warren Beatty the wrong envelope, delivering the wrong message can have embarrassing consequences.[21]) Accountants need support so that they can bring us useful messages. In a shameless bid to win the professionals over to the cause of this book, here is a plea: give them more money and power.

The UK contributes about £127 million each year to the particle accelerator at CERN, the European Organization for Nuclear Research in Geneva. "For that, we get a share in measuring the mass of the Higgs boson to I don't know how many decimal places," says Nick Oulton of the London School of Economics, referring to the elementary particle. "All very exciting stuff. But the Office for National Statistics' budget—and that's not just for GDP, of course, that's for registering births, marriages and deaths and to track migration, employment, unemployment, all the components of GDP as well as GDP itself—its budget this year is £173 million. The natural sciences have convinced everyone that if you want answers, you have to spend a lot of money."[22] The same should be true of cracking the conundrums raised in this book. If GDP was the Manhattan Project of economics, then it is high time for its Moon landing and its Mars mission.

As well as money, national accountants need political cover. Statistics are controversial. They don't always bring convenient news. Attempts in the US during the Clinton administration to introduce regular "green accounts" were stymied by a Congress responding to the interests of big business, including the coal industry.[23] Bill Clinton said, "We need not choose between breathing clean air and bringing home secure paychecks. The fact is, our environmental problems result not from robust growth but from reckless growth." Congress thought otherwise. The Bureau of Economic Analysis was threatened with a 20 percent funding cut should it pursue green accounting—which was quietly sidelined. "Statisticians really can't be expected to carry that kind of water," says one bureau insider, still bruised by the encounter two decades later. "This has got to be a societal decision to do these things. The statistical agencies can do all their homework, advance a proposal. But if democracy says no, then it's no."[24]

The gap between what economists tell us and our own experiences—the one that Nicolas Sarkozy said was so dangerous— is twofold. It is also somewhat contradictory. On the one hand, GDP may actually be underestimating how well off we are. Because it is poor at measuring innovation, bald figures on income and production cannot capture the huge advances that have been made in health, technology, comfort, and access to knowledge. GDP may be making us all more miserable than we have any right to be by underrepresenting what we already have. On the other hand, GDP overestimates some aspects of our lives. Though the economy is supposedly in constant forward march, many feel left behind, marginalized, abandoned, and trapped in a never-ending race to pay for the goods and services that are supposed to define our lives. In these circumstances, simply increasing the size of the economic pie and then hoping we'll each grab a decent slice is not a satisfactory or sustainable policy.

If we need better numbers, there's an opposite and equal truth. We cannot govern by numbers alone. Rulers rule with rulers: they measure. But not everything can be costed and quantified. Not everything looks better because it is adorned with a dollar sign. That is one of the lessons of the recent political backlashes in which voters have rejected politics-as-usual.

The invention of GDP has given rise to a class of technocrats and economists who implement policy for the good of the economy, but not always for the good of the rest of us.[25] They have inherited a Newtonian view of what an economy is, as though it were a rational and predictable system, "a singular entity with well-defined mechanical relationships between different moving parts connected by metaphorical pipes, cogs and levers."[26] Too often it is thought of as something outside human experience. As one unorthodox thinker wrote, "Mathematics brought rigor to economics. Unfortunately, it also brought mortis."[27]

Before the invention of GDP, the word economy never figured in political discourse, something almost unimaginable today. No one thought about it as a separate entity. Until 1950, the idea of an economy never once appeared in a UK political manifesto with its modern meaning. All that changed with the invention of GDP. GDP was like a back door through which economists sneaked on to the public stage—and into the halls of government and bureaucracy.

Economists can bring valuable discipline to policymaking. But theirs is not the only view. There are competing ways to govern. It should not be necessary, as the venerable British Library has done, to justify its activities on the basis that, for every £1 it receives in public funding, it creates £4.40 for the economy.[28] Nor should a well-known children's charity need to encourage dads to read to their children on the basis that improved literacy will add 1.5 percent to GDP by 2020. Some things—safe streets, good jobs, clean air, open spaces, a sense of community, a sense of security and well-being—are good in themselves. So is the love of books and reading. Sometimes more income will help us achieve what we want. Sometimes it will not. But more income—more GDP—should never itself be the goal. At most, it should be the means by which we achieve our ends. As Simon Kuznets himself asked, "What are we growing? And why?"

Our priesthood of economists depends on "the idea that there are economic laws we cannot contradict any more than we could contradict physical laws: that however much we should like to, we cannot go against the logic of 'the economy.' "[29] And yet, sometimes we can. And sometimes we must. The economy is not real. It is merely one way of imagining our world. Gross domestic product is not real either. It is just a clever way of measuring some of the stuff that we humans get up to. Growth was a great invention. Now get over it.

NOTES

THE CULT OF GROWTH

1. See Pankaj Mishra, *Age of Anger*, Farrar, Straus and Giroux, 2017; Ed Luce, *The Retreat of Western Liberalism*, Little, Brown, 2017.

2. Borrowed from Diane Coyle, *GDP: A Brief but Affectionate History*, Princeton University Press, 2014, p. 124.

3. I've always attributed this phrase to Bill Emmott, former editor of *The Economist*. Whether or not he invented it, he uses it frequently.

4. "Chinese Factory Worker Can't Believe the Shit He Makes for Americans," *Onion*, June 15, 2005: www.theonion.com.

5. "The 30 Most Insane Things for Sale in Skymall," Buzzfeed, July 10, 2013: www.buzzfeed.com.

6. Joseph Stiglitz, *The Price of Inequality*, W. W. Norton & Company, 2012, p. xii.

7. Sarah F. Brosnan and Frans B. M. de Waal, "Monkeys Reject Unequal Pay," *Nature*, Vol. 425, September 2003.

8. David Card, Alexandre Mas, Enrico Moretti, and Emmanuel Saez, "Inequality at Work: The Effect of Peer Salaries on Job Satisfaction," November 2011: www.princeton.edu.

9. "The Cost of Living in Jane Austen's England": www.janeausten.co.uk.

10. Joseph Stiglitz, Amartya Sen, and Jean-Paul Fitoussi, *Mismeasuring Our Lives: Why GDP Doesn't Add Up*, The New Press, 2010, p. ix.

11. Walter Berglund, the lawyer and environmentalist in Jonathan Franzen's novel *Freedom*, expresses similar ideas.

12. In nominal terms Japan's economy hardly budged from 1990 to 2017.

In real per-capita terms it performed much in line with most Western economies by virtue of falling prices and a dwindling population.

13. It is true that suicide rates were high.

CHAPTER 1: KUZNETS'S MONSTER

1. These are the findings of economic historian Angus Maddison. Only with the Great Depression, triggered by the Industrial Revolution in Western Europe, did China and India's share of the global economy fall sharply, reaching a nadir of around 9 percent in 1950. Today it has risen to around 30 percent. See "The Economic History of the Last 2000 Years in 1 Little Graph": www.theatlantic.com.

2. Benjamin Mitra-Kahn, "Redefining the Economy: how the 'economy' was invented 1620," unpublished doctoral thesis, City University London, p. 18.

3. Ibid. These ideas are all covered in Benjamin Mitra-Kahn's brilliant thesis.

4. There had been many earlier attempts to survey a country's assets, including the Domesday Book of 1086. However, unlike Petty, who tried to incorporate flows of money into his calculations, earlier efforts had concentrated almost exclusively on assets, mainly land.

5. Mitra-Kahn, "Redefining the Economy," p. 4.

6. Ibid., p. 24.

7. The Kuznets curve posited the theory that, as an economy advances, inequality first rises before subsequently falling. The theory has come under significant criticism in an age of inequality, with some economists saying they see no statistical evidence for Kuznets's theory.

8. For a good description of Kuznets's character and methods see Robert William Fogel, *Political Arithmetic: Simon Kuznets and the Empirical Tradition in Economics*, University of Chicago Press, 2013.

9. Ehsan Masood, *The Great Invention*, Saqi Books, 2014, p. 15.

10. Kuznets originally conceived of gross national product rather than gross domestic product. The latter calculates production inside a

nation's borders. Kuznets's measure counted what was produced by US companies and individuals, whether at home or abroad.

11. Dirk Philipsen, *The Little Big Number: How GDP Came to Rule the World and What to Do About It*, Princeton University Press, 2015, p. 99.

12. Mitra-Kahn, "Redefining the Economy," p. 14.

13. Ibid., p. 27.

14. James Lacey, *Keep From All Thoughtful Men: How US Economists Won World War II*, Naval Institute Press, 2011.

15. Mitra-Kahn, "Redefining the Economy," p. 210.

16. Ibid., p. 237.

17. Masood, *The Great Invention*, p. 31.

18. Quoted in Mitra-Kahn, "Redefining the Economy," pp. 239–40.

CHAPTER 2: THE WAGES OF SIN

1. The decision was taken in 1995 under Eurostat's updated European System of National and Regional Accounts 95 (ESA95).

2. That is because the amount each member country pays in the European Union is determined by the size of its economy, measured by gross national income, or GNI, a close cousin of GDP. Of course, this was before Britain took the decision in a referendum to leave the European Union altogether.

3. "I think you'll find this annoyingly dull," said Gareth Powell of the UK Office for National Statistics when quizzed on the methodology. "They did most of the work in the office using already published data." Telephone interview with author, March 2016.

4. For a detailed account of their calculations, see Joshua Abramsky and Steve Drew, "Changes to National Accounts: Inclusion of Illegal Drugs and Prostitution in the UK National Accounts," UK Office for National Statistics, May 29, 2014.

5. Their figures excluded male prostitutes, who amount to 42 percent of all UK sex workers. Stuart Jeffries, "Time to Tax? Prostitution and

Illegal Drugs Add £12.27bn to the Economy," *The Guardian*, October 5, 2014: www.theguardian.com.

6. See later in this chapter for more detail on value-added.

7. David Lang, "Percentage of GDP Is a Strange Benchmark for a Defence Budget," Letter to *Financial Times*, March 3, 2015: www.ft.com.

8. Matthew Bristow, "Drugs Fade in Colombian Economy," *Wall Street Journal*, April 3, 2010: www.wsj.com.

9. William Echikson, "Il Sorpasso Has Italians Riding High," *The Christian Science Monitor*, May 8, 1987: www.csmonitor.com.

10. "Australia Carbon Laws Fail to Pass Senate," *Financial Times*, December 2, 2009: www.ft.com.

11. Simon Briscoe, "Britons Highly Sceptical Over Data," *Financial Times*, December 29, 2009.

12. Kate Allen and Chris Giles, "Statisticians Face Hard Facts," *Financial Times*, September 5, 2012.

13. Estimate from Darren Morgan, interview with author, London, June 2016.

14. Net domestic product would deduct the wear and tear of the machinery that makes the goods, something known as depreciation. Working out depreciation is not easy and so gross domestic product is the preferred measure.

15. The production method is sometimes called the output method.

16. This example is used by Ha-Joon Chang in *Economics: The User's Guide*, Bloomsbury Press, 2015, p. 212.

17. It is often rendered C + I + G + (X - M) where C is household spending, I is business investment, G is government spending, X is exports of goods and services and M is imports of goods and services.

18. Author interview with Umair Haque, London, June 2016.

19. In the now more frequent case of deflation they do the same if prices fall.

NOTES

CHAPTER 3: THE GOOD, THE BAD, AND THE INVISIBLE

1. Janice's real name was not used in Steven Brill's superb exposé, "The Bitter Pill: Why Medical Bills Are Killing Us," *Time*, February 20, 2013: www.uta.edu.

2. These details are taken from ibid.

3. Figures from World Health Organization for 2014.

4. World Health Organization, 2015.

5. Bryan Harris, "South Korea Set to Take Japan's Life Expectancy Crown," *Financial Times*, February 22, 2017: www.ft.com.

6. Chris Conover, "5 Myths in Steven Brill's Opus on Health Costs," *Forbes*, March 4, 2014: www.forbes.com.

7. According to the Center for Responsive Politics, quoted in Steven Brill, "The Bitter Pill."

8. These numbers are taken from ibid.

9. In fact Japan's economy had not been performing quite as badly as commonly assumed. Nominal GDP had stalled, but adjusted for prices and a shrinking population, real per-capita growth in Japan was reasonable.

10. Leo Lewis, "Japan, Women in the Workforce," *Financial Times*, July 6, 2015: www.ft.com.

11. Sarah O'Connor, "America's Jobs for the Boys Is Just Half the Employment Story," *Financial Times*, February 7, 2017.

12. This example was provided by Angus Deaton during a conversation with the author.

13. Katrine Marçal, *Who Cooked Adam Smith's Dinner?: A Story About Women and Economics*, Portobello, 2015.

14. Ibid.

15. Jonathan Franzen, *The Corrections*, HarperCollins, 2013, p. 288.

16. David Pilling, "No Formula Can Better a Mother's Milk," *Financial Times*, March 6, 2013.

17. Julie P. Smith, "Lost Milk? Counting the Economic Value of Breast-milk in GDP": www.researchgate.net.

18. J. Steven Landefeld, Stephanie H. McCulla, "Accounting for Non-market Household Production Within a National Accounts Framework," *The Review of Income and Wealth*, September 2000: online library.wiley.com.

19. Benjamin Bridgman et al., "Accounting for Household Production in the National Accounts, 1965–2010," *Survey of Current Business*, Vol. 92, May 2012.

20. "Household Satellite Account (Experimental) Methodology," UK Office for National Statistics, April 2002.

21. "Unpaid Household Production," UK Office for National Statistics, January 2004.

22. The list includes Australia, Canada, Finland, Germany, Hungary, Mexico, and Nepal.

23. Benjamin Bridgman et al., "Accounting for Household Production in the National Accounts," Bureau of Economic Analysis, May 2012: www.bea.gov.

CHAPTER 4: TOO MUCH OF A GOOD THING

This chapter's title is adapted from John Kay, *Other People's Money*, Public Affairs, 2015, p. 3. This is a brilliant book on financialization.

1. Kimiko de Freytas-Tamura, "Secret to Iceland's Tourism Boom? A Financial Crash and a Volcanic Eruption," *New York Times*, November 16, 2016: www.nytimes.com.

2. Ibid.

3. Richard Milne, "Olafur Hauksson, The Man Who Jailed Iceland's Bankers," *Financial Times*, December 9, 2016.

4. Michael Lewis, *Boomerang*, W. W. Norton & Company, 2011.

5. Ibid.

6. Ibid., p. 17.

7. David Ibison and Gillian Tett, "Iceland Feels the Heat After Years of Growth," *Financial Times*, November 24, 2007.

8. Kate Burgess, Tom Braithwaite, and Sarah O'Connor, "A Cruel Wind," *Financial Times*, October 11, 2008.

9. Ibid.

10. Author Matt Taibbi's delicious description of Goldman Sachs.

11. Andrew Haldane, Simon Brennan, and Vasileios Madouros, "What is the contribution of the financial sector: Miracle or mirage?," chapter 2 in *The Future of Finance, The LSE Report*, London School of Economics and Political Science, 2010.

12. According to *The Banker* magazine, reported in ibid.

13. China, like other Asian success stories before it, conducted what is known as financial repression by siphoning up savings and distributing them to favored industries through the state-owned banking sector. For years China ran huge current account surpluses, investing the money in US treasuries and the sovereign debt of other Western countries.

14. Kay, *Other People's Money*, p. 1. It is worth noting that, in the upside-down world of banking, assets are not quite what you might expect. They are the money the bank has *lent* out to other people. They are assets because theoretically the banks can get them back one day. Liabilities, on the other hand, are the monies deposited with a bank, which one day it will have to give back.

15. Andrew Haldane, "The $100 Billion Question," 2010: www.bankofengland.co.uk.

16. Haldane, Brennan, and Madouros, "What is the contribution of the financial sector," p. 92.

17. Diane Coyle, *GDP: A Brief but Affectionate History*, Princeton University Press, p. 99.

18. Haldane, Brennan, and Madouros, "What is the contribution of the financial sector," p. 88.

19. Coyle, *GDP*, p. 102.

CHAPTER 5: THE INTERNET STOLE MY GDP

1. Sir Charles Bean, "Independent Review of UK Economic Statistics," Cabinet Office, HM Treasury, March 2016.

2. This does not appear in GDP. The ad fees are added to the revenue of the site supplying advertising space, but are deducted from the revenue of the advertising company as an expense. From an accounting perspective, they cancel each other out.

3. Rwanda actually wants to ban the import of secondhand clothes so that it can build up its own clothing industry.

4. The method the commission employed is called hedonic accounting, which seeks to take into account questions of quality.

5. Brent Moulton, who as head researcher for the Bureau of Labor Statistics worked on the Boskin Commission, told me the exercise was very political. That was because many state benefits were linked to inflation. If inflation were lower, then benefits would be lower too.

6. For a discussion see Bean, "Independent Review of UK Economic Statistics."

7. "How to Quantify the Gains That the Internet Has Brought to Consumers," Net Benefits, *The Economist*, March 9, 2013: www.economist.com.

8. See Bean, "Independent Review of UK Economic Statistics," p. 84.

9. Interview with author, September 2013. See also David Pilling, "Lunch with the FT: Ha-Joon Chang," *Financial Times*, November 29, 2013: www.ft.com.

10. Murad Ahmed, "Your Robot Doctor Will See You Now," *Financial Times*, January 13, 2016: www.ft.com.

11. "Why the Japanese Economy Is Not Growing: Micro-barriers to Productivity Growth," McKinsey Global Institute, July 2000.

12. This hilarious example is taken from Rory Sutherland, "Life Lessons from an Ad Man," TED Talk, July 2009: www.ted.com.

13. From a telephone interview with the former head of the Bureau of Economic Analysis, Steve Landefeld, or Mr. GDP as I like to call him, February 2017.

14. Adam Sherwin, "Welsh Town Moves Offshore to Avoid Tax on Local Business," *Independent*, November 10, 2015.

15. Brian Czech, *Supply Shock*, New Society Publishers, 2013, p. 26.

16. If we did that though we would also have to acknowledge that much of the pollution we currently attribute to countries like China is actually pollution caused by Western companies who just happen to be operating in China.

17. Gordon Mathews, *Ghetto at the Center of the World: Chungking Mansions*, University of Chicago Press, 2011, p. 109.

CHAPTER 6: WHAT'S WRONG WITH THE AVERAGE JOE

1. African Americans were not actually plotted on the graph, but the rate of decline of their deaths was actually higher, at 2.6 percent a year over the 1999–2013 period.

2. IMF in current prices, accessed from knoema.com.

3. According to the US Bureau of Economic Analysis, GDP in constant 2009 prices was $16.5 trillion at the end of 2015 against $12.7 trillion at the end of 2000: www.multpl.com.

4. In 1970 the size of the US economy was $4.7 trillion, which had risen to $16.5 trillion by 2015 (US Bureau of Economic Analysis, GDP in constant 2009 prices). These figures do not account for population increase. In 2015 the US population was 321 million against 205 million in 1970, according to the US Census Bureau.

5. Edward Luce, "The Life and Death of Trumpian America," *Financial Times*, October 9, 2016.

6. "The Decline of the Labor Share of Income," IMF World Economic Outlook, cited in a blog on Bruegel: bruegel.org. As the post points out, the share has recovered marginally since the global financial crisis.

7. "Mortality and Morbidity in 21st Century America," Brookings Institution, March 23, 2017.

8. Jeff Guo, "How Dare You Work on Whites," April 6, 2017: www.washingtonpost.com.

9. "For Most Workers, Real Wages Have Barely Budged for Decades," Pew Research Center, October 9, 2014: www.pewresearch.org.

10. Edward Luce, "The New Class War in America," *Financial Times*, March 20, 2016: www.ft.com.

11. Angus Deaton, *The Great Escape*, Princeton University Press, 2013.

12. Ibid.

13. Albert Hirschman, "The changing tolerance for income inequality in the course of economic development," *World Development*, vol. I, issue 12, December 1973. Angus Deaton alerted me to this idea: www.sciencedirect.com.

14. Angus Deaton in conversation with the author, July 2016.

15. Martin Wolf, review of Branko Milanovic, *Global Inequality: A New Approach for the Age of Globalization*, Harvard University Press, 2016, in *Financial Times*, April 14, 2016.

16. Inequality of wealth (see chapter 9) is almost always higher than inequality of·income because advantages and disadvantages accumulate over time.

17. Milanovic, *Global Inequality*.

18. Milanovic calls this "citizenship rent."

19. Martin Wolf, review of Milanovic, *Global Inequality*, in *Financial Times*, April 14, 2016.

20. See Edward Luce, *The Retreat of Western Liberalism*, Little, Brown, 2017.

21. "Income Inequality and Poverty Rising in Most OECD Countries," October 21, 2008: www.oecd.org.

22. Denmark and Australia were examples of countries with high social mobility, the report said.

23. The curve is based on the work of labor economist Miles Corak and was popularized by Alan Krueger, former chairman of the Council of Economic Advisers.

24. Table 1: Key indicators on the distribution of household disposable

income and poverty, 2007, 2012, and 2014 or most recent year: www .oecd.org.

25. Larry Summers told me in a telephone interview, March 2017, "I think the statistics are wrong because I don't think they take nearly enough account of quality improvements of various kinds. We need to make adjustments for quality increases."

26. Chrystia Freeland, "The Rise of the New Global Super-Rich," TED Talk, 2013: www.ted.com.

CHAPTER 7: ELEPHANTS AND RHUBARB

1. "Bright Lights, Big Cities, Measuring National and Subnational Economic Growth in Africa from Outer Space with an Application in Kenya and Rwanda," Policy Research Working Paper WPS7461, World Bank Group, 2015.

2. Morten Jerven, *Poor Numbers*, Cornell University Press, 2013, pp. 17–20.

3. Ibid., p. x.

4. David Pilling, "In Africa, the numbers game matters," *Financial Times*, March 2, 2016.

5. Jerven, *Poor Numbers*.

6. See "If the GDP Is Up, Why Is America Down?" *Atlantic*, October 1995.

7. GDP per capita in PPP terms, IMF for 2015. See knoema.com.

8. Jeffrey Gettleman, "As Grasslands Dwindle, Kenya's Shepherds Seek Urban Pastures," *New York Times*, November 14, 2016.

9. The study found that ruminants contributed 319 billion shillings to the economy versus only 128 billion shillings in the official GDP statistics. "The Contribution of Livestock to the Kenyan Economy," Intergovernmental Authority on Development Livestock Policy Initiative Working Paper 03-11, p. 6.

10. Miles Morland, "Notes from Africa 2: Kioskenomics," private note to his clients, June 2011.

11. Telephone interview with author, February 2016.

12. Jamil Anderlini and David Pilling, "China Tried to Undermine Economic Report Showing Its Ascendancy," *Financial Times*, May 1, 2015.

13. Jerven, *Poor Numbers*, p 57.

14. Remarks to author, February 2016.

15. Based on author interview with officials from Liberia Institute of Statistics and Geo-information, Monrovia, March 2016.

CHAPTER 8: GROWTHMANSHIP

1. World Data Atlas: knoema.com.

2. Akash Kapur, *India Becoming*, Riverhead Books, 2012.

3. International Monetary Fund figures for 2015, adjusted for local prices. In dollar terms the difference is even starker: South Korea is eighteen times richer per capita.

4. Jagdish Bhagwati and Arvind Panagariya, *Why Growth Matters*, Council on Foreign Relations, 2013, p. xviii.

5. Partly based on various personal conversations with Jagdish Bhagwati, most recently in New York in March 2017.

6. Cited in Bhagwati and Panagariya, *Why Growth Matters*, p. 23.

7. That owed as much to China slowing down as to India accelerating. In fact, India's growth also slowed somewhat, and the headline number may be flattered by a 2015 rebasing of GDP.

8. See Amartya Sen, *Development as Freedom*, Anchor Books, 2000, p. 8.

9. Ibid., p. 3.

10. James Lamont, "High Growth Fails to Feed India's Hungry," *Financial Times*, December 22, 2010.

11. Jagdish Bhagwati disputes many of Sen's figures on malnutrition. See Bhagwati and Panagariya, *Why Growth Matters*.

12. "Indian Tycoon Hosts £59m Wedding For Daughter Amid Cash Crunch," *Guardian*, November 16, 2016: www.theguardian.com.

13. Amartya Sen, "Bangladesh Ahead of India in Social Indicators," *Daily Star*, February 13, 2015: www.thedailystar.net.

14. David Pilling, "India's Congress Party Has Done Itself Out of a Job," *Financial Times*, May 7, 2014: www.ft.com.

15. Rajiv Kumar of the Centre for Policy Research, Delhi.

16. Sam Roberts, "Hans Rosling, Swedish Doctor and Pop-Star Statistician, Dies at 68," *New York Times*, February 9, 2017.

17. He objected because he said his observations were based merely on data.

18. When I asked him about the other 20 percent, he said, "That's why we have public health. That's the reason for my existence."

19. There is at least one country that breaks Rosling's rule: Equatorial Guinea, where the elite has grown fat on oil money courtesy of Exxon Mobil, has a GDP per capita of $30,000 adjusted for local prices. But two-thirds of its population lives in abject poverty, and the infant mortality rate, at 67 per 1,000, is higher than in Eritrea, a country 20 times poorer as measured by GDP.

20. The World Bank defines lower-middle-income countries as those with a per-capita gross national income of between $1,026 and $4,035, calculated by the Atlas method, which tries to smooth out differences between countries caused by exchange-rate fluctuations. Upper-middle-income countries are defined as those with a GNI per capita of between $4,036 and $12,475.

21. These numbers come from Rosling.

22. "Why Ethiopian Women Are Having Fewer Children Than Their Mothers," BBC, November 6, 2015: www.bbc.com/news.

CHAPTER 9: BLACK POWER, GREEN POWER

1. Chris Buckley 储百亮 (ChuBailiang).

2. Edward Wong, "Air Pollution Linked to 1.2 Million Premature Deaths in China," *New York Times*, April 1, 2013: www.nytimes.com.

3. Javier Hernandez, "Greed, Injustice and Decadence: What 5 Scenes From a Hit TV Show Say About China," *New York Times*, May 27, 2017.

4. See Frank Dikötter, *Mao's Great Famine*, Bloomsbury Publishing, 2010.

5. Li Keqiang, who went on to become Chinese premier, warned in 2007 that Chinese GDP figures should not be taken too seriously. He recommended looking at three other numbers: electricity production, rail cargo, and bank loans. See David Pilling, "Chinese Economic Facts and Fakes Can Be Hard to Tell Apart," *Financial Times*, September 16, 2015.

6. Paul A. Samuelson, *Economics*, McGraw-Hill Book Company, 1948, p. 10.

7. Lorenzo Fioramonti, *Gross Domestic Problem*, Zed Books, 2013, p. 151.

8. Leo Lewis, Tom Mitchell, and Yuan Yang, "Is China's Economy Turning Japanese?," *Financial Times*, May 28, 2017.

9. Jonathan Watts, "China's Green Economist Stirring a Shift Away from GDP," *Guardian*, September 16, 2011: www.theguardian.com.

10. Ibid.

11. Geoff Dyer, "Chinese Algae Spreads to Tourist Resorts," *Financial Times*, July 12, 2008: www.ft.com.

12. Jonathan Watts, *When a Billion Chinese Jump*, Simon & Schuster, 2010, chapter 11.

13. Jared Diamond has argued that the Rwandan genocide of 1994 had a Malthusian element of overpopulation.

14. Pilita Clark, "The Big Green Bang: How Renewable Energy Became Unstoppable," *Financial Times*, May 18, 2017.

15. Aibing Guo, "China Says It's Going to Use More Coal, With Capacity Set to Grow 19%," Bloomberg, November 7, 2016: www.bloomberg.com.

16. Yuan Yang, "China's Air Pollution Lifts in Coastal Cities, But Drifts Inland," *Financial Times*, April 20, 2016.

17. Yuan Yang, "China Carbon Dioxide Levels May Be Falling, Says LSE Study," *Financial Times*, March 7, 2016.

18. Gabriel Wildau, "Small Chinese Cities Steer Away from GDP as Measure of Success," *Financial Times*, August 13, 2014.

19. Arthur Beesley et al., "China and EU Offer Sharp Contrast with US on Climate Change," *Financial Times*, June 1, 2017.

CHAPTER 10: WEALTH

1. This is something Martin Wolf of the *Financial Times* told me. Personal conversation, September 2016, London.

2. For companies there's even a third set of accounts, called the cash-flow statement, which measures the ·actual cash position of the company—the liquidity at its disposal—and is thus different again from the profit and loss accounts.

3. Many advanced economies do measure what is known as produced capital, the stock of physical assets such as roads, buildings, and ports.

4. Partha Dasgupta, "Getting India Wrong," *Prospect Magazine*, August 2013.

5. This example comes from a conversation with Partha Dasgupta, September 2016.

6. Partha Dasgupta, "The Nature of Economic Development and the Economic Development of Nature," *Economic and Political Weekly*, vol. 48, issue 51, December 21, 2013.

7. This account is taken from Jared Diamond's article "Easter's End" in *Discover Magazine*, August 1995: courses.biology.utah.edu.

8. Ibid.

9. Author interview with Partha Dasgupta.

CHAPTER 11: A MODERN DOMESDAY

1. J. A. Giles and J. Ingram, *The Anglo-Saxon Chronicle*, Project Gutenberg: www.gutenberg.org.

2. Dieter Helm, *Natural Capital*, Yale University Press, 2015, p. 96.

3. Robert Costanza et al., "The Value of the World's Ecosystem Services and Natural Capital," *Nature*, May 1997: www.nature.com.

4. Partly based on a discussion with Partha Dasgupta, September 2016.

5. Robert Costanza et al., "Costanza and His Coauthors Reply," Heldref Publications, March 1998, vol. 40, no. 2: ftp://131.252.97.79/Transfer/ES_Pubs/ESVal/es_val_critiques/responseToPearce_by Costanza.pdf.

6. Helm, *Natural Capital*, p. 8.

7. Former Norwegian prime minister Gro Harlem Brundtland was given no less a task by the United Nations than convincing the world's governments to commit to a form of growth that did not destroy the planet. In 1987 the commission released its report, "Our Common Future."

8. The same law could be applied to other forms of capital, including infrastructure and even institutions.

9. See Helm, *Natural Capital*, pp. 99–118.

10. In practice such theories run into the problem of the "tragedy of the commons," whereby everyone extracts as much as possible of a resource because the alternative is that someone else will.

11. Agnes Kalibata, president of the Alliance for a Green Revolution in Africa, says climate change is the single biggest challenge for Africa's impoverished farmers, who are almost entirely dependent on rain-fed agriculture in an era when rainfall has never been so unpredictable. Interview with author, Nairobi, April 2017.

12. William Davies, *The Happiness Industry*, Verso, 2015, p. 65.

13. Andrew Simms, "It's the Economy That Needs to Be Integrated into the Environment—Not the Other Way Around," *Guardian*, June 14, 2016: www.theguardian.com.

14. This is the brilliant idea of Andrew Simms in ibid.

15. Simms, "It's the Economy."

16. George Monbiot, "Can You Put a Price on the Beauty of the Natural World?," *Guardian*, April 22, 2014: www.theguardian.com.

17. See the Global Footprint Network website: www.footprintnetwork
.org.

18. Ibid.

19. Interview with author, March 2017.

20. These ideas are based on a discussion with Martin Wolf, my esteemed colleague at the *Financial Times*, September 2016.

21. Glenn-Marie Lange et al., "The Changing Wealth of Nations," World Bank, December 2011, p. xii: www.worldbank.org.

22. Angus Maddison, a pioneer in calculating GDP over time, was professor at the University of Groningen from 1978 to 1997, and a founder of the Groningen Growth and Development Centre.

23. Oil, natural gas, hard coal, soft coal, bauxite, copper, gold, iron ore, lead, nickel, phosphate, tin, silver, and zinc.

24. The bank's most recent methodology makes some attempt to factor in the hunting, fishing, and recreational value of forest land.

25. These figures are from Lange et al., "The Changing Wealth of Nations," p. 7, for which the latest data on comprehensive wealth are from 2005. The bank publishes more regular numbers for related wealth measures, such as adjusted net savings.

26. Table 1.1, p. 7, in "The Changing Wealth of Nations": documents .worldbank.org.

27. The account of Viken comes from "Discover How Norway Saved Its Vanishing Forests," BBC, November 4, 2015: www.bbc.co.uk.

28. Tore Skroppa, "State of Forest Genetic Resource in Norway," March 2012, p. iii: www.skogoglandskap.no/filearchive.

29. Its formal name, changed in 2006, is actually the Government Pension Fund Global, a slightly confusing name given that it is not really a pension fund but a sovereign wealth fund.

CHAPTER 12: THE LORD OF HAPPINESS

1. In 1975 pounds.

2. "Jeremy Bentham Makes Surprise Visit to UCL Council," *UCL News*, July 10, 2013: www.ucl.ac.uk.

3. Jeremy Bentham, *An Introduction to the Principles of Morals and Legislation*, 1789.

4. William Davies, *The Happiness Industry*, Verso, 2015, p. 10.

5. Ibid., p. 61.

6. Ibid., p. 17.

7. This is based on a lecture by Jeffrey Sachs, director of the Earth Institute of Columbia University, at the London School of Economics, December 2016.

8. George Ward, "Is Happiness a Predictor of Election Results?," Centre for Economic Performance, April 2015: cep.lse.ac.uk.

9. John F. Helliwell, et al., World Happiness Report, 2012: world.happiness.report/download.

10. World Happiness Report, 2016, chapter 2, "The Distribution of World Happiness": world.happiness.report/download.

11. IMF data for 2015, with GDP per capita expressed in purchasing-power parity terms.

12. Ibid.

13. Results cover 90,000 people in 46 countries. Richard Layard, *Happiness*, Penguin Books, 2005, p. 65.

14. Ibid., p. 64.

15. Ibid., p. 79.

16. "Carrie Fisher's ashes carried in Prozac-shaped urn," January 7, 2017: www.bbc.co.uk.

17. Author interview with Richard Layard.

18. Layard, *Happiness*, p. 233.

19. Ibid., p. 154.

20. Layard cites research from Robert Sampson and Byron Groves of Harvard University, "Community Structure and Crime (1989)": dash.harvard.edu.

21. Paul Ormerod, "Against Happiness," *Prospect Magazine*, April 29, 2007: www.prospectmagazine.co.uk.

22. Richard Layard, "Paul Ormerod Is Splitting Hairs," *Prospect Magazine*, June 2007.

23. Cited in World Happiness Report, 2012, p. 111.

24. Gardiner Harris, "Index of Happiness? Bhutan's New Leader Prefers More Concrete Goals," *New York Times*, October 4, 2013.

25. Ibid.

26. According to 2016 IMF figures, it has a GDP of just over $8,227 in purchasing-power parity terms, which adjust for local prices.

27. All figures from Unesco.

28. Bill Frelick, "Bhutan's Ethnic Cleansing," *New Statesman*, February 1, 2008: www.hrw.org.

29. Bhutan's 2015 Gross National Happiness Index, Centre for Bhutan Studies and GNH Research, November 2015: www.bhutanstudies .org.bt.

CHAPTER 13: GDP 2.0

1. Tobin became most famous for his proposed tax on foreign exchange transactions to reduce risky and what he considered useless speculation.

2. "Against the Human Development Index": econlog.econlib.org.

3. Minus net investment is when the value of new investments is less than the value of depreciation.

4. Interview with author, February 2017.

5. From a conversation with Steve Landefeld, February 2017.

6. "Canadian Index of Wellbeing, Executive Summary," 2016: uwater loo.ca.

CHAPTER 14: THE GROWTH CONCLUSION

1. Author telephone interview with Joseph Stiglitz, April 2017.

2. Partly based on a conversation with Jagdish Bhagwati, New York, March 2017.

3. In an interview with the author, Larry Summers said GDP tended to track other things we might be interested in, including environmental protection and health, thus limiting the need to come up with different measurements. In other words, in his opinion GDP is not a bad proxy for well-being. "When some other welfare measure grows fast, that tends to be the period when GDP grows fast, and vice versa. When you do it across countries, I think the correlation between growth in alternative welfare measures and growth in GDP ends up being relatively high, not relatively low. So that all makes me a little less bowled over with the efficacy of these kinds of alternative calculations."

4. Jonathan Soble, "Japan, Short on Babies, Reaches a Worrisome Milestone," *New York Times*, June 2, 2017: www.nytimes.com.

5. Hans Rosling projected the world's population would peak at about 11 billion in 2100, when he estimated there would be 1 billion people in the Americas, 1 billion in Europe, 4 billion in Africa and 5 billion in Asia. Lecture at Davos, Switzerland, January 2014.

6. Most though not all economists see a clear trend of increased inequality in the majority of rich countries.

7. Sometimes it is expressed on a scale of 0 to 1.

8. Gini Index (World Bank estimate)—Country Ranking, Index Mundi website: www.indexmundi.com.

9. The coefficient can be calculated before or after government redistribution, including tax and benefits.

10. Data source: C. DeNavas-Walts, B. D. Proctor, and J. C. Smith, September 2013, US Census Bureau, Current Population Reports, P60–245, Income, Poverty, and Health Insurance Coverage in the United States: 2012 (Table A-2).

11. "Income Inequality Remains High in the Face of Weak Recovery," Centre for Opportunity and Equality, OECD, November 2016, Table 1: Key indicators on the distribution of household disposable income and poverty, 2007, 2012, 2014, or most recent year: www .oecd.org.

12. Interview with author, Washington, March 2017.

13. Calculating net domestic product requires a number of assumptions,

most important of which is over how many years does an asset depreciate. You might decide, for example, that the value of a building falls to zero over twenty years. So even though the building is still standing in twenty years' time, in national accounting terms it would be valued at nothing. If different nations apply different assumptions to different assets, comparing national domestic products internationally becomes difficult. But it does provide a rough guide of how well or badly an individual nation is doing in maintaining its assets and therefore how sustainable its growth is likely to be.

14. Telephone conversation with the author, April 2017.

15. As Stiglitz points out, CO_2 might not be the best measure in all situations. In China for example you could make a case that immediate health issues associated with chronic air pollution are more pressing. In that case it might be better for Beijing to measure fine particulate emissions.

16. So-called U6, the broadest measure of unemployment, includes "discouraged workers" who want work but have stopped looking because job prospects are so dim, and part-time workers who would rather work full time. See Bureau of Labor Statistics, Table A-15: www.bls.gov/news.release.

17. Partly based on conversation with Joseph Stiglitz, April 2017.

18. See OECD Better Life Index: www.oecdbetterlifeindex.org.

19. Stiglitz says that hourly wages in the US have stagnated over sixty years. For people to maintain their standard of living, they've worked longer and longer hours per household. In Europe hours worked per household have come down over the same period. If his numbers are right, Europeans have traded some income for leisure, while Americans have prioritized making money, even if they have no time to enjoy it.

20. Kenneth Boulding, quoted in Lorenzo Fioramonti, *Gross Domestic Problem*, Zed Books, 2013, pp. 145–6.

21. Faye Dunaway announced *La La Land* as Best Picture, but the card should have read *Moonlight*, the real winner. "Moonlight, La La Land and What an Epic Oscars Fail Really Says," *New York Times*, February 27, 2017.

22. Telephone interview with author, February 2017. Incidentally, Oulton wrote a terrifically spiky defense of GDP in "Hooray for GDP! GDP as a Measure of Well-being": voxeu.org.

23. According to officials at the Bureau of Economic Statistics.

24. The official spoke anonymously out of concern for retribution even after all this time.

25. Joe Earle, Cahal Moran, and Zach Ward-Perkins, *The Econocracy: The Perils of Leaving Economics to the Experts*, Manchester University Press, 2016.

26. Ibid.

27. Kenneth Boulding, quoted in "An A–Z of Business Quotations," *The Economist*, July 20, 2012.

28. Earle et al., *The Econocracy*.

29. Author interview with Joe Earle, July 2016.

ACKNOWLEDGMENTS

Too many people helped with the writing of this book to be mentioned by name. I have been discussing the ideas behind it with friends, family, colleagues, and professionals, not to mention my two boys, Dylan and Travis, for years.

In addition, I conducted dozens of interviews in person or by telephone with practitioners, academics, economists, and thinkers in Europe, America, Africa, and Asia. Many of those who helped form the arguments appear in the text of these pages or in the notes. To all of them, I thank you profusely for your kindness and for your wisdom.

A few people deserve special mention. Staff at the Office for National Statistics patiently helped to explain the guts of GDP and how it was calculated. This book argues for more statistics, not fewer, so thank you for all your hard work and dedication, Luke Croydon, Darren Morgan, Sanjiv Mahajan, and Gareth Powell, to name but a few. Thank you also to all those at the US Bureau of Economic Analysis past and present and to the dedicated statisticians in Kenya, Nigeria, Liberia, and Tanzania with whom I spoke, as well as those in other parts of Africa who are trying to make sense of their countries' economies in often trying circumstances.

At the *Financial Times*, I'd like to thank the editor, Lionel Barber, who has always been a friend and supporter. The *FT*, like the world's best universities, allows its writers to pursue their own interests wherever they may lead them. The *FT* has published several of my articles on GDP—a practice run for this book—in the magazine, the Life and Arts section, and in opinion slots. The *FT*'s precious system of sabbaticals gave me some much-needed time off to write the first draft of the book. In addition to Lionel, I'd like to thank Gideon Rachman, a wonderful colleague, and Thomas Hale, who read an early draft and made helpful suggestions, as well as William Wallis and Andrew England, who have been great and supportive friends when it was most needed.

Other readers of early drafts or chapters include Akash Kapur and Geoff Tily, whose ideas and critiques proved most valuable. Joe Earle, a gifted young economist and one of the founders of the Post-Crash Economics Society, also read a draft and helped to assure me that I was on the right track.

Danielle Walker Palmour of Friends Provident Foundation, which supported the writing of the book, was endlessly encouraging. Alison Benjamin, who read early drafts, also cheered me on and made excellent suggestions. If they had not prodded me into action in the first place, this book would never have been written.

Likewise, my agents, Felicity Bryan and Zoe Pagnamenta, who saw me through my first book on Japan, believed in this one from the outset, even though it was on a totally unrelated subject and outside my usual sphere. At Bloomsbury, Alexis Kirschbaum, and in the US, Tim Duggan of Tim Duggan Books, were quick to see the potential of this project.

Thanks too to the dedicated publicity and marketing team in the UK—Natalie Ramm, Emma Bal, and Genista Tate-Alexander—as well as to Jasmine Horsey and Sarah Ruddick, who have been incredibly helpful. In the US, though I haven't met them yet, thanks to William Wolfslau, Aubrey Martinson, Dyana Messina, Lisa Erickson, and Becca Putman for your true professionalism.

ACKNOWLEDGMENTS

I would also like to thank Ha-Joon Chang, with whom I discussed the book at conception stage and who encouraged me to believe that this was something I could do.

This book was written during a difficult period of transition in my life and I'd especially like to thank my mum, Doria Pilling, for being there for me when I needed her most. She edited her own, far more ambitious book on social care around the world while I produced this one.

Thank you finally to Kimiko, who heard all the arguments in rough formation, winkled out invaluable snippets from the Internet, and encouraged me throughout. This book is dedicated to you—and to us.

INDEX

INDEX

INDEX

ABOUT THE AUTHOR

DAVID PILLING is an associate editor at the *Financial Times*, where he has reported on business, economics, and politics from London, Chile, Argentina, Tokyo, and Hong Kong. He is currently the Africa editor, based in London.